Blind Awakening

Blind Awakening

Tamura Arthun

© 2018 Tamura Arthun
All rights reserved.

ISBN: 1984370391
ISBN-13: 9781984370396

My Story

I WAS BORN AND RAISED just south of Seattle, Washington, with one younger brother and two older ones. As far back as I can remember, I have always been a person who likes to help others. From the time I was in grade school and all the way through high school, I defended anyone who was being bullied, and I befriended those kids who were left out.

I was an independent child and didn't shy away from those people who acted or looked different from me. I had a deaf friend, a friend who was from Vietnam and didn't speak English, and a friend who had an intellectual disability. Though I had friends who were considered "normal" or "typical," I preferred to spend my time helping my friends who otherwise might have been left out or alone. I am not sure what it was that drew me toward them, but as I matured, my desire to help others only grew.

When I was about ten years old, I experienced death for the first time. My old dog, Fuzzy, had to be put down because of health issues. I felt so sad and alone without my constant companion. I cried for a whole week, despite my parents telling me that "it was his time" and that "he's in a better place." I learned that death meant that my dog would never return to me.

In my senior year of high school, I worked for my grandmother's next-door neighbor, Barbara, and her husband, Earl. They had no family in the area, and since Barbara's breast cancer had returned, she needed some help with household chores. I was happy to help her, and the fact that they wanted to pay me was a bonus. My hours of work increased as Barbara's health declined. When she could no longer stay alone at night—and because Earl worked the graveyard shift—I spent the nights with her. I would leave for school just as Earl was returning home from work.

Barbara rang a bell in the middle of the night whenever she needed my help, and inevitably we would end up talking about her cancer and likely death. She wasn't afraid to die, just sad to leave her husband and me.

A year after Barbara's death, during my freshman year of college, my mentor and closest friend, Toni, was diagnosed with metastatic breast cancer. She was twenty years older than I was, and she considered me to be like her little sister. I cleaned her house, helped with her teenage son and daughter, and took her to chemotherapy appointments. She fought with every bit of her soul, and we both believed she would win her battle with cancer. In fact, I had absolute faith that God would heal her. She was not ready to die, and I couldn't imagine my life without her.

We celebrated her remission at the beginning of my sophomore year. At the end of my junior year, Toni's cancer had returned with a vengeance. As her body deteriorated, I drove home from college several days a week to help care for her. We tried many types of treatment options, from coffee enemas to primal therapy. During her last week of life, I spent every night with her. I begged God to perform a miracle—to cure one of the most important people in my life. Toni died on her son's fifteenth birthday, just two months before my wedding. I was at work, and I didn't make it in time to be with her when she passed, which only added to my angst.

Devastated and angry that God hadn't answered my prayers, I felt lost. My faith was shaken to my core because I couldn't comprehend how my loving God could take Toni from her children and allow my heart to be ripped into pieces. I wanted to help Toni's children cope with the loss of their mother, but I had no idea how I could help, especially when I was so sad myself. I didn't know how to grieve her death—to come to peace with the very thing she herself couldn't accept.

Throughout my schooling, and while helping Toni, I was also working as a private caretaker for two severely head-injured patients. One was a seven-year-old girl who had suffered a severe head injury when she fell off a swing at three years old. She was blind, wheelchair bound, and unable to speak. She required tube feedings and many medications to keep her alive.

The other was a twenty-four-year-old man who had been head injured in a car crash when he was eighteen years old. My husband (twenty-two years older than I) was his physical therapist. The young man was also wheelchair bound and wasn't able to speak, but he could communicate through hand and eye gestures. Despite his condition, he was medically stable, unlike the little girl, who was much more fragile.

After finishing my schooling, I got a job at a subacute rehabilitation center. I worked with severely head-injured and comatose patients on one floor of the facility and with dementia patients on another. The contrast between the two floors was vast—the patients on the head-injury unit were fighting to live, while the dementia patients were waiting to die. I was responsible for helping both achieve their goals while helping their families through the process.

Eight years later, married with two beautiful daughters ages six and seven, I returned to school to get a master of social work. It was at that time that I chose to do my practicum at Evergreen Cancer Center and Hospice Center. I worked throughout the hospital, learning a great deal about a variety of illnesses and diseases. My primary focus, however, was to learn all I could about cancer and grief. I participated in patient-care conferences with physicians and other medical staff, where I gained a much better understanding of cancer. As part of my education, I ran a breast cancer support group and provided support and resources to patients diagnosed with cancer.

During the last year of my practicum, I was assigned to the hospice center. I was required to go through the bereavement program as part of my curriculum. It was the first time I experienced what it was like to openly talk about my grief. I learned how to emotionally, spiritually, and intellectually process my own losses—as well as how to help my patients.

I eventually was given my own caseload of terminally ill patients to manage. I helped them and their families talk about the dying process, provided resources and services to help them with their physical needs, and was often present when they took their last breaths.

At the same time that I was doing my practicum, my favorite grandmother suddenly became ill with chronic obstructive pulmonary disease. Though I was learning about grief, I was not prepared for another death—especially not my sweet grandmother's. Even though she was seventy-three and facing death, she was surprisingly focused on all she still wanted to do before she died. As her condition declined, she seemed to finally accept that her death was inevitable. My grandmother saw visions of her relatives who had passed before her, and that brought her peace, which brought me a bit of comfort. I visited her at the hospital as often as I could but ended up missing her final breath while I was driving to see her. I was struck with guilt and regret that I didn't make it in time to say goodbye.

It was less than a year later that my grandfather suffered a stroke, and we were told he would not survive. Somewhat educated about the medical side of his condition and much more comfortable with the dying process, I was the best suited in my family to advocate for him. Because he couldn't communicate his end-of-life wishes, and he and I had always been very close, I helped my mother and aunt make the decision to remove his life support.

Shortly after his death, I graduated from the University of Washington with my master of social work and was immediately hired by Evergreen Hospice. I was becoming quite comfortable with helping people die and helping their families work through the grief process, and I learned to help myself with my own grief along the way. Only a year after my grandfather passed away, my last living grandparent was diagnosed with terminal stomach cancer. My father's mother agreed to sign on with the hospice program, and I was designated to be her power of attorney and overseer of her care. My family and relatives took turns staying with her and helping with her care. When the end was close, I stayed with my grandmother twenty-four hours a day, and she died peacefully in my arms. For the first time in my personal experience, I felt it was a death done well.

A year after my graduation, I took a job in the critical care unit at a different hospital, Valley Medical, because I needed a more predictable schedule. I developed an insatiable curiosity about all the medical procedures, diseases, and illnesses that affected my patients. As an integral member of the medical team, it was my job to advocate for the overall needs of my patients, not just to focus on their illness. It was my role to help them with financial issues, insurance concerns, arranging caretakers or services for their return home, and addressing their emotional needs as well. I also educated patients and families about end-of-life decisions and helped them openly discuss their wishes. I sat with many patients as they passed away, and more often than not, found the experience quite peaceful.

In addition to my critical-care role, I became a member of the hospital's ethics committee, along with a small group of doctors and nurses. We discussed and ruled on various cases, including medical procedures, end-of-life situations, and issues of morality. I would never have imagined that my experience from this group would come in handy in my future.

I also started a support group for kids with a parent or grandparent who had been diagnosed with a terminal illness. It was a six-week course in which I taught children about cancer or other pertinent illnesses and provided them the opportunity talk about their feelings or concerns. The groups proved to be very enlightening and rewarding.

It was during this time that I met a very special friend, Keith, who was diagnosed with terminal brain cancer. He, his wife, and their four young children attended my church. I was happy to include his kids in my support group, as well as provide support to him and his wife for several years. Keith taught me a great deal about grief, and he was able to bring much comfort to my brother. I was grateful that I was able to help him die with dignity. I experienced great loss with his passing but was so blessed to be a part of his journey. I was thankful that his children may have had a chance to grieve his death differently than Toni's did.

I was so grateful for my critical-care job and all that I was doing with the kids and the ethics board, but it all came to a screeching halt when I was unexpectedly laid off. My disappointment in having to leave all my coworkers and patients was only slightly alleviated by being hired back to Evergreen on the same day I was laid off from Valley Medical. Amazingly, there was a critical-care position available, and my old boss was excited to have me back. It took only a few weeks to feel as if I had never left.

I not only loved my job; I was passionate about it. I believed that all my past experiences had prepared me to do exactly what I was doing—helping people through the most difficult times of their lives. Facing death is the one thing we all have in common, and I enjoyed counseling people as they came to that realization. In fact, several family friends called on me to help them as they faced the end of their lives. Whether it was a patient or a friend, I was always honored to be a part of that person's journey. More often than not, I found the human spirit to be resilient, and most people experienced peace at the end.

But I would have one more difficult job to perform, and it would require all my training and experience to get through—helping my youngest brother, Jeff, to die.

I was able to make some sense out of all the pain and loss that I had gone through, and I even developed a renewed faith. I was finally able to understand that death did not mean that God had failed us or that we lost the battle; it was simply a part of living.

Contents

My Story · v
Introduction · xv

Chapter 1	Jeff's New Job, 1999 ·	1
Chapter 2	The Invader ·	6
Chapter 3	The Diagnosis ·	12
Chapter 4	Pre-Op ·	14
Chapter 5	Valentine's Day ·	21
Chapter 6	The Critical-Care Unit · · · · · · · · · · · · · · · · · · ·	27
Chapter 7	Lights Out ·	33
Chapter 8	Time to Transfer ·	38
Chapter 9	Going Home ·	44
Chapter 10	Going Home Again ·	49
Chapter 11	New Growth ·	55
Chapter 12	On Being Blind ·	58
Chapter 13	The Unspoken Routine · · · · · · · · · · · · · · · · · · ·	66
Chapter 14	Tammy's New Job ·	70
Chapter 15	The Change of Summer · · · · · · · · · · · · · · · · · ·	73
Chapter 16	The Crash ·	78
Chapter 17	Sharing the News ·	85
Chapter 18	The Media Flurry ·	94
Chapter 19	A New View ·	101
Chapter 20	Family Update ·	103

Chapter 21	The Secret	106
Chapter 22	Jeff's Cancer Scare	111
Chapter 23	Road to Recovery	113
Chapter 24	Sharing the Duty	120
Chapter 25	Tammy's Thoughts	124
Chapter 26	Burn Man and Blind Guy	127
Chapter 27	The Holidays	131
Chapter 28	Let's Go Swimming	145
Chapter 29	Transitions	151
Chapter 30	Blind School	154
Chapter 31	Road to Independence	164
Chapter 32	Telling the Girls	173
Chapter 33	Sunday Service	177
Chapter 34	First Sack Lunch Sunday	184
Chapter 35	Lake Sammamish, June 2002	189
Chapter 36	Blind Bowling	194
Chapter 37	Fall 2002	198
Chapter 38	Where to Go from Here	204
Chapter 39	Back to School	208
Chapter 40	The Fair	211
Chapter 41	Sick and Tired of Being Sick and Tired	216
Chapter 42	Cancer Update	228
Chapter 43	Movie Time	231
Chapter 44	Brothers	235
Chapter 45	Serving the Homeless	239
Chapter 46	A Grateful Heart	244
Chapter 47	The Ups and Downs	251
Chapter 48	God's Healing	256
Chapter 49	Video Debut	260
Chapter 50	Cherished Gifts	269
Chapter 51	Celebrations	273
Chapter 52	Three-Year Anniversary	280
Chapter 53	Funeral Plans	289

Chapter 54	Trying Times	293
Chapter 55	Fish Lake Reunion	295
Chapter 56	Dying Thoughts	310
Chapter 57	A War Zone	312
Chapter 58	A Night of Horror	315
Chapter 59	The End Is Near	324
Chapter 60	Goodbye, My Little Brother	330
Chapter 61	Another One Bites the Dust	335
	Epilogue	351
	Acknowledgments	353
	About The Author	359

Introduction

As soon as Mom sat us down in the living room, I knew something was wrong. My brothers and I glanced at one another, wondering who was in trouble and why our youngest brother, Jeff, was not there. Mom caught our glances and immediately interrupted our silent communication.

"You know I took Jeff to the doctor last week to get the brown spots checked out? The doctor said they're called 'cafe au lait spots' and said they could be from a disease called neurofibromatosis. He called it NF for short. He sent us to a specialist to have Jeff tested for it."

We nodded, silently waiting for her to continue.

"The specialist, a neurologist, ordered that MRI of Jeff's brain last week because Jeff was going through puberty so young." She took a heavy breath before continuing.

"We got the results from the scan today, and it shows Jeff does have NF. And it has caused a tumor in his brain, on his pituitary gland, and they can't remove it." She paused, wrenching her hands together. "If it continues to grow, Jeff will die." Her lips quivered as she stared over our heads and out the living room window.

My siblings and I looked at one another, puzzled. We thought the brown spots were just birthmarks, not a sickness that could make him die.

Questions blurted out of my mouth. "What the heck is that disease? How will we know if it grows? Does it hurt? So when will we know if he's going to die? What else did the doctor say?"

Sniffling and eyes watering, she impatiently answered only a few of my questions before cutting me off. "I need to go lie down for a while."

My brothers were not outwardly upset by the news and quickly took off, returning to their normal activities. Terry was eight years older than Jeff, Gary was six years older, and neither had much in common with him. I was four years older and hung out with Jeff a lot. I loved to take care of my little brother; I felt like his second mother.

Worried, I ran off to find Jeff. He was watching his favorite cartoons in the rec room, seeming like his normal self. I wouldn't have guessed that he had just been told by the doctor that he could die.

"Mom just told us what the doctor said. How're you doing?" I sat next to him and put my arm around his shoulder, wishing I could make it all better.

Jeff shrugged. "Fine, I guess. I don't know what to think." His attention was directed at his show, and I could tell I would not be able to get much out of him.

I wanted to throw questions at him but didn't. Was he OK? Was he worried? Could I do anything? What exactly did the doctor say? But I knew bothering him in the middle of cartoons would not get me what I wanted.

"OK, well, I'll be up in my room if you want to talk about it."

"I might come see you when my show's over," he said without looking up from the TV.

After dinner, Jeff came into my room and flopped on my bed. He stared in silence at the ceiling for a moment. Finally, he spoke. "So what's heaven like?"

I wasn't ready for Jeff to be thinking about his own death. Talking about God was common because God was a big part of my life, but the real possibility of Jeff going to heaven confused me.

In my fourteen-year-old wisdom, I said, "I know it's a happy place where bad things don't happen. It's like Disneyland. Maybe there's lots of ice cream and rides and you can do whatever you want. You won't be sick anymore, and no one can tease you. You'll be able to see Jesus for sure."

Jeff suddenly got a worried look on his face. "Will I be able to talk to you anymore?"

My heart was pounding as I thought about it. Would I be able to talk to *him* anymore?

"You might be able to hear me when I pray, but I won't be able to hear you. But it'll be OK. God will take care of you. And I'll definitely see you when I get there," I said.

"Will it hurt to die?" he asked, picking at his nails.

"Nope. Jesus will make sure that you won't feel anything," I said with authority. "Are you scared about dying?"

"Yeah, a little."

"It'll be OK. Whenever you feel scared, you can always pray and ask Jesus to make you feel better. In fact, let's just pray right now." I grabbed his hand, and with our eyes squeezed shut, we asked Jesus to help him and to make him be OK.

Remarkably, Jeff's tumor never grew, and eventually it disappeared. I believe Jesus healed that tumor. But twenty years later, it was a different tumor and a different diagnosis—terminal cancer. As a child, Jeff wondered what it would be like to be in heaven, while I prayed he wouldn't have to find out; now he wondered if he was even worthy enough to get there, while I prayed that he would be healed of all his doubt.

Tamura Arthun

CHAPTER 1

Jeff's New Job, 1999

THE SMALL VIDEO SUPPLY STORE held my brother hostage for far too many years. They underpaid him, demanded he work overtime whenever they wanted him to, and took advantage of his fear of being jobless. After six difficult years, Jeff finally took me up on my offer to help him find a new job.

At first, Jeff struggled to complete job applications because he lacked the confidence that he could even find a better job. Eager to make a change, he was still easily overwhelmed by the process. He had few job skills and had received only a high school diploma; therefore, he usually judged himself unqualified before even trying.

Finally, Jeff invited me into his sparsely furnished apartment to help him with job applications. I had only visited his house two other times because his compulsive routines often conflicted with my schedule.

"I figured we could work at my kitchen table…if that's OK?" he asked, pointing to a little round table. A neatly folded newspaper, two notepads, and a few pens were painstakingly set out to make a work space.

"Works fine for me. Looks like you have everything ready." I pulled one of the wooden chairs away from the table and sat.

He opened the fridge door and peered inside. "Do you want something to drink?"

"No, thanks." I shook my empty cup. "I just had a latte."

"I didn't think to get snacks or anything." He opened the cupboard. "Are you hungry?"

"No. Really, I'm fine. I didn't come over to eat; I came over to find you a new job."

"I know, but I should've thought to get muffins or something." He closed the cupboard and settled into his own seat, a can of pop in one hand. For about a half hour, we scoured local newspapers and followed up on other job openings he had heard about but previously ignored. I did most of the pushing, organizing possibilities, and suggesting various jobs as I saw them.

"Did you think about trying to get on at Boeing?"

"I don't want to work there. I heard you have to start by doing graveyard shift, and I don't want to work nights."

"What about that job where Frank works?" I asked.

"No. I'd have to drive to the north end…" He took a swig of pop and sighed. "There's too much traffic, and I wouldn't want to waste that much time just driving back and forth to a job."

"It might just be worth it if they pay you well enough."

He shook his head slightly while chewing on his lip. "Not to me. It wouldn't be worth the stress."

"It was just a suggestion. We don't have to think about it right now," I said.

I was on the verge of giving up for the day when something in the classifieds caught my eye. "I think this job would be perfect for you." I slid the newspaper across the table, pointing to the description.

"Yeah, right. I don't know how to drive a forklift." He grimaced, tossing the paper onto the pile of other rejected opportunities.

"Would you just read on?" I glared and pushed the paper back. "It says they'll train you, and no experience is necessary. It pays five bucks more an hour than you're making now."

"I don't know." He slumped, his eyes scanning the small print. "What if I can't do it?"

"And what if you can?" I leaned across the table. "You have some of the other skills they've listed, so why not give it a try? The only way you're gonna know is if you give it a shot."

"Fine, but if I don't like it"—he paused, biting on his fingernail—"then I'll just have to start all over again."

If my mom had been with us, that would've been the point at which she would've lost her patience with Jeff's negative attitude, and she would've told him to just stay in his current job and be miserable. Frustration started to build in me, but unlike my mom, I never would've shown it, because I felt sorry for Jeff.

I reached across the table and patted his hand. "I know you're scared of change, but you have to try. The job you have is terrible, and you'll never get ahead if you don't try something new. Let's just fill out the application and see what happens. What do you say?"

"OK. I guess it doesn't hurt to send in the application. I need to do something." His scowl gave way to a slight smile as he scooted himself up to the table.

We chatted as we completed the last of the applications. We attached his resume and sent them out, finally overcoming the first step of potentially changing his life.

"I'm really proud of you for hanging in there. I know it's hard for you to push yourself. Now we just have to wait for one of them to call you back."

"Thanks for helping me, and I'm sorry for getting snappy. Sometimes it just pops out."

"No worries. I understand. Just make sure you let me know when one of them calls you for an interview."

"You mean *if* they call me." He rolled his eyes.

"Stop it." I playfully punched his arm. "You have to think positive."

"Yeah, yeah, yeah. That's what I have you for." He pushed my arm away. We hugged. He thanked me and sent me on my way.

Two weeks passed before I received a call from Jeff.

"Hello," I said. "How's it going?"

"Hey, remember those applications I sent in? I didn't get two of the jobs, but a guy for the forklift job just called." Talking fast, he continued before I could get a word in. "I have an interview with them tomorrow."

"That's great."

"I know, but I'm super nervous."

"You can do it," I said. "Just say a prayer before you go into the interview. I'll be praying for you the whole time."

"I just…I just don't know if I can do it, and—"

"Enough! You have to stop focusing on the negative. Now, what time is your interview?"

"Umm, it's at three in the afternoon, and I took a vacation day so I can get there early in case traffic is bad."

"You're going to do just fine. Just remember, they'll teach you everything you need to know."

"Well, I guess the worst thing that could happen is that it doesn't work out."

"Seriously, you are pushing my last nerve. We're trying to think positive here," I said. "Just get some rest, and try not to worry too much."

"OK. I'll call you after I'm done. Love you. Thanks again for all your help."

"Love you too. Don't forget to pray."

I paced back and forth across the kitchen floor, waiting to hear all about Jeff's interview. He should have called an hour ago. I was certain that he would notice all my missed calls. I called my mom, but she had not heard from him either, leaving both of us quite concerned.

I dialed his number again and pressed the phone against my ear. Four long rings passed before he picked up.

"Hello." He sounded as if he had been sleeping.

"Finally…I was starting to get worried."

He cleared his throat and said, "Sorry. I didn't mean to worry you. I'm just having a hard time and wanted to compose my thoughts before I called you and Mom."

My stomach dropped. "What happened?"

"Just sick with nerves."

"So did you do the interview?"

"Yeah. They offered me the forklift job—"

"That's awesome," I said. "So why are you nervous?"

"Well, don't be mad at me"—a heavy sigh echoed through the phone—"but I declined it and took a different job there."

"OK…what's so wrong with that? Why do you think I would be mad about that?"

"I got so nervous just thinking about all the pressure there could be with the forklift job that I puked all over the parking lot. So I went back inside and told the guy I didn't think I could handle the stress of the forklift job, and he offered me a job on the assembly line instead."

"OK, but I'm still not seeing what's so wrong."

"Well, you know how the forklift job paid five dollars more than I make now? The assembly line job only pays two dollars more an hour."

"It's still better than what you make now. I'm sad your anxiety got so bad, but I would never get mad at you for something like that anyway. I'm super glad you landed a new job. They obviously liked you."

"I'm worried Mom's going to be disappointed that I didn't at least try the forklift job." He took a deep breath. "But it's just not worth the extra money for me to feel stressed every day."

"I'm sure she'll be happy you're finally getting out of the video store. Just give her a call."

CHAPTER 2

The Invader

SEVERAL MONTHS LATER, I WAS sipping coffee and catching up with colleagues in our shared office at Evergreen Hospital, where I was a social worker. At any one time, I could be responsible for helping a cardiac arrest patient, doing a psychiatric evaluation for a suicidal patient, or helping with a drug overdose case. But I usually ended up with the cases that involved death because helping patients at the end of life and their families was my passion.

Our days typically began with a group discussion of the cases, so the room was noisy as the tasks were being divided up. Before we left the office, our supervisor interrupted the chatter.

"Hey, Tammy? It's your mom," she called across the room.

I felt a jolt of adrenaline as I hustled over to the phone. My mother would never call me at work.

"Hi, Mom. Is everything OK?"

"Jeff…" Her voice quivered. "Jeff has a mass."

"What?"

"He went to the doctor this morning, and the doctor noticed something, so he sent him right over for an ultrasound, and they saw a mass."

"Don't worry, Mom. It's gonna be OK. Not all masses are cancerous—we just need to wait for more tests," I assured her. Several coworkers watched in concern as I started to pace, tears filling my eyes. "Where's he now?"

"I tried to get him to come over here, but you know your brother. God forbid he misses work. He's certainly not going to stay home and take care of himself like he should. I even told him that a mother sometimes just needs to see that her kid's OK, but he insisted that he was just fine."

"At least he's not too upset to work. I know this is hard on you, but we just have to support him right now."

An overhead page from the critical-care unit was calling for me.

"I gotta go, Mom. I'll call you later."

I hung up and stood motionless, staring at the dreary December weather outside my window. My colleagues stopped chattering and moved closer to me—they recognized this reaction from working with families in crisis.

"My brother has a mass. It's not good. He's been bruising a lot, some as big as my hand, and he's had some unusual stomach pains."

I tried not to break down, but I couldn't keep my composure. Vaguely, I heard my supervisor send another social worker to answer my page, and then she suggested that I take the rest of the day to be with my family.

My job as a critical-care social worker required me to comfort patients and families as they faced fear, loss, and grief. Now I was the one being comforted, and it disoriented and confused me. I accepted the offer and rushed out of the office, desperate to talk to my brother and determined to come up with a plan. As I drove away from the hospital, with my windows rolled up, it finally felt safe to scream.

"I can't believe this is happening. God, why does it have to be Jeff? It's not fair to him—he's been through enough. Let him be all right, please. Heal him like you did with the brain tumor."

My teary eyes made it difficult to focus on the gray-and-white lined highway ahead. I needed to regain my composure, or there would be more than one tragedy today. I could do this. I had to do this. I couldn't help Jeff if I was out of control. I needed to call Jeff, even though he would get annoyed that I called his work. Who in the world goes to work after receiving a diagnosis like this anyway?

I pulled off the highway and dialed his work number. "Can I speak to Jeff Longley, please?" I asked the operator. I took several slow, deep breaths as I waited, trying to control my nerves. I could do this. I needed to stay calm and matter-of-fact so Jeff would not be alarmed by my panic.

Pretending to be calm, I said, "I heard the doctor found a mass."

"Yeah. Lucky me. I guess I won the lottery with this one," he said.

I swallowed, trying to clear the lump in my throat. "Did the doc tell you where he thinks the mass is?"

"Somewhere in my stomach. They said it's near my adrenal gland, but they're not exactly sure."

His apathy left me wondering if he was downplaying the problem. He always ignored his health problems, hoping they would go away if he left them alone. For that matter, he avoided dealing with anything that caused him stress.

"OK, so what's next? Do you need to see a specialist? Are you going to make an appointment?" Rapid-fire questions poured out of my mouth before I could stop them.

"I don't know what I'm doing next. But don't worry; it'll be OK. I'll call you after work—I'm in the middle of something, and I need to go."

"OK. I'll be at Mom's house, so just come over there the minute you get off."

I felt Jeff was taking it far too lightly, but I was reassured knowing I would see him after work. I pulled back onto the highway, now eager to see my mother, comfort her, and be comforted by her. When I arrived at my parents' house, Mom was curled up on the couch, crying. I sat next to her, wrapped my arms around her, and cried too.

A few moments passed before she muttered softly, "I'm surprised to see you. I thought you needed to work."

"I did, but I want to be here instead."

"You didn't have to come. I'll be OK. Did you talk to Jeff?"

"Yes. He said he was going to come over when he got off work," I said.

"I don't know what I'm going to do if something happens to him." She slowly rocked her head side to side, gazing blankly out the window. "I just can't take it…I just can't take it. This cannot be happening to me." She repeated it like a mantra.

I wanted to interrupt her so that we could talk about Jeff, but I felt I would be dismissing her feelings. It was a familiar pattern between us:

Jeff developed a problem, Mom took it on as if it were happening to her, and I tried to help Jeff fix the problem while making my mom feel better in the process.

Trying to divert her attention, I asked, "Have you called Dad yet?"

"Yes, but he said that work was really busy, but he would try to get off early."

"I can run to the store and get stuff for dinner if you want," I said.

She looked at me with sad eyes and pouty lips. "You don't need to do that. I hate to have you go through all that trouble. I'm sure I can throw something together."

"Mom, it's not a problem. I would be making dinner if I were at home, and besides, Jeff will probably want dinner when he gets here."

When Jeff walked in the front door, Mom launched herself off the couch to meet him. They embraced and cried together for a minute.

Fully composed, I hugged him and then got down to the business at hand. "So do you have the names of the specialists that the doctor recommended?"

"Yeah. I need to call and make an appointment." He sighed. "But I can't afford to miss work, so I don't know when I'm supposed to do that. The last thing I need is to be fired because I'm using too many sick days."

"They're not going to fire you because you're sick." My eyes met his. "Do you want me to try to get something set up?"

"You can if you want. You probably know what to say better than I do." Jeff sat heavily into the recliner, glancing at the clock. "What are we doing for dinner?"

"Tammy's making spaghetti," Mom said.

I ignored Jeff's attempt to deter my questioning. "I'll help you get through this and will do whatever it takes to get you to the best doctors in town."

"Thanks," he said, scrubbing at his face with his hands. "I don't even know where to start."

Both of my older brothers called me shortly after I left Mom's house to hear exactly what I thought was happening with Jeff. Mom had called each of them earlier to give them the news, but they were reluctant to take her words as fact, given how emotional she was during the calls. I arranged a family dinner to take place at our parents' house over the weekend so that we could spend time together and get caught up.

As I pulled up the gravel driveway to my parents' house, I was surprised that my brothers had not yet arrived for our family dinner. I was welcomed at the front door by barking dogs and the comforting aroma of Mom's famous roast beef. Dad was half-asleep in his overstuffed recliner, the blaring television unable to keep his attention. Mom was chopping lettuce, tomatoes, and cucumbers in the kitchen.

Dad lifted his chin up toward me as I leaned down to kiss his cheek. "How you doing?" he asked.

"Hi, Tammy," Mom called out.

"Hello," I hollered and then turned my attention back to Dad. "I'm doing fine. What about you?"

"Well, I got up this morning, so I can't complain." This was his typical response whenever someone asked him that question.

I went into the kitchen, sat my bag of rolls and a pie on the counter, and gave Mom a quick hug. "How are you doing?"

"I'm OK. I didn't sleep at all last night. I'm really struggling with this whole thing. Dad's been having a hard time too." Her sullen tone left me scrambling for words. Fortunately, the barking dogs provided a perfect distraction as they welcomed Terry at the front door.

"Hey," he bellowed as he reached down to scratch the dogs' heads, his upbeat voice drowning out the still-blaring TV.

"Hello," I said.

"Is that a new recipe I smell?" He razzed Mom as he leaned his husky chest down to give her a hug.

"I made my roast beef. Is that OK?" she hesitantly asked, even though she knew it was a family favorite.

"Of course. I'm just teasing you. You know I love your roast." Terry rolled his eyes as he left the kitchen.

Looking out the front window, I waved at Gary, who was strolling up the driveway. He lived just a few houses up the street from Mom and Dad.

He cautiously opened the front door to avoid bumping into the jumping dogs. "Hi," he said, visually surveying the room, taking note of the emotional temperature of each of us, especially Mom.

He kissed my cheek and then asked, "How are you doing?"

"I'm hanging in there."

"Jeff just pulled in," Dad said, turning off the TV.

Moments later, Jeff flung open the front door. "Come on, Rusty," he called over his shoulder, patting his hand against his thigh. Rusty, Jeff's beloved cock-a-poo, rushed through the door and bounced up and down on the other dogs.

"Well, well, if it isn't the honored guest," Terry joked. We all laughed.

"I'm honored, all right. That roast smells good, Mom," Jeff said.

"She made it special just for you," Terry said. "You know—nothing like Mom's roast for your last supper."

Laughter erupted, as it usually did whenever Terry was around.

"Terry!" Mom slapped him on the arm.

"It might just might be." Jeff's grin disappeared. "And go figure that my stomach is too upset to eat it." I couldn't remember the last time just my brothers, my parents, and I had sat at a dinner table. Growing up, it was part of our family routine to sit together for dinner—six o'clock sharp every night, except weekends. But things changed once we moved out of the house and moved on with our lives.

That night, however, we sat around the table just like old times. We talked and joked about anything and everything—Terry's job, Gary's wife, Dad's racing, Mom's garden. It was wonderful, except that we ignored the great big elephant in the room—Jeff's tumor. Somehow, we managed to avoid it for the entire dinner. After an hour of chatting, my three brothers got ready to leave. To my great surprise, they hugged one another before walking out the door. My brothers do not hug one another—ever. Terry and Gary assured Jeff that they would be there to support him in any way he needed. I believed them.

CHAPTER 3

The Diagnosis

As soon as I decided to take charge, I started frantically making calls. At last, the MRI, the labs, the specialist, and all the other necessary medical appointments were scheduled. Jeff was obsessive about many things, but his health care was, ironically, never one of them. I, on other hand, became obsessed, seeking every bit of information I could pry from the doctors.

Mom, Dad, and I went with Jeff to the first specialist appointment, an oncologist, where our fears were confirmed that the mass was cancerous. The oncologist had never encountered adrenal cancer before—most adrenal tumors are benign and treatable. Additionally, it had already spread to multiple organs.

Although that appointment left us feeling hopeless, I had scheduled an appointment with a surgeon for just an hour later to give us a second opinion. This surgeon worked with me in critical care, and I had seen him successfully take on many challenging cases. My hope was that he could help; Jeff was less optimistic.

When we entered the room, the nurse had Jeff sit on the edge of a white exam bed. He clenched his hands in his lap, legs dangling as he tried to manage his stress. Mom and Dad sat fidgeting while I shamelessly paced back and forth. Finally, the surgeon lightly knocked and nudged the door open.

"Hello, Mr. Longley. I am Dr. Jones. Do you go by Jeff or Jeffrey?"

"Jeff is fine."

"OK." He smiled at me. "Good to see you, Tammy. And is this your mom and dad?"

"Yes, this is my dad, Ken, and my mom, Pat."

Pleasantries out of the way, my hand grasping Jeff's, the surgeon went straight to the details. "I have reviewed all of Jeff's MRI reports and scans, and I am afraid it is worse than I initially thought." His eyes moved away, staring at the blank wall behind us, clearly uncomfortable with giving the bad news.

"The tumors are too large and dangerous for me to remove. I agree with the oncologist that it is the rare type of adrenal cancer, adrenocortical carcinoma, and Jeff needs to be seen by a special surgical team at the University of Washington. However, there is no guarantee the team will attempt to remove the tumors, because they have invaded the main vein leading back to his heart, his liver, and possibly his kidney."

My parents stared intently at the floor, listening quietly as the surgeon spoke. None of us dared to make eye contact for fear he would utter the words: Jeff was dying.

"I am truly sorry, Jeff. This cancer is something I've never seen before. In fact, this type is so rare that I can't even begin to give you a prognosis. I will do my best to get you an appointment at the UW as quickly as possible." The surgeon looked apologetically around the room, nodded at me, and quietly dismissed himself. We sat in silence for a moment, wondering what was next.

"Well, sounds like I'm screwed," Jeff said.

"Who knows? The other surgeon may have a different view of the situation," I said, not really believing my words but attempting to reassure my family.

"OK, let's just wait and see what he says. If nothing else, it has made for an interesting day." He laughed, hopping off the table.

I laughed as well, not knowing how else to respond. Mom kept her eyes away, gazing out to nowhere in particular. She finally reached her arm out to give Jeff a pat on the back. Dad had no words. He followed a few steps behind as I led the group out of the hospital.

CHAPTER 4

Pre-Op

After Jeff's diagnosis, I called him daily and saw him a few times every week. Each visit he looked a bit worse, as if he was fading away bit by bit. Dark circles encompassed his eyes, and his skin had turned a dusty gray. As he deteriorated, his body bloated and his face appeared swollen. Nausea and vomiting disrupted his daily routine, causing him to miss work. Unlike minor illnesses, these were symptoms Jeff could not push himself through. There was no denying that the tumor was growing, and slowly my family began to accept that death was possible.

When Jeff and I were young, we used each other as sounding boards, discussing the events of our day and any problems we encountered. It helped us feel better. But since the cancer, our conversations were short and limited. Some days he was even too sick to engage at all. Sadly, he was never too sick to think about the possibility of his death.

It was difficult to watch Jeff ride the roller coaster of life and not be able to stop it or help him off. At times the helplessness overwhelmed me. Questions constantly spun in my mind, one after another, never leaving me enough time to come to any closure. I reverted to a childhood work-around, journaling. And once I did, each page began to hold my sanity together.

I encouraged Jeff to do the same, to write his symptoms, feelings, and thoughts in a notebook, as way to help him cope too.

Jeff's Journal—January 29, 2000

Well, here we go. This is the start of a journey, and I don't know where it will take me. Finding out you have cancer is a blow mentally. Physically it's day by day. I am scared and numb. Some days it's like normal, but others it's just wacky. The support I've gotten has been incredible. The spiritual support is really flattering. I need all the prayers I can get. Right now I question my faith. I want to be a much stronger Christian. You know, have a real relationship with Jesus. If I stand outside myself, I don't see God in me. I see a hypocrite, lots of words, but no actions. Now I am working on changing while I still have time. I don't want to be a religious nut, but there is more there. I don't know where this road is going, but at this point it doesn't matter. I'm along for the ride, and where I end up, we will have to see.

Tammy's Journal—February 4, 2000

Journal 1—The past five weeks have been difficult, at best. Sadness has consumed me like a vulture devouring a fresh carcass. My heart is aching, and I am overwhelmed by my thoughts and emotions. I am starving for answers, yet don't know where to find them.

My dear Jeff, my heart is already aching just knowing you will likely die. And why you and not me? I have done nothing to deserve life more than you. Yes, I have been frustrated with your negativity, but surely that can't be the reason for your illness. What stopped you from having a better life, to have true happiness? Your suffering may soon be over, but I will still be left to contemplate your journey. I can't imagine what has been going through your head, yet I know there is more depth than what meets the eye. I will be here each step of the way, no matter the sacrifice.

It was an overcast day when Mom, Dad, Jeff, and I silently made the drive to the University of Washington to see the surgeon. We each attempted to begin a conversation, but silence had become our new language—platitudes and reassurances weren't working anymore. Eventually, we all gave up and sat, wondering if this surgeon could really help Jeff.

We entered the waiting room, which was filled with wooden chairs covered in busy fabric. My friend Midge, reliably prompt and always steady, sat facing the entrance door. As we walked in, she rested her magazine on her lap and smiled warmly. She not only brought moral support, but she also had my favorite coffee resting on the magazine table. Jeff and I went to the front desk, where a woman in her midtwenties helped us. Not long after we took a seat, a nurse called out Jeff's name and motioned him to follow her. My parents and I stood up with Jeff, and together we walked down the wallpapered hall into a small room.

There was an exam table covered with white paper, slightly angled away from the wall, where the nurse instructed Jeff to sit. She took his vitals, informed us the doctor would be in shortly, and closed the door behind her. A large luminescent picture of Mount Rainier attempted to brighten the otherwise drab room. The hum of the heater, along with muffled noises outside the door, could be heard through our silence. Finally, a brisk knock on the door startled us. The doctor entered, wearing a traditional white coat with *Dr. Smith* stitched above the pocket. I examined him carefully—this man could be the one to save Jeff. Dr. Smith had dark skin, a slightly graying goatee, warm brownish-black eyes, and thinning black hair. He shook Jeff's hand, then each of ours. Before he even began to speak, we were all close to tears, anticipating the next piece of bad news. "Jeff, I reviewed your films, and I also consulted with several other physicians on your case." Dr. Smith spoke directly to Jeff.

Barely making eye contact with the rest of us in the room, he continued. "As you know, you have adrenal cancer, which is extremely rare; only one case in a million per year. I believe I can get most of it with surgery, but the cancer has spread to your liver and inferior vena cava. It will clearly be a life-threatening surgery, but without the surgery, you will likely die within six months."

"Is there a chance you can remove all the cancer—I mean could he be cured?" I asked, fighting to contain my emotion while searching for any bit of good news.

"Let's just say we can buy him some time—perhaps five years or so." Dr. Smith answered.

Jeff's face was wet and pale, and his voice shook. "Well, I guess we don't have a choice. Let's do what we need to do. Five years is better than six months, I suppose." With Jeff's words, Dr. Smith turned, picked up the phone, and called the scheduling nurse. The nurse escorted my parents and Jeff back to the waiting area. I stayed to ask a few more questions and to work out scheduling details. I also asked Dr. Smith whether proceeding was the right thing to do under the circumstances. We discussed quality of life, and he assured me it was the best thing to do, despite the real possibility Jeff might not survive long enough to reach the recovery room. We settled on a date for the surgery, February 14. The procedure was expected to take twelve to fourteen hours and would require three different surgeons.

When I returned to the waiting area, I noticed Mom crying in Midge's arms. I instinctively searched the area for Jeff. After a moment, I saw an odd sight through the waiting room window: Dad and Jeff clinched in a hug. After a few moments, they let go of each other and reached up to wipe their eyes before they turned toward the entry door. I had never seen my brother and father embrace before that day. I knew they loved each other, but the men in my family were not affectionate with one another. A pat on the back or punch to the arm might be as physical as they got. Never a hug, never like I saw between Jeff and Dad at that moment.

As the surgery date approached, each day began to feel darker, made more ominous as Jeff's overall health continued to decline. Mom and I looked for ways to manage our fears. Both of us had the same hope—that Jeff could finally find peace, either through his death or hopefully through the miracle of his recovery. If he survived the surgery, he might have a new appreciation for his life and for his relationships with others. If he died, then his struggle would finally be over.

Jeff, on the other hand, started down a somewhat surprising path to find his peace: he began seeking assurance of his salvation. He met with several different Christians to discuss their interpretation of the scripture related to salvation and heaven. But he looked most forward to meeting my friend Keith, who had brain cancer and was facing death himself.

"I am excited for you to meet my brother," I told Keith as we drove to Jeff's house.

He smiled. "I'm glad I can give back. I remember going through the phase where I questioned my own salvation. I know what it's like to wonder."

And he did. Being diagnosed with terminal brain cancer was one thing, but having four children under the age of eight made his situation even more tragic. Jeff opened the front door, unintentionally stared at the large scar across Keith's bald head, and then extended his hand. "Hi, I'm Jeff. Come in."

Jeff hugged me as I passed through the door in front of Keith.

"It's nice to meet you. I've heard a lot about you." Keith sat down on the couch next to me.

"I'm sure you have," Jeff joked. "You know my sister; she likes to talk." They both laughed.

"So Tammy tells me you've been struggling with your faith?" Keith wasted no time getting to the purpose of our visit.

"Yeah, it's been a struggle ever since I got diagnosed. I just get worried that maybe I…" Jeff lowered his eyes to the floor and cleared his throat. "I might not go to heaven or something."

"I know that feeling." Keith paused, waiting for Jeff to look at him before he continued. "I even had the thought that God might be punishing me by giving me brain cancer."

"How'd you get through it?" Jeff asked, his eyes a little desperate. I listened carefully, but as much as I tried, I could not relate.

Keith told Jeff about his journey and all the ways he sought comfort from others. He talked about how God had answered his prayers and finally gave him peace about his own likely death. "I brought you a journal to write in if you want to—it really helped me to put my thoughts down on paper." Keith handed Jeff a yellow journal that had a handwritten note on the inside cover:

"Remember it is HIS faithfulness, not your faith that holds you up. It is HIS love for you that secures your place in heaven. And it is HIS grace toward you that allows you to live free in Christ. All the pressure is on HIM, not you."

"Wow, you didn't need to do that. Thank you. I just started journaling the other day, in fact." Jeff welled up. "I sure hope I get to that place of peace."

"You will. It just takes time. I just want you to know that I'm always here if you need someone to talk to. I know how hard it can be to have cancer and to struggle with your faith."

Jeff read those words each day as he got sicker. He was trying to find salvation, but it became a more difficult task than he expected. Helplessly, I watched Jeff frantically search for his salvation—for his personal peace. I too searched—for a peace of a different kind.

Tammy's Journal—February 9, 2000

Journal 2—As I stand still in the sunlight, listening to birds go about their business, I wonder why the world won't stop for my aching heart. Is Jeff's life and my pain truly so insignificant? Only five more days before God reveals his plan for Jeff's life, and only then will the answers to my many questions become clear. I find it difficult to enjoy my own life knowing that Jeff's in such pain, both physically and emotionally. I am becoming overwhelmed with anger toward what I see as the failings of most everyone around me. Why are they not as consumed with Jeff as I am? I feel so alone, even though Mom and Dad are in this with me; they are struggling to keep themselves afloat. I can barely stomach the fact that my brothers haven't been there for me, but it feels unbearable that they can't support Jeff at such a time as this, especially knowing that it means so much to him to know they care. We promised that we would support one another through this as a united family. If they don't even have the time to make a call or stop by for a visit, then what else is worthwhile? I am angry and discouraged because when he is gone they will never know what his life stood for—what was important to him—who he became. I am uncomfortable harboring such hurtful feelings toward those I love, but I know it would only be damaging to say them out loud.

Why do so many avoid this, yet never stop to realize that by running away, they are still running the race of life—just in the wrong direction. This is real life—the pain, the uncertainty, the contemplation, the sorrow, the compassion, the hope, and even the death. We must embrace all these emotions for they are all that we will know as the truth. Even if you try to bury them, you will still carry them in your soul. Please God help me. Despite knowing that You are in control, I still feel the agony and sorrow. Please let Jeff feel the sunlight on his face and know that it is YOU healing his heart, his soul. Oh God, let me feel your presence.

Jeff's Journal—February 13, 2000
I know these could be the last words I write. I know it is all up to God. I am medicated most of the time, and I sleep a lot. Yesterday was so emotional because both of my brothers called, and I sort of lost it, crying on the phone with each of them. I know they love me, and it is hard to see the family go through this. Just like me, they are along for the ride. Mom made me mashed potatoes and fried chicken for dinner; hopefully it won't be my last meal.

CHAPTER 5

Valentine's Day

By five in the morning on February 14, all four of us were awake. Jeff and I spent the night at our parents' house because we had to leave so early in the morning, but none of us slept much, if any. I gave up trying when the smell of coffee wafted into my bedroom. This could be my baby brother's last day alive; there was no way I could face it without coffee. Dad sat with my mom in dead silence. I filled my cup and joined them, silently watching the clock. Jeff was not allowed to eat or drink, so he rested nervously in bed. Our raw emotions were so close to the surface that we could barely speak without our eyes filling with tears.

"Well, let's go get this done," Jeff mumbled, shuffling into the living room dressed in blue sweatpants and a gray sweatshirt. Mom, Dad, Jeff, and I silently climbed into the car and rode to the hospital. The only sounds in the car that morning were my mother's sniffles and my fidgeting. The hospital was about twenty minutes away, almost an eternity when tension in the air was so thick. Jeff silently stared out the window, biting on his fingernails. I attempted to pray, but that led to crying, so I quickly stopped.

Just as Dad turned off the car, Jeff spouted a final reminder to Mom. "Now don't forget to pay my bills. And don't use any pens besides the blue one when you write in my checkbook. You know how I am. I like things to stay neat."

"I got it, Jeff. We've been over this at least five times. Don't worry. I think I can handle the job." She smiled involuntarily. Jeff's organized life left him with only four household bills, so managing his finances was not exactly challenging.

There were several friends and family in the lobby as we entered the hospital. Only a few of them accompanied us to the surgery pre-op area.

"Jeff Longley?" a friendly nurse called from the swinging doors, approaching us when she saw his timid wave.

"Hi, Jeff. My name is Lori. I will be the nurse preparing you for surgery. Please come with me."

"You're coming with me, aren't you, sis?" As he looked at me, it felt as though I was looking at an injured puppy.

"Can I come with him?"

"Absolutely. That would be more than fine," she said.

We walked down to a small room with the standard white hospital bed and wooden chairs. "Here's your gown. It closes in the back." The nurse's instructions were simple and direct. "Take everything off and place it in the garment bag in the closet. I need to take a few vitals, and then the rest of your family may join you until the surgeon arrives to answer any final questions you or your family might have. Do you have any questions now?"

"No. Do you, Tammy?"

"Not now." The routine was very matter of fact—a nice distraction from the emotional trauma fighting to get out of his head. Once the nurse finished her duties, she invited the rest of the family into the presurgery room with us.

Dad made little eye contact with anyone as he paced the room. Mom sat next to Jeff on the bed and held his hand. Gary tried to lighten the room with small talk, while Terry attempted to pretend that none of this was really happening. I sat on the other side of Jeff doing my best to appear in control—if not for Jeff, then for myself. I would not fall apart today. Not now. Dr. Smith arrived shortly and assured everyone that he anticipated the procedure would turn out well. He reminded us to expect that Jeff would be in surgery between twelve and fourteen hours and asked us to be patient. His staff would do their best to keep us up to date regarding the progress of the surgery.

He put his hand on Jeff's shoulder and asked, "Well, Jeff, are you ready to get going?"

The doctor's simple question opened the door that held Jeff's fears and emotions inside. Jeff could no longer pretend he was OK. He began to sob.

I grabbed his hand to comfort him, but what could I say? His eyes reflected his terror—he was petrified, completely terrified of dying. Weeks of meaningless reassurance made it laughable to tell him it would be all right. I began to pray aloud, hoping God could reach him—that maybe Jeff had been able to find some peace in his salvation in the past weeks or maybe that I could help him find that peace now.

Everyone in the room had a final chance to hug Jeff and left slowly and tearfully. I stayed with him. One family member was allowed to accompany him to the surgery room. No one even thought to object, since I handled all the medical aspects of Jeff's illness—and, really, the emotional support as well. In the past weeks, I had accepted that my mom could not emotionally cope with the pressure building inside her, and it seemed best she stay behind. The nurse gently tucked a blanket around Jeff on the gurney and began the journey down the cold, stark hallway. Jeff began wailing, loud enough to create an echo as he rolled over the white tile floor. My throat tightened as I attempted to swallow my sorrow. Jeff's sweaty hand grasped mine as I walked briskly to keep up with the nurse's pace. I prayed for his strength and courage.

We turned a corner, and the rolling bed came to a stop while the nurse pushed the B button on the elevator panel. She made small talk while we waited, but the words seemed to bounce off my ears into the air. The door opened, and she maneuvered the bed into the stainless-steel elevator.

As the doors began to close, a gut-twisting scream came from my little brother. "I don't want to die. Please don't let me die," he begged, louder each time. His hollow eyes penetrated mine. "Tammy, I can't—I just can't. Please help me."

I laid my heart over his and cradled him in my arms, my tears washing over his, but I couldn't speak.

The nurse confidently said, "You have one of the best surgeons in the hospital. If I had to trust someone with my life, it would be him. I will be here when you wake up, and Tammy will too. We will get you through this." Tears poured down her face, but she gave Jeff the words that could not get past my grief.

The elevator doors opened to the basement floor, and we were on the move again down a drab, windowless hallway. The gurney came to a quick halt at silver double doors with signs saying Authorized Personnel Only.

"OK, this is where you need to say goodbye." Her warm eyes met mine.

I bent over and looked straight into his swollen eyes. "I love you, buddy, and I trust that God will bring you out of this safely. I will be praying nonstop. It's time for us to walk our talk and give it up to God." My arms embraced his cold body, and I held him tightly for maybe the last time, not wanting to let go.

His countenance changed, and he relaxed. As if to comfort me, he said, "I love you too. Everything will be OK. You're right; we just have to believe."

I stood back, let go of his hand slowly, and forced a smile as he rolled away from me, through sterile doors to an unknown world. As the doors slammed shut, I dropped to my knees and buried my face in my lap. My strength was gone, and I could no longer pretend otherwise. My stomach felt hollow, and my heart cracked into tiny pieces. My back leaned against a wall, arms braced against my bent knees; I tried to quiet myself, worried someone would hear me. Normally, it would be a social worker like me extending a hand to a grieving person. But this was not my hospital, and I was not a social worker that day. I was alone and scared. In a moment, I realized this really was happening to me, to my brother, to my family. It was a dreamlike feeling to find myself, a wreck on the floor, on the other side of the crisis. I took some deep breaths, wiped my burning eyes, and composed myself enough to return to my family.

Outside the surgical unit, there was a small, dimly lit waiting room, accent lights highlighting pictures on the walls. I looked down the hall, past the group of family and friends, to focus on my mother. My mom stood as I entered the room, and we hugged.

"They said surgery would be starting within the next half hour. He was doing OK when I left," I told the group.

My mother somehow sensed what I had just experienced and did not ask for the details of my goodbye with Jeff at the operating room doors. It was too intense, too personal, too painful.

We spent the first part of the day trying to pass the time as best we could, speculating, laughing, making small talk, and waiting. The clock moved slowly, and we waited. We watched the silver doors as though waiting for God himself to come through. In fact, we would have greeted anyone with any information on Jeff as if Jesus had returned. We continued to sit, starving for answers.

Four long hours passed, until a doctor came through the door. "Longley family?"

"How is he? Is he OK?" I spoke for all of us. Everyone else waited, barely breathing, as if the sound would make them miss the doctor's words.

"Jeff is doing fine, but this is a very complicated surgery, as you know, and we do expect that it will go for the full fourteen hours. He is hanging in there, though." And as quickly as the doctor had come, he was gone.

"Well, he's still alive, so that must be good for something," someone said. Terry attempted a cheer, but our fear quickly stifled it, and we returned to our vigil.

The day was long and tedious, punctuated by a different surgeon coming out every few hours. Each said as little as possible, yet somehow met the obligation of keeping us informed. A few of us never left, while others came and went. Some brought food and words of encouragement; others merely sat vigilant with us.

Around the fourteenth hour, I finally saw Dr. Smith slowly push through the operating room doors. This was our sign the surgery was finally over. He barely made it into the room before we crowded around him. He let out a deep sigh.

"Well, I think we got it all. At least, we got everything we could see. He's still not out of the woods and has a long road ahead." He took another breath. "There were some complications with his blood pressure, but we were able to stabilize him. We are moving him up to the critical-care unit, where he will likely stay for several days."

"Is he going to live?" Mom boldly asked, speaking for all of us.

"I do believe he will make it," Dr. Smith replied in a cautious tone. "I cannot promise anything, but he is doing as well as we can expect."

He responded to our questions with as few words as possible, appearing exhausted from the fourteen-hour surgery. When I was convinced I would not get any more details from the doctor, I excused myself from the group to search for the CCU where Jeff would be taken. I needed to see him for myself; I was not going to accept someone else's interpretation of the situation, even the surgeon's professional opinion. I entered the CCU, hoping that if I remained calm and confident, someone would give me Jeff's "real" condition. Luckily for me, the nurse preparing Jeff's room had a smile on her face when I walked up to her. As she pulled the blanket back from the bed and began setting up monitors, I introduced myself and told her a bit about my work in critical care. Jeff's soon-to-be nurse became chatty while she worked. I told her about Jeff and his illness, hoping she would know him as someone special and not just another patient.

We talked for a while about Jeff's cancer and how scared my family was about his prognosis. I asked her if she had siblings, and she shared with me that she had a little brother but that he had died. He killed himself, and she was still devastated that she did not get to say goodbye. As she spoke, I warmed up to her and realized she was a special person too, not just another nurse on the floor. It was through our brothers that we bonded as sisters dealing with our shared personal experiences.

We were interrupted by a voice on the intercom. "Your patient is on his way up."

"So do I need to leave?" I asked, hoping I could stay.

"No," she whispered with a shake of her head. "As long as you sit quietly in the corner, I'm OK with you being here. I wish I could have been with my brother."

CHAPTER 6

The Critical-Care Unit

I GASPED AS THEY WHEELED the gurney by me. I was certain they had the wrong person. His face was so swollen that his cheeks extended beyond his ears. His eyelids puffed out, making it impossible to recognize his eyes. This person's body was stretched and distended. There was nothing about him that looked like my brother.

"This is Jeffrey Longley," a male nurse reported to the charge nurse, handing over a clipboard. My eyes widened in shock.

"His pressures have been all over the place. We weren't able to close him up, so he'll have to go back down to surgery in a few days."

He continued to speak, but all I could do was stare at the body on the gurney. Activity had overtaken the room as nurses and doctors worked to get Jeff settled. I moved to a window ledge in the corner of the room and hoped nobody would notice me. While they spoke candidly, I began to understand that Jeff was barely alive and they were apprehensive about his survival.

Burgundy bags of blood slowly fed into his arm while nurses attached monitors and wires to his headboard. I covered my mouth, unable to ignore the gravity of his condition. His body was saturated with sixty pounds of fluid that had kept him alive during surgery. In addition, a ventilator pushed air into his lungs via a tube, a requirement in order to maintain proper air flow.

The skin on his abdomen could not be stretched to close the wound; instead, a plastic wrap–like covering stretched tightly across the gaping hole, exposing whitish-colored intestines. I searched desperately for something familiar in the chaos, and then I saw his blond hair, matted but recognizable.

I went out to the waiting room to update my family on Jeff's condition. The words couldn't leave my mouth fast enough as I gave them the details. I assured them I would be holding vigil until Jeff was out of critical care. To my relief, no one fought me.

My aunt Robin lingered, patting my shoulder, and said, "You should call Clark. He'll want to know."

Clark was very supportive as I tried to get the words past my tight throat a few minutes later. He told me to focus on Jeff for now; he would take care of the girls.

By the time I got back to Jeff's room, a cot had been set out. I lay down on it and attempted to make sense of all that was happening. The monitor and ventilator filled the room with dim lights and white noise. Instead of drifting off, I began to pray that God would either heal Jeff or take him home.

Jeff's condition vacillated between serious and critical during the first forty-eight hours postsurgery. I was hypersensitive to each movement, beep, or comment, trying to predict what might be next.

The doctors remained optimistic that Jeff would recover; I wondered how they could see anything through the multiple issues plaguing him. It amazed me to think Jeff could withstand the severe pain caused by such a radical surgery.

I wanted to reach out and take him to safety and somehow end his suffering. But there was nothing I could do other than sit next to the bed, his swollen hand lying limp in mine. I felt alone, wondering what part of me would be lost if Jeff died. Maybe through my pain God would allow me to help others understand their own pain.

Once the nurse left after her first night check, I cried helplessly until my phone buzzed, startling me back into the present. It was one of Jeff's acquaintances. As soon I heard the words "Jeff will be fine," I knew I didn't want to talk to Jason. He didn't even know Jeff that well, nor did he know a great deal about the surgery. Still, he had the audacity to say, "Jeff will be just fine. Don't worry. I'm praying for you." I wanted to scream. How could he know God's plan when none of the rest of us did? In fact, Jeff wasn't fine—his guts were hanging out of his belly, *and* he was getting ready for another life-threatening surgery. And as if that weren't enough, he had terminal cancer. People only needed to say, "I am thinking of you."

I knew it was hard for others to support someone who was sick, perhaps because they themselves felt helpless, but I didn't care. My brother was fighting to live. I wanted to shelter him from their pressure; he didn't need to worry about letting those people down. Other people just needed to let him be sick so he could get well—either here or in heaven. I trusted that God would do what *he* chooses to do in the end.

The next day, my family and I once again had to confront the possibility of Jeff's death. The surgeon had determined that Jeff was finally stable enough to attempt closing his gaping wound. The longer they waited, the higher the risk of complications and infection. Of course, Jeff was completely unaware of this next risk. His body was alive because of medications, machines, and the grace of God. It was as though Jeff was a silent bystander in his own fight for survival. He returned to the CCU hours after they whisked him away to surgery, his skin stretched so thin it could barely contain the contents of his abdomen despite the many staples keeping it in place.

Each day had something new in store—shortly after the second surgery, Jeff developed pneumonia and a bacterial infection. Lack of sleep and emotional trauma left me with no sense of where I ended and Jeff began. The line separating us got blurrier by the day.

Only eight days after his surgery, Jeff's lung collapsed. In order to keep his lung inflated, the doctors inserted a tube into his side. I stayed with him day and night, waiting for any response but only hearing beeping, whirring machines.

My aunt Robin kept vigil with me and watched Jeff when I left the room for short times. She persuaded me to let her stay for a night so I could go home for a real night of sleep and to see my family. She was like a second mom to me, and growing up I was often at her house. I trusted her. She was always a support to me. I was terrified that if I left the hospital room for even a night, Jeff could take the death turn at any time, and I might not be there. I had missed my best friend Toni's death by an hour, and it had left me feeling empty. I didn't want to take the chance of not being there if he passed on.

But I desperately needed some sleep. My loss of weight and the dark circles under my eyes were bringing unwanted attention from my parents and other family to the fact that I was sleep deprived and not eating well. So I accepted Aunt Robin's offer and anxiously drove home, praying and trusting Jeff would be there when I returned.

Eleven days after the surgery, the doctors decided to remove his breathing tube. They slowly eased him off sedation so he would be awake enough to breathe on his own. He was restless as he came off the medicine, pulling at the tube in his mouth and the IVs in his arm. The nurse restrained his hands, but he continued to struggle. He did not make eye contact or give any indication he knew where he was or was aware of anything happening around him. I had seen this in my patients in the hospital before, and I had often assured family members what to expect and not to worry. My skin still crawled as I watched him gagging on the tube lying uncomfortably deep in his throat.

After a full day of weaning him off his medications, the respiratory therapist received orders to finally remove Jeff's breathing tube. She gently peeled off the white tape holding the tube firmly against his chapped lips. Then with one swift movement, she pulled the tube out, and Jeff was suddenly left to breathe on his own. Jeff's head was thrashing side to side as he violently jerked his arms and legs, trying to free them from the restraints. The therapist's words couldn't penetrate his panicked efforts to escape. Between Jeff's struggling and the loud warning beeps from his monitors, the room became complete chaos.

I sat on the edge of his bed with his restrained hand resting in mine, and I whispered, frantic, "Lord, he has to breathe. Maintain his oxygen—let him be free of this. Please help him breathe on his own."

"Take a deep breath. You need to breathe," the respiratory therapist ordered.

The green numbers on the monitor changed quickly, indicating Jeff's oxygen level was dropping rapidly and his blood pressure had increased dramatically. These alarms were routine for me at work, but they never filled me with the sense of helplessness I felt at that moment.

"What's going on in here?" A nurse rushed in from the hallway.

"Call the doctor—he's not ready."

"You'll be OK, Jeff. Don't worry. You just need a little more time." I continued to pray as my hand tightened.

Raspy grunts came from his throat as he thrashed, unable to cough or clear a passage for air to flow into his lungs. A doctor rushed into the room, and a new breathing tube was urgently threaded down his throat. The alarms shrilled for a few minutes longer, until Jeff's vitals normalized. Once again, he was deeply sedated. The room slowly calmed as the sedation relaxed Jeff.

As the nurse and I cleaned his sweaty body, we noticed a rip over his scarred abdomen. He must have ripped his stitches during his struggle to breathe.

Jeff's return to the ventilator was a setback for my family as well. Dad and Mom had been traumatized when both of my mom's parents died after they were placed on a ventilator. Both of my parents were superstitious and believed being placed on a ventilator was a sign of death. So they had made a pact with Jeff that if he had to go on a ventilator, they would not visit him until the ventilator was removed.

They did come to the hospital but went only as far as the waiting room. There they could have some distance from their past, and present, nightmares.

Prior to surgery, Jeff went along with it as his way of protecting them. Of course, none of them anticipated the pact might last for days, let alone weeks.

The routine was slowly becoming more manageable—in a strange way, even peaceful. Our family and friends kept their vigil in the waiting room. The doctors and nurses did their jobs, shift after shift. And I mostly remained at Jeff's bedside, with visits from Aunt Robin whenever she was around.

A week after the first attempt to take Jeff off the ventilator, the doctor decided it was time to try again. It had been weeks since I had heard Jeff's voice and seen his hazel eyes. I wanted so desperately to talk to him, to reassure him, to be part of his life again.

My cot was pushed snug to the wall under the window—all my belongings tucked away, the chairs neatly folded. Still, the little room felt crowded as nurses and doctors filled the room, ready for the big event. A nurse waited on each side of Jeff near the head of the bed. The respiratory therapist turned down the air pressure on the ventilator. The doctor stood at the foot of the bed, arms crossed in front of his chest. A medical tech watched the blood pressure and oxygen machine. I stood a few feet from them, praying in my head.

"Let's do it," the doctor commanded. And with that, the tape was peeled away from his pale skin and the tube yanked out of his throat.

"Jeff, I need you to take some deep breaths for me," the respiratory therapist firmly directed.

There were a few weak coughs and then a garbled whisper. His voice was nearly impossible to hear. He tried again to clear his raspy throat.

"Can you turn the lights on?"

The staff and I looked from one to another as though we had all missed the punch line to one of Jeff's jokes. This seemed like a silly request considering the bright lights shining directly on his face.

A bit louder, he asked again. "Can you turn the lights on, please?"

CHAPTER 7

Lights Out

SURPRISED, THE DOCTOR LEANED OVER the metal bed rail, flashlight in hand, shining the light first into Jeff's right eye, then the left. He glanced up at the nurse on the opposite side of the bed, and he repeated the process—this time, lifting up Jeff's eyelid as he shined the light directly into his pupil.

"What are you doing, Doctor?" Jeff asked.

"He's not tracking." The rest of the doctor's words were drowned out as I rushed to his bedside. "Not tracking" meant that his pupils were unresponsive. As an ER counselor, I was very familiar with this; it could indicate damage to Jeff's brain.

Ignoring Jeff's questions, the doctor sent the nurse outside. Hurriedly, he explained. "Jeff, we need to take you down for an MRI of your brain. It looks like something is going on in your head, and we won't know what it is until we see the scan."

Seemingly unaffected, Jeff remained quiet. Attempting to reassure us both, I said, "Don't worry; I'm here with you. They'll figure out what's happening."

A whirlwind of fellows entered the room within minutes of Jeff's examination. I overheard the unimaginable mentioned—Jeff might be blind. His bed and machines were quickly unplugged, and he was pushed out the door, fellows in tow.

I stood in shock, not believing things could go from bad to worse in such a short time. It was one thing to be sick with cancer and a very different thing to wake up blind. And even more unfathomable, he was going through it with severe depression and anxiety. How much suffering could one human being endure?

As they wheeled Jeff out, my favorite nurse, Kathy, entered. She gave me a brief hug, thankfully not saying anything.

"I need to go talk to my parents, but I don't know what to tell them," I said.

An emergency call dragging her out the door, she said over her shoulder, "I would wait until the doctor returns with the MRI results. It's best to have all the facts before talking to them."

I stared at the floor as I thought about what this all could mean. How do I explain this? How do I even figure it out for myself? What kind of plan could this possibly be?

An hour of soul searching went by before the medical tech rolled Jeff's bed through the door, monitors in tow, leaving a trail of eerie silence. Jeff had tears seeping out the corners of his eyes.

Reaching for his arm, I said, "I'm here, Jeff."

His hand grabbed mine, I leaned over the rail, my cheek next to his, and we sobbed together.

"I'm here, and I'm not leaving. I promise." Words couldn't soothe pain like that; I just wanted him to know that I was there with him.

I forcibly calmed myself down and pushed up from the bed, my eyes searching the room for hope, for reassurance. But no one looked my way. No one's eyes met mine, and my soul felt the darkness that Jeff now knew.

"What about Mom and Dad?" he whispered. "Do they know yet?"

"No, but I'll go down and talk to them. You rest and remember your only job is to stay off that ventilator. God will take care of the rest. Never lose faith."

I looked around the room again; this time the doctor motioned me toward the door.

"May I have a moment to regain my composure?" I asked, knowing he was waiting to accompany me to the family room.

"Of course. Take your time. I'm so sorry." His words evoked no emotion, as the news of Jeff's blindness had seared my senses.

I left Jeff's room a few steps behind the doctor, rehearsing in my head what to say to my parents. He paused at the family room door, his white coat swishing from side to side, motioning me to enter first. Mom's fingers abruptly stopped tapping on the round wooden table where they were sitting. She jumped to her feet and took a step toward us.

"Were they not able to take the tube out?" she asked the doctor.

"Yes, they got the tube out OK, but—"

"Oh my God, oh my God. What happened?"

"We just learned that Jeff suffered a stroke on his optic nerve during the operation. For the time being, he has lost his sight. Until we know more, it will be impossible to tell whether his sight will return."

"No, no. How could this happen?" She fell to her knees, her face in her hands.

"We aren't exactly sure at this time. We will be running some further tests." He looked at me and my dad helplessly.

Looking toward my mother, he said, "I'm sorry. I have never had something like this happen to a patient before. As I said, we will be doing further testing. Are you going to be OK?"

Dad moved closer to Mom, silently resting his hand on her head and covering his eyes.

"Yes," my mother replied. "I'm sorry. I just wasn't prepared for that."

I gave them another moment. "Mom and Dad, we need to go see Jeff. He needs to know that you guys are OK. Right now, he's more worried about both of you than himself."

Dad reached his arm under Mom's, and I tucked mine under the other, helping her to her feet. She wiped her eyes and straightened a bit.

"Are you ready to go see Jeff now?" I asked.

"Yeah, I need to see him."

The three of us walked into Jeff's room, hand in hand. As soon as they saw him, their composure cracked, their sobs reaching Jeff before they did.

"Are you guys OK?" Jeff asked.

Unable to speak, they sat on the edge of the bed. Mom tightly pressed her wet cheek against his while Dad squeezed Jeff's hand, both sniffling quietly.

"God will not leave us," I said, trying to ease the agony.

I had no real concept of what those words meant. I had always felt that Jesus would be with me, but at that moment I was not feeling his presence. I said the words, hoping that I would also be reassured. I wondered if God's plan included the celebration of a miracle or the celebration of a life passed before us.

Hours after the family left, I was exhausted, not having slept since this nightmare began. Lying in the corner of Jeff's dimly lit room, machines humming in the background, I finally dozed off. Within minutes, I was woken up by the nurse who came in to silence the beeping monitor. It was three o'clock in the morning; Jeff was sleeping deeply with the help of medications, while my mind spun endlessly.

I snuck out of the room, pushed through the double doors of the CCU, and walked down the quiet hallway, trying to find some peace. I paced back and forth. I hadn't been home in two weeks, my head hurt so badly I could barely think, and all I wanted was some time alone. I tapped my index finger against my forehead repeatedly in an effort to disrupt the pain. Involuntary sobs released some of the pressure as my sinuses drained.

I walked to the end of a deserted hallway and curled up in the corner. My heart was shattered—first cancer, now blindness? A steady stream of tears rolling off my chin, I began to pray. He would be better off in heaven. How would he cope with terminal cancer and now blindness? This was hell. He deserved better than to waste away.

I rocked back and forth, trying to console myself. My brother deserved so much more than this. I began to whisper, voice strangled, "Please take Jeff home. He can't get through this. Please, I trust you. Please take him home." I returned to the room and released the last of my emotions in my journal.

Tammy's Journal—March 3, 2000, 3:30 a.m.
Journal 3—He certainly has been through a day of battle. I don't understand why he, and all of us, must suffer such pain. A part of me feels sorry for myself, but if I tell that to anyone, they might suggest I stop. I don't want to stop and even if I did, I wouldn't know

how to stop. It's like asking me to stop living. I believe I bring my brother comfort like none other, and that's what he needs more now than ever. Nothing else seems more important to me than every moment I am watching over him making sure he is well taken care of. I feel special, confident, and needed. My girls and husband miss me desperately and I miss them. I know they're doing their best to be supportive, but clearly long not only for my presence, but some sense of normalcy. I feel guilty about being away from them. I feel guilty if I think of leaving Jeff. I feel guilty for not being at work. How can I be everything to everybody? It makes me sick to be anything less. I wonder how much longer I can endure this agony.

The next morning brought more doctors, more tests, and more unanswered questions. Despite the chaos around us, Jeff was calm. He seemed to have an unusual sense of peace about him.

"You know that Ray Boltz song, 'Thank You'? Do you think you could play it for me?"

The medications caused him to forget, so he repeated himself frequently. He didn't realize that he had asked us this same question at least twenty times that day.

"Isn't that the most beautiful song? I love the words," he whispered in a soft voice before dozing off to sleep again.

I was surprised that he knew the song so well and equally intrigued by how it touched him. It was as if he rejoiced in the words. He seemed so different that day. Even his voice was different—not only softer, but sweeter. I never knew him to be so sentimental and funny. He cracked jokes throughout the day, even about being blind.

"Hey, Mom, you know when I was a little boy, how you told me that if I touched my penis, I would go blind? I believe you now."

We all laughed and experienced our first moment of relief in weeks.

CHAPTER 8

Time to Transfer

JEFF SEEMED TO COPE WITH his blindness better than the rest of us. I wasn't certain whether it was denial or something more. Each day he made small steps to recovery, such as strengthening his muscles so he could breathe better and discovering ways to locate things with his hands instead of his eyes.

After three weeks, he was finally ready to transfer out of the CCU and into a regular room. Although this was seen by the medical staff as progress, we as his family felt extremely frightened and vulnerable. The nurses in the CCU had become like family to us. They were affected by this tragedy as well and had taken care to make Jeff's time there as comfortable as possible.

Jeff was rolled down to the new floor in his hospital bed. Kathy, his favorite nurse, took extra time to get Jeff settled. She assured us that she would let the charge nurse know how unique Jeff's condition was so that she would keep an extra eye on him. His room was intentionally located near the nurse's station. Once he settled in, Jeff said a tearful goodbye to Kathy.

"Don't worry, Jeff. I'll be back to check on you whenever I'm working. You can't get rid of me by moving floors."

"I hope you do," he whimpered. "Thank you for all you did for me."

With Jeff resting in his new room, Mom and I hung signs above his bed that read, "Jeff is blind. Please announce who you are when entering, and say goodbye to him so he knows you are leaving."

"Mom and I are going to run down to get some coffee. We'll be back quickly. I'll let the nurse know we're stepping out for a minute."

"OK. I won't go anywhere." He looked amused with himself for being clever.

While we were gone, a busy nurse's aide set Jeff's lunch tray on his table and quickly hurried off to the next room. Jeff not only had to discern what was on his tray, but also figure out how to get the food onto his fork and into his mouth. It sounds so basic—until you suddenly can't see. Not to mention his wasted muscles had difficulty coordinating the simplest of movements, including picking up a utensil and moving it to his mouth.

Jeff felt around the bed for the nurse's call button, which proved to be a formidable challenge since the aide might have forgotten to hook it to the bed.

"Hey, where is that button?" he asked loudly.

Terrified, he panicked, shouting louder, "Where is the button? Hello…is anyone out there? I need help. I can't find the button—please help me."

We returned from our quick coffee break to find Jeff shaking and sobbing.

We rushed to his side, concerned he was hurt or in pain. "Jeff, what's wrong? What happened?" I asked.

"Why did you leave me?" His words caught in his throat as he struggled to regain composure.

"We just went for coffee. What happened?" I dabbed his wet eyes with a tissue.

Quivering like a lost child, he said, "Don't do that again. I couldn't find my food or call the nurse—nobody was coming to help me. I was so scared."

"We're here now. I am going to talk to the head nurse to figure how this happened. It's going to take some time, but we *are* going to figure it out. But for now, let's sit you up and get you fed."

It was in that moment that Jeff discovered how helpless the blindness and his weakened body had left him. He was launched into a full panic attack. It wasn't that he needed to eat lunch immediately; it was the realization that he couldn't, even if he wanted to. He couldn't see to wave someone down in the hall; he couldn't get out of the bed; he couldn't scream loud enough to be heard. He was in fact physically trapped, which left him frantic.

The whole ordeal left me with an even stronger sense of responsibility and determination to make sure he never had to feel that vulnerable again.

My assurance seemed to lift Jeff's spirit, and he shifted a bit in apparent anticipation of being served lunch. I didn't know exactly how I could fix the nurses' and the aides' inability to take Jeff's blindness seriously, but I could at least feed him lunch.

"I want to try to feed myself," Jeff said, perhaps wanting to gain some independence after his scare.

"Great. Here's your fork." I placed it in his left hand. "On your plate is turkey, mashed potatoes, and green beans, but you will have to learn how to find it on your plate. Your fork and spoon need to become an extension of your fingers, so start moving it around the plate to see if you can feel which is which."

"OK," he said. He gently used his fingers to figure out the size of the plate and then slowly raked the fork through his food.

"I can feel the turkey," he said. "It's bigger than the beans and harder than the mashed potatoes."

He tried stabbing the turkey with his fork, hooking a piece with the tines. Slowly, he took the shaking fork to his mouth, his anticipation shifting to disappointment as the fork arrived empty.

"Screw it. I'm just going to use my fingers."

"Don't do it. You've almost got it," I said. "Come on, try it one more time."

"OK, I think I got it this time." His mouth opened wide, but once again the fork arrived empty. "Sis, could you just help me out here?"

"Don't worry, Jeff. It *will* get easier. It's just going to take some time," I told him. "Here comes a bite of potatoes."

While I fed Jeff, Mom and I discussed how we could take shifts caring for him so he wouldn't be left alone. We set up a schedule that would give each of us the flexibility to be there when we could and leave when we needed. I would be there the majority of the time. My mom wanted to help, but I felt as if caring for Jeff was my responsibility, since I knew the most about medical stuff.

It was painful to watch Jeff struggle, but despite wanting to help him, I didn't know how to help him. I figured if I tried eating blindfolded myself, I would understand a bit about the difficulty of accomplishing simple tasks, and maybe I could find a way to make it easier.

Therefore, I decided to try to eat my dinner blindfolded.

"Good luck." Jeff chuckled. "It's harder than you might think."

I covered my eyes with a towel, and feeling confident that I would be able to feed myself just fine, I picked up the fork. Next, I located the edge of the plate and began stabbing away. I moved the fork carefully to my mouth. But nothing was there.

"Dang. I thought for sure I had it."

Mom laughed at me in the background.

"It's not so easy, is it?" Jeff snickered, seemingly pleased that I was having as much trouble as he had.

I tried a few more times and then got discouraged. Much to my surprise, I took an empty fork to my mouth more times than not. Taking off my blindfold, I was reminded that my game was over, while Jeff would struggle for the rest of his life.

The routine at the hospital got easier. Mom, Dad, and I took turns staying with Jeff. I spent most every morning and night with him, while they came during the afternoon. We dressed him, cleaned him, fed him, took him for strolls in the wheelchair, and entertained him. A physical therapist worked with Jeff daily to strengthen his weakened body.

He entered the hospital weighing 170 pounds, weighed 230 pounds after surgery, and now weighed a mere 130 pounds. He was emaciated and gaunt. His blond eyelashes and eyebrows contrasted with the brownish color of his entire face. The skin covering his hands and arms was lying directly on the bones with no muscle or fat to provide support.

Jeff wanted desperately to leave the hospital. After all, it had been almost seven weeks since his nightmare had begun, and he just wanted to go home. However, he still required a great deal of care and had a number of complex medical issues.

Typically, it would be appropriate for someone with Jeff's medical complications to stay on the rehabilitation unit, which was the doctor's recommendation. However, blindness limited his ability to manage independently on that unit, since rehabilitation units are primarily set up for physical rehabilitation, not blind rehabilitation. Even after seven weeks, the staff still seemed to forget that Jeff couldn't see. It was all too common for a nurse to ignore the signs and hold something like a thermometer in front of Jeff's face, waiting for him to open his mouth.

"Uh, you have to instruct him about what you need him to do. He can't see what you're holding."

We often reminded them, and we were constantly reminded that the hospital staff could not meet Jeff's needs without a family member there to supervise. This certainly made it difficult for us to leave him alone. He really was dependent on me and our parents.

Over the past seven weeks, I had been away from Jeff only a few times. I understood his medical issues and believed I could manage most of them. I was much more comfortable dealing with his needs than my parents were, so it only made sense that Jeff would come to live with me and my family.

Even though my parents were quite willing to take care of him, they recognized that I had a genuine desire and need to take care of him. Also, I would be going back and forth to my parents' home if Jeff lived with them. I believed his care would overwhelm our mom, and that would only cause me additional stress.

I talked to Clark, Chelsey, and Kendra about caring for Jeff at our house. The girls had some apprehension about how the decision would affect their lives but eventually accepted the idea.

Clark enjoyed his home so much that he often referred to it as his castle—his place to escape from others. He didn't usually like a lot of company, so this transition would be a huge sacrifice of privacy on his part. In addition to Jeff, there would certainly be lots of family and friends around. Despite his discomfort, he considered it an opportunity to reciprocate, since I never turned away his family. I had raised my stepson, Bobby, for ten years before he moved into his mother's home, and I had provided years of day care for my stepdaughter's children.

Though it would clearly be a major disruption to our family, they all agreed that it was the only option we could accept. They all worried about what the actual impact of Jeff's presence would be but supported my desire to care for him. Jeff seemed relieved that he would be cared for by family rather than having to stay in the hospital. Knowing that there was no cure for the cancer, our hope was that we could get him healthy enough to enjoy his life until the cancer returned.

CHAPTER 9

Going Home

WE ARRIVED IN THE DRIVEWAY of my house and were quickly greeted by Clark and the girls. Jeff was barely able to walk due to weakness and difficulty with balance, so my dad and I hooked our arms under his to support and direct him as he very slowly made it to the front door. Clark and Mom followed with all his belongings. Jeff was exhausted from the drive home, so we took him straight to the other thing he had anticipated so much: his own bed.

The king-size bed, head facing the door, rested on a plain metal frame. Fresh sheets, several blankets, and a new blue comforter were folded back, waiting for Jeff to crawl in. On the left side of the bed, there was a white two-drawer nightstand piled high with bandages, syringes, medications, and other supplies. A tall, heavy oak dresser sat against the wall between the window and large closet. The bare, off-white walls reflected the sunlight shining through the wooden blinds. Not exactly a cozy-looking room, but certainly functional and better than a hospital room.

"OK, Jeff, we have four more steps to reach your bed," I said. "Now turn and reach back, and you can sit."

"Ah—my bed. My blankets, my pillow. Wait." He gently ran his hand over the top of the blue comforter. "This doesn't feel like my old comforter."

"It's not. I had Clark pick you up a new one at Costco. Your other one was pretty worn out."

"Thanks, Clark."

"No problem. Welcome home," Clark said from the bedroom door.

"Let me get your shoes off and scoot you up against the wall so we can bring Rusty in here," I said. I quickly pulled off his slippers and tucked pillows up behind him.

Jeff was thrilled to see—or rather touch—his best friend, his dog, Rusty. He and Rusty had been inseparable companions for several years. Jeff found him in the local want ad paper, the *Little Nickel*. This devoted blond cockapoo was not just a dog to Jeff—he was more like Jeff's child.

"I can't wait. I hear him scratching to get in," Jeff said.

"Here, let's put this pillow over your stomach, because I'm sure Rusty's going to jump all over you. We have to be careful he doesn't tear your wound."

Chelsey stood on the other side of the door, holding Rusty's leash as he squealed and jumped, impatiently trying to get to Jeff.

"OK, Chelsey, we're ready. Bring Rusty in," I hollered.

"Come on, boy. Where are ya?" Jeff called, reaching out his hand.

Trembling, Rusty gently jumped on the bed and sniffed all around until his black wet nose met Jeff's hand. He burrowed, lay down on Jeff's good side, and then rolled over onto his back. Jeff's arm tucked under Rusty's neck, the dog's four paws pointing up to the ceiling. Rusty filled the room with loud whimpering and several long coyote-like howls.

Tears dripped down Jeff's cheek as he pulled Rusty even closer. "I think he's happy to see me."

Passing the tissue box around, I said, "I think happy is an understatement. I've never witnessed something so amazing."

Normally, Rusty jumped all over everyone and everything, hardly able to stay still. Today, he was content to just be near Jeff, overjoyed by his return.

The week following Jeff's arrival was filled with many challenges as I learned my new role as his caretaker and returned to my cherished role of mother and wife. I struggled to balance long-overdue quality time with my family and meeting Jeff's every need. The oblong, ten-inch wound across Jeff's abdomen still required packing twice a day. He needed blood-thinning shots twice a day and was on over twelve different medications. He couldn't control his bowel and bladder, so he needed his adult diaper changed at least ten times a day. Each day presented me with a new symptom that left me scrambling for answers.

Toward the end of the week, Jeff started feeling a funny sensation in his shoulder, and then he was unable to move his right arm. He also was having some general weakness and dizziness. My parents and I took him back to the doctor, and since they couldn't figure out what was causing his new symptoms, they decided he needed to stay in the hospital for further testing. Jeff was devastated and terrified of what else might go wrong. All of us were worried about him—he had come so far, only to be readmitted to hospital.

After many MRIs and CAT scans, the news of Jeff's condition could not have been worse: a new diagnosis of cancer. The doctor told us that he likely had a cancerous mass in his shoulder—as well as tumors in his brain. None of this made any sense to me. I knew enough about cancer to know that it follows a path, and it did not seem normal for adrenal cancer to follow the path the doctor reported. Accustomed to challenging doctors on behalf of my patients, I questioned the doctor about his diagnosis. I felt especially confident since the ultrasound technician shared with me that the shoulder "mass" looked more like dried blood in the tissues than a tumor.

Dr. Smith seemed irritated that I was second-guessing him and remained adamant about his diagnosis, leaving me with little hope of finding the truth.

Jeff was trying to take it all in stride, but he had no emotional reserve to help him. Each day that passed, he seemed to be getting sicker instead of better. He couldn't move his arm, and his dizziness was getting worse. After seven days in the hospital, gaunt and emotionless, he more than ever looked like death itself. He couldn't keep food down, and he had horrible diarrhea. Jeff wasn't saying much, which left me to believe that his body and soul had been through enough, and he was preparing to die.

The doctor called us into the conference room to explain the results of Jeff's recent tests. He told me and my parents that Jeff had only about six weeks to live and that his cancer had spread to his brain. Normally, he would have discussed a treatment plan, but Dr. Smith informed us that Jeff's body was too weak to recover. He apologized for how things had turned out, and while we were all churning this reality in our minds, he silently stood up and left the room.

I sat stunned and confused, not believing what he was saying. It made no sense to me. I had seen many people die of cancer, and this just didn't fit the typical pattern. Then again, nothing about Jeff's illness had been typical.

After a silent pause, I spoke. "I want Jeff to return home with me. It's the place he wants to be, and since I do this for a living, it makes the most sense that I should be the one to help him die. I comforted Grandma and Grandpa through their last days, and this is what I need to do for my brother. I can do this."

Prepared for pushback, I got none. The next step was to share the news with my husband and our girls. It was one thing to bring Jeff home for rehabilitation, but another so he could die.

CHAPTER 10

Going Home Again

As soon as I arrived home, I gathered my family to discuss Jeff living in our home for his last weeks. Clark immediately agreed to the plan, but the girls resisted the idea.

"I don't want Jeff to die here—it would freak me out just knowing there was a dead guy in our house." Kendra scrunched her face while shaking her head side to side.

"I have to agree, Mom. I would be worried his ghost would haunt us or something. I have goose bumps just thinking about it," Chelsey said, shrugging her shoulders up to her ears and squirming in the chair.

"First of all, Jeff doesn't have to actually die in our home, because when he gets too sick, we can move him to the hospice center—"

"And besides, no ghost is going to haunt you," Clark said.

Chelsey looked to Kendra for her reaction. Disgust spread across her turned-up lips.

"What if one of you was sick? Wouldn't you want to be around your family who loves you?"

The girls nodded in unison.

"I know it's a lot to take in, and if it gets too hard on you, then we can talk about doing something different."

"OK. As long as he doesn't actually die here," Kendra said. Chelsey nodded her head in agreement.

I hugged them each and kissed their foreheads, then quickly gathered my purse and keys.

"It's all going to work out," Clark whispered into my ear as he hugged me tight.

By the time we had finished our family discussion, it was 2:00 p.m., and I didn't want Jeff spending another night in the hospital. Because discharge planning was a regular part of my job, I knew getting things done in the few hours left would be challenging. I immediately contacted my old social work preceptor at hospice, Christine, to request services for when we got home. She was a gentle, unassuming woman, but as a seasoned social worker, she was very competent to help me set up an urgent home visit.

Trusting she would have a hospice team waiting for us, I requested the doctor discharge Jeff that evening. An ambulance was arranged, and Jeff was once again on his way home. When we arrived at home, the hospice nurse was already there and preparing Jeff's room.

The room was quickly converted into a mini hospital: oxygen tank, bedside commode, wheelchair, medication bottles, wound dressing kits, and bed pads. It was a stoic reminder of the many issues the hospice team would need to help manage. They were not only the most qualified people to help Jeff make the journey from this life to the next; many of them had been my hospice coworkers when I was a graduate student.

Unlike last time, Jeff was unable to walk into the house, so the ambulance crew carried him on a gurney. The nurse introduced herself to Jeff as she helped me get him comfortable in his bed. She explained the hospice program to him, showed me a few things about the oxygen tanks and medications, and then said goodbye until the morning.

While organizing the medical supplies and paraphernalia on top of his dresser, I heard Jeff's weak voice.

"You didn't have to do all of this for me. I hope it won't be too much on you."

"No worries. I wouldn't have it any other way," I said. "I want to spend as much time with you as I can."

"Thank you. I can't imagine being anywhere else."

"I don't think the doctor is right about the cancer, but there is clearly something going on that's making you worse. I figure the hospice team will help me sort it all out."

"I sure hope so," Jeff said.

His spirit seemed to be the only part of him that was not sick. From the moment he got back, Jeff acted different. A quiet sense of acceptance and peace had come over him, replacing the fear and uncertainty that had dominated him for most of his life.

The next day my parents moved their motor home onto our driveway so they could be close to Jeff and help with his care. Even though our homes were only thirty minutes apart, the idea of my parents having a private respite in my yard made good sense with what we were facing. Not knowing how long Jeff had to live, all of us were forced to live one day at a time.

Rusty startled me as he launched off Jeff's bed toward the front door. "Come in. We're in Jeff's room," I hollered from the bedroom, where I was finishing changing Jeff's bandages.

"It's just me," Mom announced.

"Hello. You guys don't have to knock, you know."

"Well, I typically don't just walk into someone's house without knocking," Mom said.

"Seriously, I would hope you know better. I never knock at your house."

"OK, OK." She set her canvas bag on the floor.

She immediately leaned down to give Jeff a kiss on his forehead and was met with Rusty's wet nose against her cheek.

"What's the matter, Rusty?" She wiped her cheek. "You need some attention?"

"Yeah, he's pretty needy these days." Jeff smiled.

"Where are the girls? I brought them a few treats."

"Oh, I was wondering what was in your bag. I think they're upstairs," I said.

Mom left the room but didn't go upstairs, and I didn't hear the girls come downstairs. The silence confused me, so I left Jeff's room to find out where Mom had gone.

A slightly guilty look spread across her face as she was folding the laundry that was on the couch.

"Mom, what are you doing? You don't have to do our laundry."

"I know, but it's the least I could do, since you have so much with Jeff and all."

"Clark and the girls will help out."

"I know you're a lot like me in that you like to take care of things on your own, but I'm going to need to do something while we're here. I handle all Jeff's stuff, so at least let me clean and do laundry." It was more a demand than a question.

"I get it. Your granddaughters aren't going to let you leave if you do all their chores." I smiled as I left the room. Mom could be a little dramatic, but it was great to have the help.

"I hope Clark will let your dad help him around the yard or with house projects. He'll go crazy if he doesn't have something to do."

"Well, you know how Clark is." I rolled my eyes. "He isn't one to ask for help. But if he's at work, he won't be able to tell Dad not to mow the lawn or fix things. I'll let him know Dad needs things to keep him busy."

"I really do appreciate all that you and your family are doing for Jeff. I know he's so comfortable here. This is all just so hard for me. I not only worry about Jeff, but I worry about you. I don't want this to be too much on you guys." Mom looked for reassurance that I did not mind Jeff staying with us.

"It's going to work out just fine. We will make it work," I told her. I had made it clear that I wanted to have Jeff here, but it would take a little time for Mom to adjust.

We all had different things to offer Jeff, and the more support he had, the better it would be for all of us. And although there would be many other family and friends who offered support, we knew the job would ultimately be mine and Clark's.

That next night we took turns reading to Jeff to help pass the time. His favorite book was about a famous wrestler who overcame hardships in his life. It also shared some of the behind-the-scenes trivia about how professional matches are staged. Jeff always enjoyed the drama of a good wrestling match.

While I was reading to him, he randomly said, without emotion or emphasis, "I'm grateful I'm not paralyzed from the neck down or brain injured on top of it all."

And once again I was reminded how much at peace he seemed.

The following days were long and hard—both physically and emotionally. Each day was a mystery, and we never knew if Jeff would be physically sick, sad, and emotional, or both. He could barely move his body from one position to another, making him utterly dependent on us. I did my best to help him cope by teasing him and making light of having to wash his body, especially his private parts. Jokingly we started calling his frequent diarrhea episodes "packages."

"Tam, I have a package for you," Jeff called out.

"I'm getting pretty tired of your 'special packages.' I'm beginning to think you're getting even for all the torture I put you through when we were kids," I teased back.

Humor was a good way for us to cope. As we quipped and bantered with each other, we were able to forget that Jeff was dying. It stayed at the back of our minds, but enjoying every moment with my brother became one of my focuses, along with meeting his needs.

But humor could only do so much, and my inability to help my brother drove me to find anything I could do to relieve his symptoms, particularly the diarrhea and vomiting. So I called Dr. Smith, hoping he could provide some answers.

"Can we do anything to stop the diarrhea? Everything he eats just goes right through him," I said.

"Well, I suppose we can order a stool sample, but I don't expect it will make much of a difference," Dr. Smith said, clearly thinking tests were a waste of energy, given that Jeff only had a few weeks to live.

"Even if we can just slow down the diarrhea, I know he will feel better." Of course, it would also make my life easier, not having to deal with as many special packages.

Dr. Smith begrudgingly agreed to order tests, and Jeff supplied me with a stool sample. I carried his package to the lab and waited to hear the results.

We finally got a phone call from Dr. Smith, who meekly told us Jeff had a bacterial infection in his gut and would need to go on antibiotics.

It took two days for the diarrhea to slow down after Jeff began the antibiotics. He started gaining a pound here and there, and he even began moving his arms normally again. He ate better and actually felt stronger, instead of deteriorating as predicted. He bypassed pudding and broth and requested a burger and fries from McDonald's. As the days passed, it appeared he would soon be strong enough to get out of bed and actually sit on the bedside commode. We anxiously awaited that day, since I was ready to be done with his packages, and Jeff was certainly ready to reclaim some dignity.

CHAPTER 11

New Growth

By the end of May, Jeff started to take a turn for the better. The natural process of regeneration was not just happening outside, as white and pink blossoms covered the trees, but inside as well. Jeff began budding new skin over his partially closed wound, filling in the gaps of his uncertain prognosis. His wound still required a great deal of care, needing to be cleaned twice a day and covered at all times to avoid an infection. Prior to every bath, it had to be taped with plastic wrap so it would not get wet. Jeff required very close monitoring, so he was never left alone. He did not seem to mind the constant company, which created some safety and was often his only source of entertainment. Though his health continued to fluctuate, the one constant was that he felt sick most of the time.

Jeff developed a problem where his body temperature dropped to about ninety-three degrees every time he ate. His body shook vigorously, and his lips and fingernails turned a bluish hue. We warmed blankets in the dryer and wrapped him up just to get his temperature back to normal.

Unfortunately, the doctors had no idea why this or many of his other symptoms occurred. Nonetheless, everyone involved in Jeff's support was thankful for the progress he was making.

Despite Jeff's progress, it was a production to get Jeff to leave the house—bathing, feeding, wound care, dressing, and transporting. A visit to the doctor took two of us to get him ready; luckily, Midge, my rock, was there to help. We first got Jeff to the side of the bed, and then we would guide him to his wheelchair. We lifted him into the wheelchair, headed down the two front steps, wheeled him to the car, loaded him up, and off we went.

When we arrived at the hospital, the three of us drove around the parking lot just to find a parking space large enough to get Jeff out of the car. Then after a struggle with Jeff's wheelchair, we finally got ourselves down the hospital hallway to Dr. Smith's office.

Dr. Smith seemed somewhat surprised that Jeff was doing so well. He examined Jeff and determined the drain in his side could finally come out. He could not be sure all the infection was gone, but he decided to take a chance. The doctor addressed some of our concerns, including Jeff's severe sweating, frequent bowel movements, and intermittent vomiting. He offered no hope for the future.

It was difficult to trust the doctor's advice, since he never addressed his misdiagnosis with the shoulder and brain cancer. I was left wondering why the so-called "brain cancer" was not getting worse, especially because Jeff was improving rapidly. It made me question everything the doctor said.

Despite his wavering health issues, Jeff's faith continued to grow. He learned all he could about his belief in Jesus Christ. He listened to the Bible on tape and loved having intense discussions with our pastor about faith and salvation. He also spent a great deal of time talking to our good friend Keith, whose brain cancer remained in remission. Jeff occasionally got stuck on the details of his faith in Jesus, as he desperately wanted to make sure that when he died, he would go to heaven. He was very apprehensive because he had already experienced the fear of death and the potential reality of meeting his maker. He struggled most with the concept of Jesus's gift of salvation, because he felt guilty about the way he had lived his life prior to surgery.

He believed he was very self-centered, selfish, and unappreciative for the things he had in his life. He became committed to making sure his faith was real and not just an attempt to avoid his fear of God's wrath. Jeff also wanted to make sure he made amends for the things he had done wrong in his past, as well as not repeat the same mistakes in his future.

This was amazing for me to witness, as the brother I had known all my life had never seemed to have such insight and personal drive. All of us were learning a new way to view life right alongside him, whether we liked it or not. It was difficult to complain about the trivial things in life when you looked at someone like Jeff, who had every reason to complain and chose not to.

His new attitude became an inspiration to all who met him. Many people seemed to embrace being with him, while few went out of their way to avoid him. The old saying goes, "The people you think will be there won't be, and the people you never expected to be there would." This certainly was true in our situation. Jeff's best friend, Allen, seldom came around, while his childhood friend, Frank, whom he seldom saw prior to surgery, stood by his side from the beginning.

One of Jeff's friends was brutally honest with him, saying he could not stand to see Jeff in his condition, and he didn't think he could handle coming around. Though this was hurtful, Jeff appreciated his honesty. In fact, he said he might have done the same thing to his friends if the tables were turned.

CHAPTER 12

On Being Blind

JEFF HAD FINALLY IMPROVED TO the point that he could sit up in bed on his own and was eager to build up his strength and endurance so he could walk on his own. He was so frail that standing up for a minute or two would leave him huffing and puffing, yet he was determined to get stronger.

My husband, Clark, was a physical therapist. He worked in home health care and enjoyed working with people in their own homes. He loved his work and was known to be one of the best, especially in helping more complex patients. During his twenty-year career, Clark never had the opportunity to work with a completely blind person and welcomed the challenge.

Jeff paused and waited for Clark to mute the TV. "Tammy told me you don't mind helping me build my strength back up."

"Yeah. I'm just the guy who can teach you everything you need to know to get better," Clark said.

"I really appreciate the help." Jeff sat up a bit straighter. "When should we get started?"

"We can start tomorrow morning if you want. I have to warn you, though—when I have my physical therapist hat on, I might sound more like a drill sergeant. Are you sure you can handle me pushing on you?" Clark asked.

Hearing the playfulness in Clark's voice, Jeff tapped his index finger against his lips. "Umm, maybe I should rethink this idea."

From the other room, I could hear Clark counting out the reps as Jeff stood up and sat down. I was proud of the way he patiently helped him through his daily exercise program; it was a welcome break from having to be the only one responsible for Jeff's progress. Clark could be gruff at times, but with Jeff he was quite patient and unusually chatty.

After a week of pushing himself up from the bed to a standing position and then lowering himself back down to the chair, again and again, Jeff was finally ready for his next task.

"It's time. We're going to get you walking today," Clark said as he strolled through Jeff's door with his coffee in one hand and a walker in the other.

"I'm not feeling well again this morning," Jeff said from his bed.

As a former marine, Clark was accustomed to pushing through tough days, and he expected nothing less from his patients.

As he set up the walker, he said, "I gave you a break yesterday, but I think you should at least give it a try today. I promise I won't work you too hard."

Jeff sighed heavily. "Fine."

Undeterred, Clark helped Jeff stand. Gently, he helped Jeff explore the walker with his hands. "I brought a walker so you can try to walk to the living room today. Just feel around so you can get a sense of how wide it is."

Clark wrapped a safety belt around Jeff's chest, just above his wound.

"What's that for?" Jeff asked.

"I have to have something to hold on to in case your legs give out or you lose your balance." He gave a little tug on the belt to demonstrate. "Not too tight, not too loose. Perfect. OK, now I want you to just push the walker a step in front of you, then walk toward it."

Clark stood slightly behind Jeff as he took his first step in over a month. Jeff slowly wobbled across the room, clinging to the walker, and paused for a break once he made it through his bedroom door.

"Wow. I'm doing pretty good, don't ya think?" Jeff asked.

"Yes, you are. I knew you could do it. Now let's turn back toward your room. I don't want to work you too hard the first day. Maybe tomorrow we will try going to the living room. Careful as you turn."

"OK," Jeff said, lifting the walker to turn around. With a sharp clack, he hit the metal leg against the wall.

"Oops. What did I hit?" he asked.

Clark pulled the walker away from the wall and pointed Jeff toward the bed. "It's not your fault. I should have described what was around you," Clark said. "OK, so it's about six steps back to your bed, and then you can have a break." It took days of practice and enormous patience for Jeff to be able to make his first solo round trip. The walls took a beating as Jeff learned how to maneuver through the narrow walkways that led to and from the family room. Eventually, he managed to get around the entire bottom floor, and we started taking his mobility for granted.

When a loud crash echoed through the house, I rushed to find him.

"I'm OK. I'm OK," he hollered from the rec room.

"What happened? Did you break anything?" I asked, ignoring the lamp lying on the floor and the walker in the middle of the room.

"I tripped and knocked something off the table. I'm sorry." Jeff sounded more sheepish than annoyed, as if I had caught him doing something wrong. "I fell onto the couch, but my walker went flying."

"Are you sure you're not hurt?"

"I'm good. It's OK. Take a deep breath," he said, wiggling his slumped body upright. "What did I trip on?"

"Chelsey's backpack. She left it next to the chair. I'm going to have to talk to the girls; we can't have this happen again. It could have really turned out bad."

Even though Jeff was well enough to get around the house, a bad fall could open his barely healed wound or cause any number of complications, given his wide variety of symptoms.

"Don't get upset with them. They didn't mean for me to fall."

"I know, but they have to learn you can get hurt. Maybe I'll have them walk around blindfolded so they can see how hard it is," I said. That would be more impressive than me lecturing them anyway.

"How did that work out for you when you tried to eat blind at the hospital?" He laughed.

I smiled as I picked up the lamp and placed it back on the glass end table. I straightened the coaster holder and put the TV remote back on the edge of table where Jeff knew to find it.

"Did anything break?" Jeff asked.

"Just the bulb in the lamp broke. No big deal. I'll get another one and be right back."

"Hey, if you're going to get a bulb, will you get one for my bathroom. I noticed it was out this morning, but I forgot to tell you."

"Sure," I said as I walked out of the room.

I returned from the garage, relieved that I was only fixing burned-out light bulbs. I walked down the hall to the bathroom and heard Jeff giggling. Unsure what was so funny, I chose to ignore him. I flicked on the bathroom light to see which bulb was burned out and quickly realized why my brother was laughing: there were no burned-out lights. Even if there had been, Jeff would have had no idea, since he didn't use the lights anyway.

"You're real funny."

"I can't believe you fell for it." Jeff sat on the couch, still laughing at me.

"I admit, your comedy routine is getting better. Just remember who makes your food, though."

Our banter was interrupted by the girls and Christopher busting through the front door. The three kids were like brother and sisters, since I had been babysitting Christopher from the time he was three months old. He was family, even as far as Jeff was concerned.

"Mom, we're back," Chelsey said.

"In the family room," I yelled back.

"What are you guys doing?" Kendra asked as she and Christopher plopped on the sofa next to Jeff.

"Well, your uncle about gave me a heart attack when he tripped over Chelsey's backpack and fell onto the couch. I heard this loud crash from upstairs and flew down the stairs."

Her eyes opened wide. "Are you OK, Uncle Jeff?" Chelsey asked.

"Yeah, I'm fine. I broke open my gut, but it's no big deal."

Chelsey was less amused, but by then we were all used to Jeff's humor.

"Hey, Chels, will you grab me a towel from the linen closet? We're going to do a little exercise to help you guys understand what it's like to be Jeff."

Expecting something fun to happen, they all stood and waited for me to give the next set of instructions. Jeff could tell by the chatter in the room that someone was near the TV. He took the opportunity to use one of his favorite lines: "Hey, do you mind getting out of the way? I can't see the TV."

"Oh, sorry," Christopher said as he moved a few steps left.

"He's on a roll today." I grinned, mockingly rolling my eyes.

Christopher looked at me with a curious expression, and then it dawned on him that Jeff couldn't see the TV.

"That was a good one, Uncle Jeff." Christopher giggled.

Still smiling, Jeff curled his legs up on the couch and got cozy before the entertainment began. A sip of his milk, a bite of a homemade chocolate chip cookie, and he was ready.

"OK, who wants to go first?"

All three shifted up and down on the sofa, wanting me to pick them.

"Chelsey, you can go first. Let's tie the towel around your head so you can't see anything. It's cheating if you can see, so tell me the truth."

After tying the towel tightly over her eyes, I put my index finger against my closed lips as I looked at Kendra and Christopher. They both nodded, acknowledging that they needed to keep quiet.

"Here we go. I want you to try to make it to Jeff's room, and try not to tear up the walls."

"OK, but don't let me fall."

She placed her hands on the walker and began to move toward Jeff's room. The left leg of the walker slightly clipped the corner of the wall as she slid between the wall and a wooden kitchen chair.

"How are you doing, Chels?" Jeff asked.

"Good so far, I think."

I put a slipper and her backpack directly in her path. Kendra and Christopher were silently motioning for me to place even bigger items in her way.

"I feel something. What is this?" she asked, her foot squashing the slipper.

"Nothing big. Just a little slipper."

Her direction was shifting to the left as the walker bumped into the backpack on the floor. The kids were trying not to laugh as they moved the dog's bed in front of her. The walker came to a sudden halt as she bumped into it. Unable to tell if it was a wall, a chair, or something else, she stopped.

"Where am I?"

"In the living room." The kids, finally unable to hold it in, laughed hysterically.

"I thought I was in the hallway."

I steered her in the right direction. "Nope. You missed the turn."

"Wow, it's easy to get turned around." She pulled the towel off her eyes to look around the family room, looking a bit disoriented to still be in the same room.

"I wanna try. Let me try now," Kendra and Christopher begged.

After a few more minutes, I took the towel from Chelsey and blindfolded the other kids, one at a time. They too struggled to stay on course, especially when obstacles were put in the way. After everyone had a chance to play, we had a few laughs and a serious conversation about the necessity of their cooperation in keeping the house safe for Jeff to get around. However, it was clear that Jeff needed help to learn how to manage his blindness. Our family would do our best, but we could not protect him from everything. He would have to be able to avoid situations like this one, for his own safety.

One day, I bought Jeff a red-and-white cane. When I suggested he use it to help him get around, he made a face as if I were asking him to wear a Post-it note on his forehead. He believed that if he didn't use a cane, people wouldn't notice he was blind; therefore, he wouldn't get unwanted attention. He believed he would stand out and therefore would be less "normal."

It was true that just looking at Jeff, many people did not initially realize he was blind. His eyes looked normal, and though he did not make direct eye contact, he seemed to look in the general direction of the person to whom he was speaking.

I needed him to be more independent if I was going to balance my many responsibilities, and I trusted he would eventually move through the grief process to the acceptance phase of his reality. The stronger his body got physically, the greater his awareness of his blindness became, and the more his anxiety plagued him. It is one thing to know you will die blind, but a whole different problem to live in darkness.

I contacted the county Blind Services Department and scheduled a visit to give us some tips on making our home more accessible for Jeff. He was not very excited about the whole idea and had no intention of using their "great cane ideas," but he was willing to oblige us and listen to their advice.

"I don't mean to harp on you, Jeff, but this is all about you getting stronger and more independent. I just want you to get better. I need your help, though. You might even learn something," I said, feeling some of my growing frustration with the amount of work it took to support him.

Sitting at the kitchen table dreading his first encounter with "the blind people," as he referred to them, he said, "I know. I want to do better, and I will listen to their advice. I promise." His shoulders dropped, and he sighed heavily.

As always, Jeff looked worried while we talked about increasing his independence, but he was also determined to help make my life a bit easier.

The occupational therapist from the Blind Services Department knocked on the front door.

"Hello, come on in." I extended my hand. "I'm Tammy, Jeff's sister."

"Hello, Jeff. My name is Mary, and I'm from the Blind Services Department. How are you today?" she asked. Her voice was very sweet.

"I'm fine," Jeff curtly replied, still slouching in his chair.

"I'm here to assess how you are getting around and managing with your blindness. I brought with me a bag of items that may help you be more independent."

"OK."

I shook my head at Mary, acknowledging Jeff's stubbornness.

Mary nodded. Undaunted she asked, "So how are you doing getting around?"

"Things are going great; I get around just fine," Jeff assertively informed her.

"Have you learned how to work in the kitchen yet or get around outside?"

"Well, not exactly. My sister prepares all my meals, and I haven't been strong enough to walk outside by myself yet."

Jeff neglected to share the complete truth with her, which would have required that he tell her that he actually liked having me take care of just about all his needs.

Mary read Jeff's emotions very quickly and understood he was still in heavy denial, an easier place to be than accepting all that he could not do. This was not good or bad; it simply was where Jeff needed to be at the time. Mary began by sharing with Jeff, Mom, Dad, and me what the benefits of her services would be for Jeff and the rest of us.

She talked about helping Jeff become independent and more self-reliant. He vigorously picked at his fingers the more she discussed being able to live independently. Before long, his body tensed and his face contorted in fear.

I placed my hand on top of his. "Jeff, don't worry. We don't have any intention of moving you out. As far as Clark and I are concerned, you can live here forever."

"I don't want to live on my own—not like this."

Mary gave us helpful tips and suggestions to make living with a blind person safer and easier. She left Jeff with a white cane, along with a quick lesson on how to use it. Jeff politely appeased her as she tried to persuade him to use the cane.

CHAPTER 13

The Unspoken Routine

LIFE HAD BEEN OVERWHELMING FOR the past few months. The therapist from the Blind Services Department worked with Jeff, but he was not very motivated to make progress. Instead of feeling satisfaction from completing the little things that used to be so routine for him, he felt frustration that they required so much effort. He was able to get around the house somewhat, but he still needed help with much of his personal care, due in part to his blindness and in part to his lack of physical strength and endurance.

Before Jeff's illness, I had taken for granted that I did daily tasks without much thought or planning. I was amazed how much detail actually went into my own process of getting ready for the day. Like many people, I started my day by using the bathroom soon after I got out of bed. This simple, mindless task often evoked a great deal of anxiety for Jeff even before he became sick, but postsurgery it was worse.

First, he had to learn to sit on the toilet, which was very a different method than he had used for the past thirty years. He tried standing up, but blindly aiming toward the toilet bowl only resulted in me cleaning up urine from everywhere surrounding it.

Second, he was still too weak to get to the bathroom on his own; therefore, he needed my help in more ways than one.

"OK, back up one step, and you'll feel the toilet against the backs of your legs," I instructed while he held on tightly to my forearms for stability.

"Can I sit down now?"

"Let me drop your drawers first." I pulled his sweats below his knees. "Go ahead. I got you."

He slowly lowered himself to the seat and adjusted himself until he was comfortable.

"OK, I'll leave you alone for a bit. Just call me when you're done, and I'll clean you up," I said matter-of-factly.

"I'll make it nice and smelly for you," he joked, which was our coping mechanism for the awkward vulnerability we had both been experiencing since I had become his caretaker.

"I'm ready," Jeff hollered. "You might want to wear a gas mask—it's pretty ripe in here." His laugh echoed through the white noise of the fan.

I swung the door open and fanned it back and forth to air out the pungent smell that filled the very tiny bathroom. My exaggerated groans, followed by a dramatic "pew," let him know I was happy to play along. We both giggled as if we were four years old again.

"OK, lean forward." I stood beside him and reached down to wipe his butt. "There. We're done."

I slipped off my latex gloves and reached for the sink.

A serious look of concern replaced his grin. "Wait. Are you sure you got it all?" he asked.

His question instantly reminded me of his past obsession with hygiene and how he would wipe his butt repeatedly, sometimes going through a quarter roll of toilet paper.

"Oh yes, I'm sure."

"OK, but did you look at the toilet paper to be sure?" he hesitantly clarified.

Did I? I wondered for a split-second because the process was so second nature that I couldn't be sure how I knew he was clean. But then I remembered. "Yes, there were no more brown streaks."

I left Jeff on his bed organizing his nightstand before he took a rest, a routine that was looking more like an anxiety ritual. I figured it would be a good time to start dinner, since he would be distracted for a while.

Not more than ten minutes later, a sharp voice came from his room. "Tammy, could you help me for a minute?"

"I'll be there in a second. I just need to put the chicken in the oven," I hollered back from the kitchen.

My own frustration boiled below the surface. I had so many things to get done, and it seemed as if every time I turned around, Jeff needed me. I didn't mind so much that he needed help with the bathroom, getting around the house, or dealing with his health issues, but his obsessive needs sometimes became irritating.

"What do you need?" My tone reflected none of my irritation.

Though Jeff could be annoying, I knew it was not his fault. In fact, he was relatively low maintenance for a blind person with terminal cancer.

"I can't find my remote. Did someone move it, or what?" He huffed.

"It's right here in the top drawer, where you like it." I gently grabbed his hand and guided it to the drawer.

"Sorry. I looked there but didn't feel it."

"It's OK. Maybe you stuck your hand in the second drawer by mistake?"

"Yeah, maybe. Are my nail clippers in that drawer too? I couldn't find those either."

"They're next to the clock." I patiently guided his hand again.

He slowly moved his fingers along the surfaces of the drawers and top of the nightstand to be sure things were in their right places. He then proceeded to meticulously straighten the talking clock, two books, the baby monitor, and a tape recorder that sat on top of the nightstand. He opened the second drawer, straightened his comb so it was parallel to the front of the drawer, and then carefully placed the nail clippers next to the comb. He slid his emergency whistle toward the back-left corner of the drawer. He closed the second drawer and opened the top. He moved the remote to the front-right corner of the drawer and then pushed the four cassettes, which held his books on tape, toward the left side. For the third time today, things were to his satisfaction.

It was the little things, such as going to the bathroom and knowing where all his things were, that caused Jeff the most anxiety. While he was able to stay positive and joke about his condition, Jeff still struggled to control his obsessive-compulsive disorder. I knew he didn't want to bother anyone with his worrying, so I learned to work with him and not push him on it. Despite my occasional irritation, I hated that I could do little to help his symptoms, so I did everything I could to make him comfortable.

CHAPTER 14

Tammy's New Job

As it became clearer that Jeff was unlikely to die as soon as the doctor expected, I had to reevaluate how I was managing my life. While I was thrilled that Jeff continued to recover, I couldn't be absent from work indefinitely. But I certainly couldn't kick my blind, sick brother out of my home house just because he wasn't dying. As a result, I needed to make some permanent changes in my life. Putting my life on hold for six weeks was one thing, but it was another to just let it keep going on for months.

I finally generated enough nerve to return my boss's call.

The secretary answered. "Hi, Sue. Is Carol available?" I nervously asked.

"Oh, hi. How are you? We were just talking about you at the staff meeting; everyone is wondering how things are going."

I cleared my throat. "We're doing pretty well. Jeff is making progress."

"It's so good to hear from you; we sure do miss you. Let me send you through to Carol."

My stomach felt a bit queasy as I waited.

"Well, hello. You were on my list of calls today," Carol said joyfully.

Guilt, mixed with worry, made it difficult to get my words out. "Yeah, I'm sorry it took me a bit to get back to you. I was trying to figure out if I could make things work, but I haven't had any luck."

"I know it's been difficult on you. I wish I could give you more time, but I can't keep putting pressure on the rest of the team to fill your shifts." I could tell by her voice that our conversation was hard for her as well.

"I totally understand. You've been so gracious by giving me so much time off, and the team has gone above and beyond for me…" My voice cracked. "I know I have to give up my position. Jeff is still really sick, but he isn't dying anytime soon. He really needs me to take care of him."

"I know this has to be so hard for you, especially knowing how much you love your job. I hope you know that everyone here will respect your decision. Your brother is blessed to have you."

Streaks of mascara dripped down my cheek. "Thank you for understanding. I do need to ask just one more favor…uh, hmm…if you ever have a night shift available, please consider me. I need to find something at least part time, because we still need my income."

"I definitely will. And if anything changes, you give me a call, and I will do whatever I can to get you a job."

We hung up, and I felt sick. I loved every part of my critical-care job. We were such a great team—my boss was so supportive, my coworkers were like a second family, and I loved working with the patients. I felt I was losing a part of myself. Of the many sacrifices I was making—time with my family being a major one—the job was one that saddened me deeply. I loved my job, but I loved my brother more.

I worried how we would make ends meet financially, considering that we needed my income to live a comfortable lifestyle. Clark assured me we could get by, but I needed to feel I was still contributing to my family. I had to find a job that would accommodate my new circumstances.

Amazingly, an opportunity presented itself shortly after I resigned from my critical-care position: an opening in the emergency room. I had never had a desire to work in the ER, but the hours worked for my situation. I would work from 7:30 p.m. to 2:00 a.m., while Clark and my mom cared for Jeff in the evenings.

Clark was not particularly happy with this change because he not only was without his wife in the evenings, but also he had become a principal caretaker as well. He was, however, relieved that I would be bringing in some extra money. Fortunately for both of us, his strong work ethic gave him the right foundation to handle this new challenge.

Though the decision to give up my beloved CCU job was one I made with sadness and apprehension, I was grateful that after working a few ER shifts, I felt as if I fit in well. However, the type of work and hours were more difficult than I had anticipated. In the CCU I had spent plenty of time with each patient and his or her family, helping them with their grief, medical crisis, and discharge plans. I felt I was an integral part of the medical team since I was able to help the staff see the whole person, not just the medical condition. In the ER, I could do this as well, but the pace was much faster. I didn't have the time to get as involved with each patient before he or she was sent home or to a different floor.

Also, in the ER I had to work with drug and alcohol assessments, rape cases, and psychiatric evaluations, none of which I had ever handled. I was most comfortable with the trauma cases and the death-and-dying cases, so it was a steep learning curve for me. My new schedule was a major adjustment for me and my family as well. I was constantly exhausted because I often did not get home until three or four in the morning, and I wanted to be up in time to see my girls off to school. I was the one who always drove them to school until Jeff's illness. I needed to keep some things consistent for them and for myself, and I needed the time to catch up with their lives.

Each passing day seemed to require a bit more sacrifice. Sometimes I lost time with my husband, other times I snapped at my girls out of exhaustion, and occasionally at work I found myself almost falling asleep over paperwork. I loved all my roles, but there simply was not enough time to do everything well.

I tried not to let my family see how overwhelmed I felt, but it was difficult holding it all together. I often found myself questioning God, trying to rely on the promises I had learned in church. But somehow the pastor had never addressed how to face a situation like this. How could I be a good mother, caretaker, wife, and social worker all at once?

CHAPTER 15

The Change of Summer

Summer approached, bringing not only sunshine but also a much-needed break from the hectic schedule of another school year. Chelsey and Kendra were apprehensive about how they would spend their summer days; they knew by now that I was consumed with my caretaking duties for Jeff. Constantly balancing the needs of everyone, I felt as though I fell short of everyone's expectations.

The girls and I had spent past summers together in endless fun and adventure. I was the mom who, year after year, took them and their friends boating on Lake Sammamish at least twice a week. We were typically very active whenever I wasn't working, but this was going to be a very different summer.

The girls tried to be understanding and supportive, but at eleven and twelve years old, it was a great deal to put into perspective. My husband would have to sacrifice his beloved fishing, since I couldn't imagine being able to leave Jeff for a day-long adventure, and Clark wouldn't think of fishing without me.

My parents were doing their best to share in the caretaking duties. The idea of taking Jeff to their house a few days a week was more appealing now that he was ambulatory and capable of helping himself more. Jeff expressed concern about whether Mom would take care of him the same way I did, since he was so comfortable with the care he got from me. Mom, on the other hand, was quite confident she could manage just fine; after all, she had been there throughout the whole ordeal.

Yet I felt very anxious. Mom had spent plenty of time watching how I did things with Jeff, but she had never had to actually do everything herself.

The time finally came for Mom and Dad to take Jeff to their house for a couple of days. Packing up all the things he needed was a task all of its own. It was like having to pack up our whole family for a month-long trip out of the country. His medications, bag of bandages and ointments, suitcase of clothes, toiletries, and dog food sat by the door waiting to be loaded. Jeff's anxiety was off the chart. Mine was not far behind—not from concern for his care as much as the feeling that my baby was spending the night away from me for the first time.

"Bye, everyone. See you in a few days," Jeff said. "Have fun while I'm gone."

"Bye. Have a good time at Grandma's," Chelsey said.

From the back seat of the car, Mom said, "I'll call you when we get him settled."

"OK. Have fun, and I'll talk to you guys in a bit." I waved at them as they drove away.

Although my body walked back into the house with my family, my mind was elsewhere. I tried to get a hold of my racing thoughts. What if she forgot his medication? What if he woke up and she didn't hear him? What if he got worse and I wasn't around?

"Mom, Mom." Kendra tugged on my arm, breaking me from my gaze. "Dad said we can go to the Mexican restaurant tonight, since Uncle Jeff isn't here." Her hopeful grin made me smile. I felt comforted—maybe I would be able to balance everything after all.

"That sounds perfect."

"Chels, Chels," Kendra shouted. "Mom said we can go out to dinner. Let's go get ready."

Chelsey exuberantly pumped her fist into the air and belted out an ecstatic "Yes," and then they both scampered upstairs to get changed.

It had been our family tradition to go to the Mexican restaurant around the corner whenever there was something to celebrate or when we felt we deserved a special night out. Clark and I loved the fajitas, and he especially liked the fact that the portions were plenty large enough to satiate his big appetite. The girls especially loved the virgin margaritas and churros for dessert.

Just as the waiter arrived to take our order, my cell phone rang. I pulled it from my purse and saw that it was my mom's number. All three of my family members glared at me as I pressed the phone against my ear. I felt conflicted—I hated that they knew I couldn't ignore it, yet their disappointment cut me to my core.

"Hello?" I discreetly answered. I felt my heart skip a few beats.

"Hi, Tammy. I just wanted to let you know that everything is going just fine. Jeff is resting right here in the chair, if you want to talk to him—"

"We just sat down at the Mexican restaurant. Can I call him back when I get home?"

"OK, honey. Have fun, and we'll talk to you in a bit."

Anticipating disappointment, the girls simultaneously released deep sighs as I hung up the phone, and they quickly resumed their bubbly chitchat.

As a result of Jeff's first visit to our parents' house, a new schedule emerged. I switched from the night shift in the ER to working during the day on Thursdays, Fridays, and every other Sunday. My parents managed Jeff most of the days I worked. He was usually home with me the rest of the time, which was comforting on one hand and strenuous on the other.

I continued to struggle with balancing Jeff's needs and my family's, and I never felt sure if I was successful at either. Jeff seemed happy with the way things were going, likely because he had the best of both worlds. He got to spend time with Mom doing the things that they enjoyed: sending e-mails, visiting with people, watching television, and such. He also enjoyed the opportunity to get to know Dad in a way he never could as a child. Jeff and Dad had had little in common when we were growing up, which meant that Jeff had spent most of his time with our mom.

As a result, Dad wasn't as emotionally affected by Jeff, and he was much better than both Mom and me when it came to pushing Jeff ahead. He really helped Jeff heal by encouraging him to do his exercises and taking him for walks. Dad also made the transportation between homes much more manageable, since he was retired.

I felt as if a piece of me was gone when Jeff was away. I wanted to feel as if the time with my family was enough, but it just felt like a tease, not substantial enough to be satisfying for anyone. Also, my girls and Clark tended to openly express their joy at having things feel normal on those days. I was left wondering if they were beginning to resent me for the decision I had made to have my brother live with us.

The August days brought warm mornings, which were great for outdoor walks. Jeff and I had incorporated a short walk into our routine at least three times a week. On this particular morning, we were attempting to increase our distance by one block. As we turned the corner and meandered down a new street, the sun bounced off our faces.

"I love the feel of the sun on my face." Jeff lifted his chin toward the sky. "But I miss not being able to see it or the trees. I sometimes have a hard time even remembering what a tree looks like. It's weird how you can see for thirty years and within such a short time forget such simple things."

"That would be weird. I can't even imagine."

"I even have a hard time remembering what all of you look like. I can remember an old family picture from when we were really young, but I have no clue what you look like now. I can't remember Chelsey and Kendra's faces at all."

Distracted by his thoughts, I guided him across the street as we successfully extended our destination by one block without him even realizing it.

"I hate that I can only see black. It gets so frustrating."

"What's it like to not be able to see yourself now?" I asked.

A grimace spread across his face. "I don't think I would want to see my scarred-up stomach. It grosses me out just feeling it."

"It's not as bad as you think. So what do you miss the most about not being able see?"

He paused for a moment. "I really miss driving and being able to just get in my car to go get a hamburger. I also miss window-shopping at the mall and seeing the water at Alki Beach. It's weird; I don't dwell on it that much. It's like God won't allow me to focus too much on it. He has taken away my ability to obsess on things, which I am so grateful for. I don't know how I could live if I couldn't ignore the reality of being blind. I know that is all God." Jeff was right. God was the reason he could view his current life with gratitude and peace. How else could he be transitioning from a lifetime of debilitating anxiety and chronic depression to a place of comfort and acceptance of his shattered life?

CHAPTER 16

The Crash

By the end of the summer, we had all settled into our new routines. Jeff spent the night at my parents' at least once a week, and I got that time to spend with the girls and Clark. Of course, it was still a struggle to hold everything together, but it finally felt as if I had a bit of sanity again.

It was August 12, the night before my birthday, and we had plans to celebrate with a family barbeque the next day. I was not sure who was more excited, me or Jeff. He had proudly picked out my birthday gift, with help from the girls, and he was eager to give it to me. I was mostly looking forward to having a relaxing time with my family. After a hectic day, I finally fell asleep, only to be startled awake by the ringing phone.

"Who would be calling at this hour?" Clark grumbled.

"I have no idea," I said drowsily. "Hello?"

"Tammy, are you watching the news?" My mom's voice was carefully controlled.

"No. Why?" A rush of adrenaline immediately cleared my foggy brain. Mom would never call me this late, especially since I was going to see her the next day.

"Well, everything is going to be OK." Her voice cracked. "Dad was in a car wreck at the track tonight."

"What?" I bolted upright. "I didn't even know he was racing this weekend. Is he OK?"

"Well, he and another driver were burned, and they're being airlifted to Harborview. But I saw him, and he's going to be OK," she said.

"Where are you? Was he awake when you saw him? What's going on?"

"Yes, he talked to me for a minute just before the helicopter took off. I'm just leaving the track and going to the hospital. Don't worry about me."

"I'll get up and head to the hospital now. I'll meet you there."

"Tammy, drive safe. He's going to be OK. I don't need both of you hurt," Mom said, still in that strange, too-calm tone.

"I have to go." I hung up and quickly grabbed the TV remote, turning on the television. I knew he was definitely *not* OK if they were airlifting him to the burn center at the regional trauma hospital. I needed more information.

"What happened?" Clark asked as I flipped through the channels searching for the local news.

"Dad was racing tonight, and his car blew up. I need to know what happened. OK, here's the channel."

The newscaster dramatically announced, "Two cars exploded in a fiery crash at Spanaway Speedway. Two men have been airlifted to Harborview with life-threatening burns." I swallowed hard.

I knew the news sensationalized things, but it looked as if no one could survive those burning cars.

I grabbed the phone and called the ER to find out what they knew about the victims.

"Hello, my name is Tammy, and my father is being airlifted there after being in a race-car crash. Can you tell me if he has arrived?"

I paced back and forth.

"One of the helicopters had to make an emergency landing at another hospital so they could intubate one of the two crash victims. We do not know at this time which one of the victims it was. The other is expected to land here within the next forty-five minutes." I listened to the detached voice with disbelief. This could not be happening.

"It's really bad news for one of the drivers," I shouted out to Clark. "I can't believe he was racing. I thought he was done with that stupid car. I hate racing. Why didn't they even tell us he was coming out of retirement? Why now, when we have so much going on in our lives?"

I frantically tried to get dressed, fumbling to find a shirt.

"Where are my shoes? I need them. Now."

"Tammy. You have to calm down before you try to drive. I'm not letting you go like this." Clark firmly grabbed my shoulders, looked me square in the eyes, and then hugged me tight.

"I will, but what do I do about Jeff? Should I wake him up and take him with me?" I mumbled.

"I would let him sleep," Clark said.

"But if Dad dies, Jeff might not be able to say goodbye." Unable to slow me down enough to think rationally, Clark just followed me downstairs. I poked my head into Jeff's room and was surprised to find him sitting up in his bed.

"What's happening?" His voice quivered.

I sat on the side of his bed and cradled his hand.

"Jeff"—I choked on my emotion—"Dad was in a bad race-car wreck, and they're flying him to Harborview. I'm going there now."

"Do you want me to come with you? I don't want you to have to go alone," he mournfully said.

"How about if I go and check everything out? I'll call as soon as I know what's happening, and Clark can bring you if you need to come."

"OK. I'll be praying," he said. "Is Clark going to stay here with me?"

"Yes, and I'll call as soon as I get there," I said, and then I fluffed his pillows before I went to find Clark.

Clark rubbed his hand across his forehead as he paced in the living room. He and my dad had fished together regularly for the last fifteen years, and my dad was one of his closest friends. I knew he wanted to go with me, but someone had to stay with Jeff and the girls.

"OK, I'm leaving. I'll call as soon as I know anything. Make sure you listen for Jeff and that the noise didn't wake the girls."

Clark wasn't happy about me leaving so quickly, but I was too upset to give him a choice.

"Please be careful. Please don't speed. Be safe," he begged as I raced out the door.

I tried to honor his request, but I just couldn't do it. I sped down the freeway and intermittently screamed at God, "You cannot be letting this happen.

Have we not had enough? What else do we have to learn? God, I can't handle any more tragedy. Please let my dad be OK. Why? Why now, after forty years of racing? Please, let me get there. I have to see him before he dies." I arrived at the hospital and frantically ran up the cracked sidewalk. Busting through the ER doors and past the security guard, I heard my brother Gary call my name. He motioned for me to enter a little room where family and friends were waiting. I couldn't hold back my emotions as I fell into my mother's arms. Stoic and unusually composed, she let me cry.

I wiped my sleeve across my burning eyes and slowly regained my composure. "What have they told you?"

"They haven't said anything yet, except Dad was the driver who had to be put on the breathing machine," Mom said.

"Have you asked the nurses? Do you know where they took him?"

Mom shook her head, and I immediately left for the nurse's station.

As I headed out the door, I overheard someone say, "I told you Tammy would find out what was going on when she got here." A middle-aged woman smiled at me as I approached the desk.

"My dad was one of the race-car drivers airlifted here, and I wonder if I could find out what is going on?"

"Let me look him up. Last name?" The woman asked me for more details as I stood impatiently. "OK, here he is. They just transferred him from the helicopter, so we don't have his paper work updated yet. I'll have more information for you once he's settled."

"I'm worried he might die. Will you please just go ask the doctor if I can see him?" I asked, starting to panic.

"I'm sorry; it's really chaotic in there right now, as they're trying to stabilize him. You can see him when we take him to the CCU," she politely, yet emphatically, told me.

I knew it could be two hours by the time they got him stable in the ER and then transferred him to CCU. That was too much time—anything could happen.

"Please, I work in the emergency room at Evergreen Hospital and have seen critically injured patients before; I understand the chaos. I will hold it together."

"I'm sorry. But the doctors prefer family to wait until the patient is stable."

"Please. My dad may die, and this might be my last chance to see him alive. You would want the same if your dad was in the ER, wouldn't you?"

She paused, lowering her eyes. "Let me ask the nurse if you can go back. I don't think they'll let you, but I can try."

A minute later, she swung back through the double doors and nodded at me.

"The doctor said you could come in quickly. Only two of you are allowed, and you have to keep it short."

"OK. Just let me ask my mom if she wants to come with me."

My mom just shook her head. She was not prepared to see my dad on a ventilator. So my brother Gary, also a race-car driver, jumped up to go with me. We walked into the room, where at least ten medical staff were urgently working on a very swollen person on the bed. A large tube was sticking out of his mouth and was attached to a machine. It was difficult to discern whether this was actually our dad, as nothing about that body resembled him.

For a moment, I was reminded how bad Jeff had looked fresh out of surgery, but this was actually much worse. His eyes were so swollen I couldn't tell the bottom eyelid from the top. I wondered if he would ever see again. His nose was charred, and much of his face had a whitish-gray hue, like a piece of seared meat. There was a shiny liquid coming from his nose, flowing down the sides of his chin. His neck and arms were a pinkish red mixed with patches of light gray.

I had a fleeting thought that maybe we were in the wrong room, but our reality was confirmed when I overheard the nurse say, "We'll be ready to transfer Mr. Longley in half an hour."

Though I had seen some pretty horrible sights in the ER, I had never seen—or, for that matter, smelled—a burn victim before that day. The stench of burned flesh permeated the room, making it smell more like a mortuary.

We were in the room for less than ten minutes before a nurse gently told us that we needed to leave—they were getting ready for an X-ray and needed the room cleared.

"I really thank you for letting us come in. We'll be in the waiting room, so please let us know if anything changes."

My brother and I stepped around the corner, scrambling to gather our emotions. We hugged, consoling each other.

"I think we should keep the details to ourselves," Gary said. "No one needs to hear how horrible he looks."

"You're right. It's just so much worse than I expected." I wiped my swollen eyes.

We got back to the waiting room and the many family and friends. We told them that Dad was critical and it didn't look good, but we purposely saved them from the horrific images we had seen. Gary's uncharacteristic silence confirmed to me the horror of what we had both seen. After being able to see my dad and understand his condition, I finally had some time to think about how this had happened. I hated Dad's racing. He shouldn't have even been racing. I glared around the room. My mom should have stopped him. Or at least she should have told me so I could have talked him out of it. Dad was stubborn, but then, so was I.

"Why was he even out there? We went to his retirement race last year. This was not going to be an issue anymore. How did this happen? Why didn't I know he was racing again?"

"Dad was just racing this one last time…a favor for his friend. He wasn't there to compete—mostly just to draw a crowd. You know how popular he was," Mom said.

I stomped around the room. "So what happened? What went wrong?"

Gary answered me matter-of-factly, attempting to deflect a bit of my anger. "It was the first lap and a car spun out in front of him, so he slowed down. Another car hit him from behind, piercing his gas tank and causing his car to crash into another car. The impact ignited their fuel tanks, and it spread so quickly they couldn't get out."

"I always knew something bad would happen," I shouted back.

Reaching for my hand, Mom said, "We just need to get through this now."

But this time I was too upset to even stand still.

"I can't believe what is happening. I don't think I can cope with this now. Maybe never." I paced the room. "I need to go home and talk to Jeff. And the girls…" I sobbed louder. "This is all too much. I don't even know how to tell them. I'm going now. I'll be back in a few hours. Call me if anything changes." Nauseated, I got to my car and called home. I told Clark the details of our nightmare. He did his best to comfort me so I could leave the parking lot. It was around four o'clock in the morning, the day of my thirty-sixth birthday. While driving home, I prayed that my dad would survive. As I finished praying, I caught myself wondering again: What good, if any, could possibly come of this horrible situation?

CHAPTER 17

Sharing the News

As soon as I got home, Clark greeted me at the door. "The girls are still sleeping," he whispered. "I haven't said anything to Jeff yet, but I think he's awake."

I quietly opened Jeff's door. He was in bed, listening to one of his books on tape. Rusty crawled over him to greet me as I sat on the bed.

"Hey, I just got home. Everyone says hi."

He pushed the stop button on his cassette player. "How's Dad?"

"He's pretty bad…" I paused; pressure filled my nostrils as I tried not to bawl. "His face and body are really burned…"

I couldn't keep it together. Jeff clung to my hand, and he too began sobbing. Clark rushed into the room; his red-raw eyes met mine as he sat next to us. Pressing his lips tightly together, Clark tried suppressing his angst. Rusty paced around the bed, nervously licking Jeff's face, then mine.

Suddenly understanding how helpless we must have felt through his sickness, Jeff said, "I'm so sorry I've put you all through so much. It seems like a terrible burden to put on people you love."

Taken aback by his words, I immediately tried to comfort him. "You haven't put anything on us. We take care of you because we love you. Besides, you didn't do anything to cause your cancer or blindness. It could have happened to any of us." "It's not your fault, Jeff. This is life. Bad things just happen," Clark said.

"I know. I'm not saying I did anything, but it's still hard knowing how helpless I am. And I hurt for Dad just knowing that he's suffering, and there's nothing he can do to help either."

A quiet moment slipped by before Jeff cleared his throat and continued. "If Dad lives, I imagine his life will never be the same—damaged and disabled in some significant way." He took a deep breath and exhaled slowly.

I reached over and gently wiped his cheeks and quivering chin. "We can only pray; it's all out of our hands." It was a poignant reflection on his own shattered life. There is nothing worse than watching someone you love go through the hell of helplessness. I could not protect Jeff from the heartache he was dealing with, nor could I do anything to make this better for him. But I believed, with all my heart, that God had a plan, and this was a part of it.

"I'm going to go talk to the girls," I said to Jeff as I stepped away from his bed. "I'll be back in a bit."

"Come on, Rusty. Let's go potty," Clark called as he stood to go with me. Rusty eagerly followed.

My head pounded as I walked up the stairs to where the girls were waiting. I opened my bedroom door and saw my girls sitting on the bed, tucked in Clark's arms, crying. They both jumped up and rushed over to me. I held them tightly.

Chelsey asked, "Is Jeff OK?"

"Yeah, he'll be OK. How are you guys?"

Kendra lifted her eyes and looked at me squarely.

"We don't want to go to the hospital. We wanna wait till things are better. Is that OK?" Chelsey asked.

"Of course it's OK. I'm just so sorry all this is happening. You girls have been through enough already."

I rested my head in my hands, rubbing my throbbing temples.

"I'm sorry, Momma. This isn't a very good way to celebrate your birthday," Kendra said, her head resting on my shoulder as she rubbed her hand repeatedly over my back.

"Thank you, Ken. I love you."

I lay on my bed, exhausted from being up all night. Riddled with angst, I couldn't relax, so after only a half an hour, I pulled myself together so I could get back to the hospital, back to my dad's bedside. Jeff decided he wanted to come with me to see our dad. I submitted to his insistence even though I wasn't sure how he would react to all the emotions and chaos.

Clark walked Jeff to the car and then helped me get the wheelchair into the trunk. He lovingly made me coffee for the road, and with sadness in his eyes, he sent us on our way. I called Midge on the way to the hospital to ask for her prayers. Her calm demeanor and relentless faith comforted me like none other. She offered to help however we needed her and prayed with us over the phone before hanging up.

Once we arrived at the waiting room, Mom immediately got up and walked over to Jeff. She leaned over his wheelchair, and they hugged. Everyone started crying all over again. Terry had an inquisitive look on his face and silently pointed at Jeff, mouthing, "Is he going to be OK?" Worried about how Jeff would handle the stress, the rest of the family quietly watched for my answer.

I shrugged.

Since Jeff relied on his hearing for information, it took him a few awkward seconds before he figured out that the silence was intentional. "OK, what's going on?" he asked. "I can tell you're whispering something."

"Terry was just worried if you would be OK. Everyone knows how sick you've been, and stress can just make it worse," I said.

"I appreciate it, but I'm fine. I want to be here with all of you."

"It's not that they don't want you here; people are just worried," Mom said, patting his shoulder.

Within minutes, a nice-looking man, maybe in his twenties, wearing a white coat, entered the little room where mostly family and a few friends waited. "Hello. I'm sorry to have to meet you under such difficult circumstances. I'm Dr. John, and I'll be taking care of Mr. Longley."

Mom jumped in. "Hi, I'm Pat, his wife. Is he still alive?" An odd question given the doctor's calmness, but Mom had a way of being dramatic.

"Yes, he is alive. Let me give you an overview of all that's happening. Mr. Longley is on a ventilator and is in a medically induced coma. He has suffered third-degree burns on his face, neck, and arms. He has first- and second-degree burns on his back as well. He will need to have surgery in few days; we will graft skin to his face, neck, and arms. His nose has been significantly damaged, so I may have to reconstruct it by using a part of his hip bone. Most likely he will be in a pressure mask on his face for up to a year and a half, and he will wear pressure garments on his arm as well."

He paused for questions.

"Could you tell us more about this pressure mask?" Mom asked. Unlike with Jeff, Mom was holding up surprisingly well.

"It's like a tight ski mask, something he'll wear twenty-three hours a day. It'll help his grafts heal. It can be very difficult to get used to, but we'll work with him to ensure the best results. Family members, especially children, can also have trouble adjusting to it, since it can look scary. It might be hard for him to go out in public because so many people would be frightened." After answering a few more of our questions, he left, and the nurse continued to answer more generic concerns.

I caught up with him just as he was leaving. "One last question. When my brother was hospitalized, my dad thought we should take pictures of him so he could see his own progress. Since my brother came out of surgery blind, those pictures obviously weren't helpful. But my mom and I believe that my dad would probably want us to take pictures of him for the same purpose. Would it be OK if I took some pictures of him?"

"We've allowed many family members do that, and I've personally talked to several patients who were encouraged by those pictures." He smiled at me, perhaps relieved that we had chosen to focus on helping my dad recover rather than worrying about his death.

Mom and I agreed nobody should see the pictures except my dad. It was his choice if he decided to show them to others or even keep them. "Would you like to go back and see him now?" The nurse looked at my mother. "We can only have two visitors at a time, and we prefer to keep visitors to immediate family members only. We also ask that you keep your visits short."

Mom and I instinctively rose from the couch together, grabbed each other's hands, and followed the nurse. We entered a large, sparsely furnished room where a middle-aged nurse tended to my dad. There were bags of medicine hanging from silver poles at the head of his bed. A ventilator, rhythmically pumping oxygen into his lungs, hummed in the background. There were two metal folding chairs neatly placed at the foot of his bed. It was what you would image a stark and sterile hospital room would be like.

Unconscious, a breathing tube smashed against his scorched bottom lip, Dad lay motionless. His swollen eyelids were covered with glossy ointment. White gauze covered his charred hands and arms. Small moist cotton pads covered his burned forehead, cheeks, nose, chin, and neck.

"Hello, I'm Mary," the nurse said. "And I'll be caring for Mr. Longley." Her warm smile and sweet voice brought me immediate comfort.

"Hello. I'm his daughter, Tammy, and this is my mom, Pat."

"I'll be done here in a minute. He seems to be doing OK right now."

"So do you think he's going to make it?" Mom asked.

Unstartled by the direct question, she stopped what she was doing, looked straight at Mom, and confidently replied, "I believe he will. He's very sick right now, but he's in the best hospital around to treat his burns."

"Have you seen people come through with burns this bad?"

"Oh yes. I've seen people much worse than him get better. We have patients come here from out of state because our burn unit is that excellent."

"I sure hope so. I don't think we can handle much more," Mom said.

"I have a question before you leave. I'm not sure if the other nurse told you or not, but we want to take pictures of my dad's burns so that he can see the progress of his recovery," I said.

"Yes, she did tell me. I think that's a great idea. I can help you now if you'd like."

"That would be great. Are you OK with that, Mom?"

"Now is as good a time as any. I'd like to see how bad it is."

The nurse put on latex gloves and proceeded to carefully lift dad's right arm, pulling the sheet away from his body. She then moved to the left side of the bed, and with even more caution, slightly lifted his left arm up and pulled the sheet down. "Why don't we start with his face, then work our way down?" Mary suggested. "His left side has more severe burns than the right side."

"Whatever you think is fine with us. Are his burns third degree?" I asked.

"He has a mixture of second- and third-degree burns. The skin with a grayish hue is most likely third degree."

She gently lifted the gauze from his face. Mom was standing opposite her at the head of the bed, looking intently at the variegated pink-and-gray-colored skin. His nose had a dark spot on the tip.

"Will he be able to see again?" Mom asked.

"We expect so. Typically, people's eyeballs don't get burned. We have a natural tendency to close our eyes. Even though his eyelids look awful, his eyes are most likely just fine."

I stepped toward the head of the bed, my camera pressed against my face. As I peered through the hole of the camera lens, the horrific sight sent chills up my body. With each click, my stomach tightened, and I swallowed hard to keep from vomiting in my mouth. I tried to conceal my agony, fearing the nurse might presume this was too difficult for me and not allow me to proceed.

"Do you know what happened to his necklace? He was wearing a gold chain with a race-car emblem on it," Mom said.

"Well, if you look at his neck, right here"—she pointed to a deep-red area just above his breastbone—"you'll see where his necklace melted. You can also see the marks from the melted chain along his neck."

Calm and emotionless, Mom said, "That's amazing. I guess I'll have to have another one made for him."

"Tammy, did you get enough pictures of his face and neck?" Mary asked.

"Yes, thank you," I said without moving the camera from my face.

"OK, let's move down to his arms."

She peeled off the coverings on his left arm and hand. The inside of his forearm was mostly gray, as was the top of his hand. As she lifted his limp arm, I saw the area closer to his armpit void of skin, leaving just raw tissue. It was a gruesome sight.

My voice controlled, I asked, "How are you doing, Mom?"

"I'm OK. I just can't believe it."

We proceeded to his right arm, which was mostly a reddish color, the color it would be if you burned your hand on a pan or oven rack. "There are some smaller burns on his back, so let me roll him on his side so you can get those too."

As I snapped more pictures, I began to wonder if this was just too personal, too private, too painful to continue. I pondered whether I needed to be doing this. Was this really what he would want? I felt done. "OK, I think we have enough. I just want to give him the chance to see where he started."

"I think he'll find the pictures helpful someday," Mary said while placing fresh dressings over his burns.

She pulled the sheet up to his chest, slightly raised the head of his bed, and pointed to a button on the bed rail. "I need to step out now, but you can push this button if you need anything."

"Thank you, Mary, for all your help and for taking such good care of my dad."

I sat next to Mom in the hard chair at the foot of his bed.

"Do you want to go out, Momma?"

"No, I'm staying with him as long as I can. I guess it's time for me to get over my ventilator issues. I need to be here with him."

"I can stay if you want me to."

"No, you need to go take care of Jeff. I'll be OK. I'm just so sorry you guys have to go through this. I'm worried about how Jeff's going to handle it. And I'm worried about how you will manage with Jeff, since it looks like I'll have my hands full for a while."

"Don't worry about us. Clark and the girls will help me. Midge will help too. I'm just sad because I want to be here with you."

"I know, but there's nothing you can do. We just have to wait and see. I'll be fine. I'm not sure why I can handle this but get so broken up about Jeff."

"It's weird, because I can hardly keep it together seeing Dad like this, but I can be strong for Jeff."

Mom decided to walk out with me to say goodbye to Jeff. More people were crowded in the small waiting room than when we had left. There was a round table with four plastic chairs occupied by friends, and four others were squashed on the couch. There were five or six people standing around talking. Jeff was slumped, his head resting against his hand, in an oversized chair in the corner. Plates of food brought in by friends and family filled the tables.

The buzzing in the room slowly quieted when we entered. "Well, how is he?" Terry asked.

"He looks bad, but the nurse said he'll probably make it. She's seen worse," Mom said.

I made my way through the crowd of people, toward Jeff.

"Hey, Jeff, are you doing OK?"

"Yeah, but I'm pretty uncomfortable," he said with a pained look on his face. "Is it OK if we leave soon?"

"Sure. Let me get our stuff together."

I didn't want to leave, but I knew Jeff needed to go. The cancer was wreaking havoc all over his body, and lying down was the easiest way for him to get comfortable. But I was torn. The next few hours were critical; if Dad was going to take a turn for the worse, it would be soon, and I was scared I wouldn't make it back to the hospital in time if his condition deteriorated. And what about Mom—would she really be OK?

I pulled Terry aside. "Call me if anything changes with Dad. And please watch over Mom. I hate that I have to leave."

"Don't worry; I got Mom. I'll call you if anything changes. I promise." He pulled me into his barrel chest and patted me on the back.

I guided Jeff to the wheelchair, placed his hand back on the armrest, and held the chair still so he could sit down. "Mom, make sure you keep me updated," I said. "I'll be praying." I kissed her cheek, hugged her tight, and fought to hold back angst.

She hugged me back and then leaned down and kissed Jeff's forehead. "OK, you guys drive safe and call me later. Love you."

Once I got Jeff settled at home, I sat the girls down to update them on their grandpa. I told them he was hanging in there, but he would need surgery on his face and would have many scars. Their eyes lowered as I described the mask he would have to wear and how it would prevent infection and secure his new skin. No longer able to contain their sadness, they both began to sob. I squeezed my eyelids shut and took in a deep gulp of air.

"Are you worried Grandpa's gonna die?"

"Chelsey, don't even ask that," Kendra snapped.

"What? I'm just asking."

"It's OK. Yes, I'm scared, but I don't think he'll die, so let's try not worry about that."

They sat quietly on either side of me. Kendra patted my thigh with her long, slender fingers, and her big brown eyes intently looked up at me. Chelsey held my hand. Her head rested against my arm as she waited for me to stop crying, but I could not.

"Why…why don't you go downstairs and see what Daddy's doing. Would you tell him to put on some coffee?"

"I'll go tell him," Chelsey said, popping up from the bed.

"You sure you're OK, Momma?" Kendra asked, her eyes still glued to mine.

My composure began to crack as I answered. "Yeah, I'll be OK." I wanted desperately to be OK.

The bedroom door barely closed, and I buried my face in my pillow. I lifted my head to blow my nose, only to hear Kendra from her bedroom next door. An all-too-familiar wave of nausea rushed through my stomach as I went to comfort her.

I pushed open her bedroom door, and there, face-down on her pink-striped comforter, I saw my precious little girl—her face buried in her pillow. I lay next to her, wrapped my arms around her, and held her tight. I wanted to be strong for her, but I just did not have it in me.

CHAPTER 18

The Media Flurry

THE OUTPOURING OF PUBLIC SUPPORT reaffirmed my faith in humanity. People extended unimaginable acts of kindness by bringing food, sending cards, and giving money. One of my dad's friends mowed the lawn every week; another said he would handle any of Dad's chores until he could do them himself. Mom's friends, knowing how much she cooked and baked, brought dishes to her almost every day.

In addition, my mother received phone calls from old friends who had seen the wreck on TV, asking what they could do to help. The media had been parked outside the hospital, eagerly waiting for any bit of information they could obtain. The crash played repeatedly on news stations around the country, and we were contacted by several reporters requesting interviews. We felt compelled to say something about how our dad was doing. After all, the fans—his fans—had helplessly witnessed a horrible fire and were conveying genuine concern for the well-being of both my dad and the other driver.

While Mom was not comfortable talking to the press, she felt strongly that the racing community deserved to hear from us about Dad's condition. He had raced for over thirty years, and many involved in racing were like extended family. It had been forty-eight hours with no update on Dad's condition, so Mom asked my brothers and me to meet with the media.

Gary and I began arranging interviews, and we asked our other brothers if they would like to be involved. Terry didn't want to be on camera and declined. Jeff, however, jumped at the chance.

Because of Jeff's needs, we arranged to have the interviews at my home.

Soon, a reporter made her way to the front door. "Hello. My name is Karen, and I'll be doing your interview," she said, stretching out her hand.

"Come in. We're set up in the living room." I pointed and stepped aside, pressing against the wall as she and her camera crew swept by.

As she entered the living room, Gary stood up and shook her hand. "Hi, I'm Gary."

"Hello," she said with a smile, shaking his hand.

"And I'm Jeff, the youngest brother." Jeff extended his hand in her general direction, taking cues from the sound of her voice. Bewildered, she shook his hand, looking around the room for context.

Catching her expression, I explained. "Oh, Jeff has cancer, and as a result of surgery, he has lost his sight."

She nodded, processing the new information. "It's nice to meet you."

As she chatted with us, the crew helped prepare her for the camera. I sat on the couch next to Jeff, fidgeting with my pen. While I was not nervous about giving updates on Dad's condition, I was not looking forward to her prying into my feelings. I was only here to give her the facts.

She opened her notebook, took out a pen, and glanced up at Jeff.

"So, Jeff, what kind of cancer do you have?"

"It's a rare type of adrenal cancer," he said. "The blindness is pretty rare, too. Guess I won the lottery." He smiled.

She grinned politely but waited for a longer explanation. We looked at each other, trying to figure out a way to break the awkward silence.

Jeff, naturally, saved us. "Yeah, I'm the guy that everyone looks at and says, 'Man, I'm glad I don't have it as bad as that dude.'"

Gary and I laughed. Karen smirked and made a few quick notes.

By now, Jeff was on a roll.

"Hey, could you lower the lights? They're a bit bright," he asked with a straight face. The cameraman immediately reached over to shut off the lights.

"Jeff, be nice," I teased. "Don't worry; he can't see the lights. He's just trying to be funny."

Everyone laughed again. The tension melted, and Karen began her planned interview.

We did our best to articulate our father's condition without sharing all our concerns. We then apologized to all the fans for having to witness such a horrific accident. We thanked everyone for all their support and ended the interview with a promise that there would be additional updates, hoping that more information would help the fans and friends cope with this experience.

Karen was compassionate and professional as she asked about the facts. I contained my emotion until she asked how we were dealing with our father's tragedy. Struggling to keep from crying, I looked away to avoid answering her unwanted question. Gary and I glanced at each other, and then he gave her a vague response making it clear we were not willing to talk about those raw feelings. She tried to ask again, but in a different way. Annoyed and feeling vulnerable, I put up my hand concluding the interview, and they left respectfully. It had been several hours since the interview ended, and we were now gathered around the TV, anxiously waiting for the five o'clock news.

Jeff laughed and kept insisting, "You look lovely."

It always took me a second or two to remember that he couldn't see me or the TV.

After the broadcast, calls poured in from old friends and coworkers. Every call was different. Some wanted to know how they could help, others wanted to talk about the last time they had seen my dad, and there were even a few who were shocked to hear about Jeff's condition. I didn't know what to tell most of them because what I needed they couldn't give me—my family's life back, my brother's health back, and certainly for my dad to have another victory trophy on his shelf instead of the burns covering his body.

Four days passed, and we were once again surprised by the miracles God performed. My dad had been taken to surgery to have his grafts completed, and the doctor believed that he saw new skin buds on my dad's face. If true, the skin buds would grow new skin, and dad's face would not need to be grafted. He also didn't have to take a bone from my dad's hip to rebuild his nose, since it appeared to be healing on its own.

This all meant that my dad wouldn't have to wear the mask after all. Dad was still in critical care, and doctors did place grafts on his neck and arms.

However, his burned back and the portion of his thighs where they took the skin for grafting were expected to heal just fine.

Jeff and I went to visit Dad. We waited for nearly an hour before the nurse would let us come in. Jeff decided that he wanted to go to Dad's room instead of just staying in the waiting room.

An unfamiliar nurse was fiddling with the ventilator when we entered the room. She was plain looking, her hair tightly up in a bun, and her uniform was more outdated-looking than the others'.

I guided Jeff to the metal chairs routinely placed out of the way at the foot of the bed.

"Hello. I'm Ken's daughter, Tammy, and this is my brother, Jeff."

She barely looked up, grumbled, "Hello," and then focused back on the machine. She reminded me of the cranky nurses at my work who hated when family was in the room.

I sat on the chair next to Jeff, trying to stay out of her way.

Jeff turned his head toward my ear and whispered, "What's that noise?"

"That's the ventilator," I whispered back.

"So Dad can't talk?"

"No, he has a tube down his throat. The ventilator is breathing for him."

"Does he even know we're here?"

"No. They have him drugged up, so he's basically in a coma."

The nurse moved past us to the other side of my dad's bed to check the monitor.

"I hate not being able to see what's going on," Jeff said. "What's he look like?"

I continued to whisper as I tried to explain to Jeff what he couldn't see. Unlike the hospital where I worked, visiting hours at the burn center were strictly monitored. I was anxious to avoid disturbing the nurse so she wouldn't send us back to the waiting room until she was done with Dad.

"Dad's arms are wrapped like a mummy. The skin on his face is very pink, although they usually have it covered with bandages. His lips are swollen, and it's difficult to tell how they will heal because of the breathing tube. His nose is much smaller than before, but it still has the shape of a normal nose. He's still recognizable as Dad, but he looks different."

"Wow. I can't even imagine it. It just sounds so awful." The nurse left the room, so I approached the side of the bed. "Hi, Dad. It's Tammy and Jeff." My voice cracked. "We love you."

Jeff blotted a tissue against his eyes and then said, "I think I'm ready to go. This is just too hard."

"OK. Let me just take a few pictures so I can keep track of his progress." I reached into my canvas bag and pulled out my camera.

As I snapped the first picture, I was startled by an angry nurse.

"What are you doing?"

I immediately lowered the camera away from my face, feeling like a child who's been caught doing something naughty.

"You are not allowed to have a camera in here," she scolded, waving her finger at me.

"Um, I received permission from the other nurses to take pictures of my dad's recovery. It's something he wanted us to do during my brother's battle with cancer."

"I'm sorry," she said. "But I need you to put that away until I go talk to my supervisor. This is unacceptable." Heavy footed, she turned and walked out.

"Is she gone?" Jeff whispered.

"Yeah, but she'll be back. I can't believe this. Just this morning the doctor asked Mom to give them permission to take pictures of Dad for their training program. It's ridiculous that she thinks it's inappropriate for us to take pictures, but they—"

The nurse interrupted me once again as she stormed back into the room, even more intense than when she left.

"I need to ask you to wait outside until we get this sorted out."

"That's fine. But it seems a bit hypocritical that the doctor just asked us this morning for permission to take pictures of our dad for teaching purposes, but we can't take them to help my dad see his progress. Something's wrong here."

I helped Jeff up from the chair, and we walked toward the door. I look back at the nurse and said, "And your rudeness will be addressed when we meet with your supervisor."

"Wow. You must be mad. I've never heard you talk to anyone like that," Jeff said, trying to keep up with my pace.

"I'm so ticked off. No family deserves to be treated like this, and besides, she has no right telling me what is appropriate or not."

I paced back and forth, my heart beating faster as my anger increased. Jeff calmly listened as I ranted through my teeth.

About an hour later, a doctor came to the waiting room to find us. He told me he had consulted with the ethics board about my request. Since my mother was the legal power of attorney for my father, and she had given me permission, then he was OK with us taking pictures. The only stipulation was that pictures could only be taken once a day so it wouldn't disrupt his care. All of this was fine by me, and I felt I had won a small battle on my father's behalf. After much discussion on the drive home, Jeff decided that he did not want to go back to the hospital until Dad had regained consciousness and could talk.

"I just wish I could do something so everyone wouldn't have to hurt so much. I thought it was bad being the patient, but worrying about Dad feels so much worse," Jeff told me as I was setting up his nighttime medications.

"You think it's worse being the family of someone sick rather than the one who is sick?" I asked.

"Yeah. First, when I'm sick, I'm too out of it to know what's going on. And second, there's nothing else I have to do but be sick.

"When you're not the one who's sick, you still have all your other stuff to do while being worried about the person who's sick."

"I can see that. The only thing I know is that it all sucks, whether you're the family or the patient."

"Agreed," he said, laying his head on the pillow as I pulled his covers over him.

"Come on, Rusty." The small cockapoo plopped down by Jeff's side, nosing around for a belly rub.

"You know, Jeff, you have so much to share with people, and after all, not everyone has the opportunity to experience things from your perspective. You really should start journaling again so that someday others can continue to learn from your wisdom."

"That sounds interesting, but obviously, I can't write. So we'll have to figure out something else."

"I could write for you if you ever want to do it," I said. I was tired, but I wanted to make sure he was heard.

"OK. I'll think about what I would want to share. Maybe another day."

"All right. Have a good sleep, and I'll see you in the morning. Call out if you need anything." I kissed his forehead and turned out the light.

CHAPTER 19

A New View

THERE WERE SO MANY CHANGES happening, but somehow, we found a way to make it all work. The warm and dry summer weather made everything a bit more tolerable. It was another beautiful August morning—a perfect day for a leisurely stroll with Jeff. I looked forward to our walks. Most of the time, Jeff just listened to me vent, letting me have some time to be myself. But some days, he made his own observations about the world, God, his illness, and anything he happened to be thinking about that day. Shoes on, Jeff grabbed my arm, and out the door we went.

"Doesn't that sun feel good?" I squinted as I raised my head toward the bright rays of sun beating down on my face.

"Oh yeah. I love how warm it is." He lifted his face toward the sky, smiling contentedly.

Barking dogs startled Jeff, as did the cars zipping by us as we walked along the edge of the road. His hand squeezed my elbow a bit tighter until the sounds dissipated, then he relaxed. The sound of crunching gravel beneath our feet filled in the occasional pause in our chatter. As usual, our discussions covered a gamut of topics.

"Hey, I've been thinking about that whole journaling idea, and I think we should try it. Maybe when we get home you could help me start writing?"

"I've got a couple of things to do right when we get home, but I promise I will make time today to do it."

A few hours after our walk, Jeff and I got comfortable on the couch. Pen and pad in hand, Jeff began to talk while I tried to capture his every word.

"Everything seemed to be going well. It's been seven months now, and as far as we know, I am cancer free. Now my father sits in the hospital from being in a race-car wreck. I pray for him every night and ask Jesus for his healing."

"Hold it; stop for a sec. I need to catch up." I scribbled quickly. "Ask Jesus for healing…OK, go."

"Every day is a challenge. Not being able to see is very frustrating, not only for me but for my family. I try to cope with humor so I can keep everyone else up. I never pray for God to take the cancer away because He never put it in me in the first place. We live in a sick world." Jeff paused, listening to me mumbling the words as I wrote them. "You got all of that?"

"Yep. I'm ready."

"I worry about my cancer coming back before Dad gets well, because my family has enough on their plate as it is now. I hate being a burden to Tammy. I know it's hard to schedule her life around me. My friends, Allen and Collin, have left me because they don't know how to deal with my illness. It's difficult that they don't visit me, but I understand them. Some days are good and others are miserable, and I want to sleep them away. Knowing that my friend Keith is going through the same thing helps me. I'm not scared to die; sometimes I do get a little nervous, though. Bye for now. Jeff."

I wrapped up the last few words and shook out my hand. "Good job. Your insight is wonderful. I bet journaling your thoughts will help me as much as you. Want to do it again tomorrow?"

"Yeah, that sounds good. Sometimes it's nice just to talk without worrying what other people think." Jeff smiled slightly, proud of his accomplishment. The twenty-minute session was enough to tire Jeff out, so he rested on the couch while I buzzed around the house getting chores done. My thoughts were all over the place but kept landing back at a place of gratitude that Jeff's faith continued to grow, despite his sickness. I remembered the night in the hospital when I asked God to let Jeff die, to end his suffering. I was so grateful he didn't listen to me. I could see all that he was doing in Jeff's life and in mine.

CHAPTER 20

Family Update

Tammy's Journal—August 2000
Journal 4—I am completely consumed with Jeff's every symptom, especially because this is a cancer I have never seen before. In fact, most of my medical friends have never worked with anyone who has had adrenal cancer either. I read as much as I can, ask questions of his doctors so that I can be somewhat prepared, but at the end of the day his symptoms are unlike most of their patients'. I too fear that the cancer may be back.

Jeff seldom complains; he worries more about how everyone else is doing, and he is very appreciative of our help. Unlike me, Jeff has never been one to go against the current. He accepts his role as "the patient" with an eerie familiarity to when he was young. Growing up anxious, he welcomes the security of having a caretaker to help him and keep him safe. I don't mind because he doesn't resist the help and is so pleasant, which makes it easier on all of us.

Though it might be better for him to become more independent, there are times I selfishly find it simpler to do things for him rather than watch him struggle to do simple tasks himself.

It has been two weeks since my dad's accident. He remains on the ventilator due to double pneumonia and concerns that he may have suffered a stroke. Mom is learning how to take care of Dad's burns since she will be responsible to be his caretaker. His grafts are healing well, and his recovery is going as planned, at least from a burn standpoint. They are concerned that he hasn't woken up and his right arm is weak. They will do further testing to assess the situation.

It is so difficult for me not to be there as often as I wish since I have to rely on others to get answers to all my questions. But I am learning that my need to handle things for my mom may not actually be necessary; she may be stronger than I give her credit for.

As the days pass, I anxiously await for my dad to be off the ventilator and able talk to all of us. I do my best to go to the hospital at least every other day so I can be around family and I can take pictures of his progress.

Jeff's eagerness to return to a routine, a part of his anxiety, is causing a bit of stress around our house. Despite his gratefulness and appreciation for help, he doesn't like that different family and friends have been helping out with the caretaking duties, he feels uncomfortable and vulnerable. Mom and I want to return to our routine, though it will be a while since she doesn't truly know what caring for my dad will be like.

Clark and I are doing our best to hold on to some normalcy during this chaotic time in our life. He, along with some friends, has been helping to take care of Jeff since my mom has mostly been with my dad. Chelsey and Kendra have been spending more time than usual doing things with their friends. Chelsey is really good about helping out with Jeff. She enjoys spending time talking to him and telling him about things going on in her life. She too has anxiety and Jeff helps her cope with it. They talk about how her anxiety makes change difficult and how it causes her to struggle with school.

Kendra tends to keep her distance; she doesn't easily express her feelings, but she has shared her sadness at times about the change in our family dynamic and that she really misses my attention. She has always been a "Momma's girl," so the loss of our time together is a real sacrifice. Whenever I am away from Jeff, she is by my side. If I'm planning on going to the store alone, she asks to come along. Kendra tries to help me get things done so we can spend more time together.

Both girls seem to understand the predicament Jeff is in and would not want him to move out. But this doesn't minimize their wish to have things back to how they were before Valentine's Day. We talk openly about what's going on, and although I ask about how they are feeling, I suspect they don't always say.

Sometimes it is difficult because Jeff wants to go wherever I do, which by the time I get him ready, it takes about three times longer than going myself. I feel badly telling him he can't go though, because he has no way of going out on his own. Sometimes I see Jeff as a victim of his own circumstances.

It is unbearable now to see my dad also be a victim, though he owns some of the responsibility since he chose to race. I sometimes feel angry that he put himself in harm's way, and even more upsetting is that I didn't know about it. I have always feared that something bad could happen to him on the race track.

I cry a lot about my dad. It makes me sick inside to see him weakened and in pain. My dad has always been the rock in our family, and now he requires help with everything. My mom is struggling as well, but mostly with the fact that she is unable to share in the caretaking duties for Jeff right now. She is doing great with learning how to manage my dad's wounds. She has even surprised herself in how strong she has been. She emotionally struggles more with Jeff, and I with my dad.

In the meantime, Jeff and I have become increasingly worried about the possibility that he may be getting worse. I fear sharing my concerns with Mom because she already has enough on her plate dealing with Dad. Although, not telling her feels deceitful since I promised that I would never "protect" her by hiding Jeff's medical information. Jeff has requested that we wait, and I agree it is best until we know for sure.

CHAPTER 21

The Secret

AFTER DINNER, JEFF JOINED CLARK in the family room to watch TV while I finished up the dishes. He gently sat down in his favorite spot on the couch, tucked his legs next to him, and tapped the couch for Rusty to sit with him.

"Hey, Tammy, what time is it?"

Sitting in his recliner next to the couch, Clark answered instead. "It's six twenty."

"Oh, OK, thanks. John should be here anytime."

"Yeah," Clark said over the loud chatter of the TV.

John, Midge's husband, came to our house every Wednesday to do Bible study with Jeff. He also seemed to be benefiting from Jeff's insight and new perspective on life. It was so helpful, as the Bible study fulfilled not only a need for Jeff, but gave Clark and me a chance to have some alone time and run errands.

"Tammy, could you bring me a pain pill?" Jeff asked.

I felt annoyed that he couldn't wait until I was done with the dishes, but then I knew that while he was not in much pain at that moment, he would be shortly. The medication would take about a half hour to work its way through his system to give him the most amount of relief. Timing was critical in pain management, so I immediately dried off my wet hands, poured his juice, grabbed two pills, and wasted no time getting it to him.

Clark's brows squeezed together as his eyes met mine. I shrugged.

"What's hurting?" I asked.

"It's my back and side again. I thought it would go away, but it seems to be getting worse." He exhaled through his pursed pale lips.

I guided his hand to the two pills in my open palm. He pinched them between his thumb and finger and slipped them into his mouth. He reached for the juice and then took a gulp.

"Thank you."

"Those should kick in within a half an hour."

"Hopefully I won't get too drowsy to finish my Bible study."

"It's OK if you do. John will understand."

A knock on the door interrupted my worry. "Come in."

Rusty bounced off the couch, excited to greet John at the door.

"We're in here, John," I shouted.

He walked in and made his way to the family room with Rusty in tow. He knelt and ruffled Rusty's ears.

"How're you doing? Jeff's excited you're here," I said.

"I'm doing good." He then nodded hello to Clark and smiled. "Ready to get started? Looks like we're doing Matthew chapter five today."

"Yep. I'm ready. But I did just take a couple pain pills, so I might get drowsy in a bit."

"No problem. If you doze off, I'll wipe the drool off your chin," John said. A big grin spread across his rosy face. John was a tall, sturdy Swedish-looking man whose humor was dry, and his demeanor even steadier than his wife's.

"Clark and I are going to go have coffee out back. Yell for me if you need something. Help yourself to the snacks, John."

I poured two cups of coffee and added a chocolate-chip cookie on each saucer, and our coveted coffee time was ready. I pushed the screen door open with my foot and smiled at Clark, who was already sitting outside. Coffee time was our special time to bond and get caught up. It was sacred time that brought both Clark and me comfort and allowed us to have some time to ourselves. The girls, and now Jeff, knew not to bother us when we were having coffee. We sat in silence for a moment, enjoying the evening and the quiet. The lush green lawn was lined with lilacs, rhododendrons, and various knee-high shrubs. Tall evergreens surrounded the perimeter of the yard, keeping out unwanted distractions. Unfortunately, despite my best efforts to put on a face of joy so I wouldn't make Clark feel the void in my heart, the silence allowed my thoughts to get carried away.

It was difficult to get my mind away from Jeff, and now my dad, as life outside seemed so insignificant. I had a hard time enjoying the things I had once enjoyed. I envied those around me who were seemingly able to live life freely, without worrying about death knocking on the door. They didn't seem to be aware of the fact that they too could be on our path at any moment. I not only lived this reality at home but saw it at work as well. I wondered if I would ever be able to live life without having to think about the frailty of our very existence.

Clark finally broke the silence. "So what do you think's going on with Jeff?"

"I don't know. It seems like he's feeling worse every day. I can't tell if his medications are off or if the cancer's back."

"Did you guys drop off his urine?" he asked, dipping his cookie in his coffee.

"Yeah. We won't know the results for a week or so. If it's not the cancer, then I don't know what to think. Something's obviously going on."

I took a sip of my coffee as I gazed at the splashing water in the pond.

"What's the word on your dad today?"

"Nothing new. Mom said he's still out of it. I just don't know what's going on. I know it's only been two weeks, but he may never wake up." My eyes started to water. I blinked hard, trying to hide my emotions. I didn't want to waste coffee time crying again.

"I thought they expected it could take a while for the meds to clear his system. Do we need to be worried?" Clark asked.

"That's what they said, but—I just don't know." The mixture of black mascara and salt burned my eyes, making it difficult to see him or acknowledge his concern.

Clark rose to his feet and came toward me with his arms stretched out. He leaned down to hug me. I responded like a child running to the safety of her father's arms and held him tight. His bearded chin rested against my forehead.

"It all seems like too much," I whispered after a few moments of resting my head against his chest.

"I know. We just have to take one day at a time."

After a moment, he released me and returned to his chair.

I used his paper towel to blot my red eyes and runny nose. Moments of silence were periodically broken with innocuous topics such as Clark's work or projects we wanted to do on the weekend. We slowly relaxed, enjoying our time together, until Jeff's Bible study ended, and we got up to say goodbye to John.

Jeff requested that I help him get ready for bed. His pain pills seemed to have brought him some relief, but they also made him a bit drowsy. It was earlier than usual to start his night routine.

"I'm going to hurry and get Jeff down, and then we'll have the rest of the evening together." I kissed Clark on the forehead and then went inside to join Jeff in his room.

I set Jeff's medications in their designated spot on the nightstand next to a fresh water bottle. "Do you need anything else?"

"Do you think we could take a few minutes to journal? I just had a few thoughts to share and figured it might help me to get them out of my head."

"Um...sure. Let me go grab the pad and pen." My stomach filled with angst as I left his room. I hated letting Clark down but worried what thoughts Jeff was harboring.

I swung the screen door open and apologetically said, "I'll be a just a few more minutes. I'm hurrying."

Clark nodded. He had heard those words many times over the past many months.

I sat cross-legged on the edge of the bed, ready to capture Jeff's thoughts. He carefully moved from side to side, trying to find the most comfortable position, while Rusty waited patiently.

"OK, I think I'm ready." He patted the comforter, and Rusty took his place next to him.

"I'm ready to go when you are." His fingers gingerly ran through Rusty's fur as he started to talk.

"Yesterday was a pretty stressful day. I went to see my dad, and it was very difficult. It took all I had not to cry so I wouldn't make a spectacle of myself. I made the decision to wait until he is clearer and able to talk before I see him again. The other hard thing today was that we dropped off my urine, which will tell whether or not my cancer is back. That's probably why I didn't sleep last night.

"I had Bible study with John tonight, and he is going through issues which make what I'm going through seem so insignificant. He has a family to support and has no job. I can't imagine having that kind of pressure. I pray for him a lot and wish him the best. I don't know what to tell him, other than that I will pray for him.

"The past few months, we've seen a lot of miracles and have seen God do many things. I never again will take my blessings for granted. I am thankful I have family to take care of me, friends who visit me, and I can walk, talk, and now move around. Most of all, Jesus has given me peace, which I never experienced before. Hopefully, he will do something for John. Good night."

Once again, I put down the pen, feeling as though I had just heard a sermon that was intended solely for me. I was reminded to focus on my own blessings instead of the sacrifices I was having to make. I found it amazing that Jeff so often thought other people were so much worse off than he was. I didn't know one person who would look at Jeff and think he or she had it worse. It was as if Jesus had taken Jeff's sight so he could actually see God through his heart.

CHAPTER 22

Jeff's Cancer Scare

It had been five months since the doctor told us that Jeff had about six weeks to live, so it was no wonder that every new symptom left us concerned that his death might be imminent. Every time I called the doctor, it felt as if I had to convince him of Jeff's new symptoms so he wouldn't minimize them, as he had in the past. Jeff's cancer was one in a million—I wanted them to think outside the box and search for why he remained so miserable.

"Have you heard from the doctor yet?" Jeff asked.

"Not yet. I was just getting ready to call again." It had only been four days since we had dropped off the sample, but we were anxious about the results.

"Oh, good. I just wanna know. I can't stand wondering if it is cancer causing this or something else."

A pleasant-sounding woman answered the phone and eventually passed it on to Dr. Smith's nurse. I held the phone between my ear and shoulder so I could take notes on all she was saying. I asked questions and gave details about Jeff's pain and other symptoms. I set a follow-up appointment for two weeks out and then hung up.

"What's the word? Am I dying?" Jeff quipped with a smirk.

"Not yet. But there's good news and bad news."

His smirk disappeared. "The good news first."

"There's no sign of the cancer."

His sweaty palm slapped against mine. "Thank you, Jesus." We both took a deep breath in and released it almost simultaneously.

"The bad news is that the cancer messed your adrenal glands up so badly that they aren't working now. It's causing you to have a different disease, called Cushing's syndrome. We need to go up on your steroids so you won't feel so cruddy and you won't get sicker."

"That's not so bad. At least I'm not dying right now. That would have been so hard on everyone. I don't care what I have to take, as long as I don't have to be so miserable."

"We'll get it handled," I said, while neglecting to share with him the plethora of other details the nurse had to say in our lengthy phone call.

"Thanks for your help. I'm going to go watch TV for a bit, if you don't mind." He pushed himself back from the table and cautiously made his way to the couch.

"By the way, I think I want to call Mom and give her update. Do you mind?"

"That's fine. She needs to know about this other thing going on." During my nightly call to my mom, I told her we had had Jeff's urine tested. She was upset that we hadn't told her we were doing it. When I explained why we hadn't, she understood, but she made me promise not to withhold information from her in the future.

Unlike Jeff, she asked me to give her all the details that the nurse had given to me. I informed her that Cushing's syndrome was not fatal; however, it had some horrible symptoms. It caused significant weight gain, stretch marks that looked like purplish flames around the abdomen, fatigue, muscle aches, hot flashes, and mood swings. It was usually diagnosed simply by the accumulation of symptoms—most of which Jeff was developing.

CHAPTER 23

Road to Recovery

ARM IN ARM, JEFF AND I gradually made our way down the hospital hallway, his heavy breathing echoing in my ears. His fingers tightened around my bicep as he labored to walk. Familiar with his grip, I slowed our pace so he could catch his breath.

We were on our way to visit my dad. The cooler days of fall had ushered in changes not only in the leaves, but in our life circumstances as well. After almost three weeks, Dad was finally off the ventilator and out of critical care. He shared a room with a man who had serious burns from an electrical shock. Mom and his wife, Tina, seemed to get along well.

"We're almost there; Dad's room is just around the corner. Are you doing OK?"

"Yeah. Just a little winded, but I'll make it." He wiped his blond brow with his fleece sleeve and then reached for my arm.

"Here we are. You ready to go in?"

"Yep. Let's do it."

The large room had two single beds separated by a curtain. Tom, Tina's husband, was in the bed closer to the window. Dad's bed was near the door. Several vases of flowers splashed the dreary room with color. A stack of get-well cards sat on the table next to several magazines and a bag of candy.

"Well, there's Tammy and Jeff now," Mom said, giving Jeff a quick hug before guiding him to the empty chair near the head of my dad's bed.

"Hi, Dad," I said, leaning over the silver metal rail to kiss his rosy forehead.

His hollow eyes lifted up to meet mine. He looked so weak. I turned toward the TV and paused quietly, intentionally avoiding eye contact with anyone in the room, especially my mother.

"Hi, sis," Dad whispered. His soft, feeble voice was haunting.

I took a deep breath and heavily exhaled, subtly wiping under my eyes before I turned back around and tried to force a smile to my lips.

"How you feeling, Dad?" Jeff hesitantly asked.

"I'm doing fine." He paused. "How are you? Have you been getting out for your walks?"

"Yeah. Tammy's doing good with all that. Don't worry about me; I just want you to think about getting better." Jeff leaned back against the chair.

I heard their words, but I was focused on how amazing my dad's face looked. Miraculously, the doctors didn't have to graft his face. It was fresh and new. The grayish-white skin was gone, and the growth of pink skin lined by rose-colored edges reflected the healing taking place. His new eyebrows consisted of brownish-black stubble, but they looked so much better than I had expected.

"I'm lucky to be alive," Dad whispered, as if he knew what I was thinking.

"Look at how well his neck and armpit are healing." Mom excitedly pulled back the sheet, revealing a raw, red area with distinct patches of flesh that resembled cheesecloth. She gently moved his arm away from his side. Dad groaned. The grimace on his face immediately made me feel sick to my stomach.

"That's OK, Mom. I'll see it another time," I said.

"Oh, he's fine." Mom continued to stretch his new skin. "The physical therapist wants us to move his arm around to create mobility."

I stepped away from the bed and looked up to the TV again. I took a few quiet sniffs, hoping to prevent the need to blow my nose.

"Dad, I think it's really important for you to eat the Jell-O they give you. Do you want me to feed you a bite?" Jeff said. A devilish grin spread across his round face.

"Oh, you're excited to make him eat his wonderful hospital foods, aren't you? Just like he made you do." Mom laughed.

"No, thanks. I'm good."

"But you really need to eat so you can heal and get strong," Jeff said, passionately reciting one of Dad's favorite lines he had used when Jeff was in the hospital.

Dad's puffy lips curled upward toward his raw pink cheeks. "Thanks. I'm not hungry."

"I'll be right back," I said, heading out the door. I stepped into the hall in search of the restroom, my head aching; I was no longer able to hold myself together. I pulled open the heavy door to the single restroom and turned the silver dead bolt to ensure my privacy. I sat on the toilet, put my head into my hands, and wailed.

I wondered why, in every other circumstance of my life, I was able to manage my emotions, but when it came to my dad, I lost all control. What was wrong with me? I didn't want to take the time to figure it out, especially not there. I just wanted to be in control of my emotions, to not continually feel so overwhelmed. I did not want to cry anymore.

After a few minutes, I blotted my eyes with a damp paper towel and wiped the mascara off my cheeks. The chrome mirror reflected a sorrow-filled red face framed with messy blond hair. I stared back at a broken me and tried to give myself a pep talk. "You can do this. You need to get it together for everyone out there. Focus on the good things."

Worried that someone would come to find me, I blew my nose one last time and exited the room, feeling only a slight bit better.

Chin up, emotions less visible, I stepped through the door and was met with expressions of concern from Mom and Dad. I shifted my eyes toward the side of the bed, where Jeff sat silently, his hands resting on his thighs, his head turned toward the direction of my movements.

"Well, Jeff, did I miss you feeding Dad the Jell-O?"

"No, he wouldn't let me."

"I'm sure there's going to be plenty more opportunities."

"Yeah, I know I'm going to have to let him feed me at least once," Dad said, resigned.

"Right now he can't open his mouth wide enough to get a spoon in it. We have to work on stretching the skin with a tool the therapist gave us. She said it will help to minimize the scar tissue," Mom said.

"I'm really sorry I've put you all through this," Dad said.

I gently dabbed the wetness around his eyes, softly kissed his forehead, and swallowed hard to force the lump in my throat to go away.

It was an unusual expression of remorse for my dad, and it took me off guard. With tears running down my face again, I said, "We're fine, Dad. We're going to be just fine. You've just got to worry about getting yourself well."

Mom came around the bed, wrapped her arms around me, and pulled my head toward her shoulder. "It's all going to be OK." She patted my back.

"I know, but it kills me to see him like this. I don't know why it's so hard for me."

"'Cause it's your daddy, and you're a daddy's girl." Her voice was motherly and soft.

Unsure what that meant, I felt better for a moment just letting out some emotion.

I looked down, and Dad's hollow, damp eyes met mine. "I'll be OK, sis."

"It—it's just hard for me to see you in this kind of pain." My voice broke.

"Well, at least the morphine seems to keep the pain under control most of the time." Mom smiled, trying to lighten the mood.

"You've got to love that morphine," Jeff said, having had firsthand experience.

Dad was focused on leaving the hospital and seemed to lack insight into his frailty. His body remained weak and required painful physical therapy so he could regain the use of his arms and hands. The physical therapist recommended that Dad transfer to an inpatient rehabilitation facility. But Dad believed that he would be better off if he just went home and worked in his garage to rehabilitate and go to outpatient therapy a few times a week.

The therapist told us that some people just have to see how hard it is for themselves. It was just who he was, and Dad had always believed hard work would get you wherever you needed to go. I believed that if anyone could recover quickly, it would be him.

But Dad simply could not do everything on his own, so he had to rely on my mom. In order for Dad to come home, Mom had to learn how to scrub his wounds and rebandage the open holes. She was apprehensive about taking him home so soon, based on the physical therapist's recommendation and the fact that he got fatigued so quickly. However, she thought that emotionally it would be better for everyone to have him home, and the rest of us agreed. She also had to help him with bathing, dressing, and exercises. She already had that part of the routine down, thanks to Jeff.

The day of Dad's homecoming finally arrived. Mom and I went to pick him up, while Jeff waited at their house with my cousin Allison. When we got to my dad's room, he was sitting in a chair, dressed in baggy gray sweatpants and a loose-fitting, short-sleeve, button-up shirt. His expression did not reflect the excitement one might expect on such a special day. The nurse was writing out final instructions for discharge.

Lightly caressing the side of his head, Mom asked, "Well, are you ready to come home?"

"Yeah. I'm ready to get into my cozy chair."

Even the slightest movement seemed to trigger a grimace on his discolored face. "You feeling OK, Dad?"

"Yep. Just ready to get out of here."

"We just finished changing his bandages and getting him dressed, so he's a bit tired. You're lucky you get to go home instead of to the rehab unit. They really work you hard up there," the nurse said as she put all the papers in a nice stack.

"Let's hope this is the right decision," Mom said.

While I packed up the remainder of Dad's things, the nurse gave Mom final instructions. She confirmed all the necessary arrangements had been made for physical therapy and follow-up care. Then she turned and smiled at my dad. "Do you have any last questions, Mr. Longley?"

"No. Thank you all for the wonderful care. I really do appreciate all you have done for me."

A nurse's aide arrived with a wheelchair to escort Dad to the car. "Hello, Mr. Longley. Are you ready to go?"

"Yes, sir."

"OK then. Do you need a little help transferring out of the chair?"

"No, I think I got it." He leaned forward, put his right hand on the arm of the chair, and tried to push himself up. His wobbly arm failed to give him enough lift. I got a pit in my stomach as I watched him rock back and forth trying to gain enough momentum to get up. I held myself back from helping him, and after one last rock forward and a weak push-off, he was up.

He stretched his shoulders toward the ceiling, glanced my direction, and gave me an accomplished nod. The soles of his slippers slid across the linoleum floor as he made his way to the wheelchair. The attentive aide held the back of the chair as I swung the chrome foot plates out to the sides. Dad turned and sat down.

I grabbed the two overstuffed white plastic bags filled with Dad's toiletries, cards, and supplies and headed to my car. As I drove around the building to the front of the hospital, I realized that just thirty-one days earlier, I believed this would be the place my dad would die. But not only was he alive, he was doing better than anyone expected.

When we arrived, Mom popped out of the car first and opened the passenger door. I released Dad's seat belt, and Mom kept it from touching his arm as it retracted. Dad slowly swung one leg and then the other out the door and planted his slippers on the ground.

"Here, Kenny, grab my hand and I'll help lift you up," Mom said firmly.

"Just wait a minute," he snapped. "Don't pull me; just let me hold on to you for balance."

Mom looked at me and shook her head, lip curled. Her silent gesture reminded me of other times my dad's resistance to help had frustrated her. Dad was certainly independent, sometimes stubborn, and occasionally he simply refused to listen to anyone. He was not a complainer; he just liked to do things his way.

He wobbled to the blue overstuffed recliner and slipped his frail five-ten frame into it. As he leaned back, Mom pulled up on the side handle to help him recline. He grunted and groaned, his eyes squeezed tightly together. I watched intently for his hand to release its tight grasp of the chair cushion.

"Welcome home, Dad," Jeff said from across the room.

"Thanks." Dad sighed heavily. "I can't believe I got so winded."

"I feel for you. I know what it's like. You ready for just one more walk around the house before you rest up?" Jeff said, looking in Dad's general direction with a wide grin on his face.

Disapprovingly, I shot a glare at Jeff that fell on blind eyes. Jeff was far too cheerful for the situation. Yes, Dad was home, but he was obviously in so much pain. But then I caught myself and smiled, thinking of the irony. Jeff, and the rest of us, had learned that humor was the best way to deal with the grief. Maybe it would help Dad as well.

Dad had always been very focused on pushing Jeff to recover, reminding him to do his exercises and telling him to work through the pain. At times, he would get frustrated with Jeff for saying he did not feel good or he was too tired to do anything. Dad's attitude toward Jeff was always one of "suck it up and get it done." Now Dad was gaining new insight into how difficult Jeff's rehabilitation had been.

I wasn't sure whether it was a blessing or a curse that they would have the opportunity to recover together. However, one thing was for sure: my dad not only looked different; he talked with more emotion than I had heard from him before. Perhaps Dad and Jeff would find new meaning to their lives as they recovered together.

CHAPTER 24

Sharing the Duty

By September, Chelsey and Kendra were back in school, doing their best to pretend that life was somewhat normal. I felt I was missing so much of their childhood, and I imagined they felt the same way. Even though we enjoyed some days together during the summer, my mind was often distracted with worries about Jeff and Dad.

Tragedy is said to have a way of robbing joy from people, and I certainly felt robbed. Clark and the girls seemed to welcome the structure of work and school. I'm sure it was a relief to escape from the drama that had taken over the last seven months of our lives.

My life calmed down a bit by not having to help the girls get back and forth to friends' houses and other activities, on top of having to work and care for Jeff. Now I had most afternoons free to hang out with Jeff, which he loved, since he could get very bored listening to the TV all day.

Although I was grateful that I could take care of my brother, it was still difficult at times. He generally tried not to be demanding, but since he needed constant help, he could only reduce the strain so much. His health continued to require regular monitoring and intervention.

Cushing's syndrome caused Jeff to sleep away much of the day, and the more he slept, the more difficult it was to get him to engage in a rehab routine. He understood that he could not change how sick he felt or how his medication affected him, so he basically resolved to put rehab on the back burner.

It had been a month since Dad left the hospital. His medical insurance ran out, so he was no longer able to go to outpatient therapy. He was still in significant pain and unable to use his hands much. Limited range of motion with his arms made it impossible for him to do simple tasks such as buttoning his shirt or cutting his own food. If he didn't continue therapy, he would be permanently disabled.

Clark and I both worked in health care, and we exhausted all the resources we thought might be available to help my dad. The cost of therapy was very expensive—too expensive for someone to come to the house as much as my dad required to fully recover.

"You know, I'm happy to go to their house before work and do his therapy," Clark said as we were driving to visit my parents.

"That would awesome," I said, feeling thankful. "I think you should be the one to talk to him about it."

"I'll mention it." After visiting with my parents for an hour and watching Dad struggle to reach for his glass of water, I brought up the topic of rehabilitation. Clark took the cue.

"So I was thinking about the insurance issue and your rehabilitation..." Clark paused and waited for my dad to look at him, and then he continued. "I would like to come over two or three times a week and help you with your physical therapy."

The words had barely left his lips before Dad shook his head. "No, thanks. I appreciate the offer, but you're already doing enough by helping with Jeff."

"I don't have to do hardly anything with Jeff. I can come on my way to work."

"Oh no. I'll be just fine. I don't need any help doing my exercises." Dad politely, yet firmly shut the conversation down.

"I really think Clark could help you, Kenny," Mom said. "And not to nag, but you're not doing your exercises like the doctor recommended."

Dad ignored Mom's comment and apathetically stared at the TV.

"I know you hurt..." Mom continued, but Dad acted as if he didn't hear her. "He won't listen to me."

"That's pretty normal—that patients don't listen to family. But they do listen to me," Clark said. Dad glanced at him. "But it's up to you. Just let me know if you change your mind."

"I really do appreciate your offer, but I think I can manage."

During our visit the following week, Dad's attitude had changed as he realized just how much work it would take to recover.

"So, Clark, if, um, the offer still stands…" Dad cleared his throat. "I would welcome your help."

"I'm ready to get started. I'll look forward to torturing you; it's one way to get even for all those times you outfished me." Unlike Jeff, Dad had always been a very physical man. Combined with his determination and strong work ethic, he enthusiastically dove into his physical therapy. He initially focused his energy on the exercises that brought about the quickest change, such as those for his arms. He did not like doing the face and mouth-stretching exercises because of the pain, but he did as much as he could tolerate.

It was fair to say my mother had never wanted to be a nurse, but she was turning out to be a good one. She did a great job of caring for my dad: scraping off dead skin from his burns, putting on his medication, and rewrapping his wounds. She bathed and dressed him every day. She became the queen of making milkshakes, as Dad's mouth would not open wide enough to eat whole food. Everything Dad ate had to go through a straw. As Dad made good progress in his recovery, Mom eventually determined it was time for her to resume her share of the caretaking duties for Jeff.

"I think I would be OK having Jeff overnight this week. I have to try it sooner or later," she told me.

"OK, how about if Clark drops him off on Thursday morning, and I'll pick him up on Friday night?"

"So what's happening on Thursday?" Jeff asked, overhearing.

"Oh, Mom was just saying she thinks it's time to have you come back for an overnight."

"Don't you think that's going to overwhelm her? It seems like a lot to take care of me and Dad," he asked, nervously picking at his fingers.

"I think it'll be fine. You're doing better than you were when they first started taking you. And if it doesn't go well, I can always come and get you."

"Yeah, I guess it's as good a time as any. And who knows; I might be able to bring Dad some comfort."

Thursday night came and went without a call from Jeff. It was Friday morning, and I called my mom as usual while on my way to work. "Hi. How did it go last night?"

"Well, the night went fine, but we had a small problem this morning." She sounded weirdly giddy.

"What happened?" I asked, starting to feel a little worried.

"I told Jeff not to get out of bed until I came in to get him up. I got your dad in the shower and was scrubbing his burns, when I heard Jeff screaming—"

"Oh God, what happened?" I interrupted, now panicking.

"He's fine. Just listen. I have Dad hollering at me in the shower, and now Jeff is yelling too. I run to Jeff's room to see what's happening, and I find him standing there peeing in the closet."

I spewed my gulp of coffee all over the steering wheel. Mom tried to compose herself so she could tell me more.

"He got turned around and thought he was in the bathroom. Jeff, *stop*—you're peeing in the closet."

I slapped the steering wheel as my deep laugh filled the car.

"He said, 'Really?' And then he started laughing while in midstream. 'I didn't want to bother you while you were helping Dad, so I thought I could do it myself.'"

"That is hilarious." I took in a deep breath, rubbing my throbbing cheeks, trying to regain my composure so I could focus on the traffic ahead of me.

"I struggled to get him settled back on the bed and ran back to your dad." Mom's story ended, but her amusement continued.

CHAPTER 25

Tammy's Thoughts

Tammy's Journal—September 2000
Journal 5—We've had some pretty funny things happen lately that remind me that we have two choices in life—to laugh or cry. Since Jeff's surgery we collectively spent more time as a family crying, but now the tide is shifting. Lately, more often than not, we tend to laugh. Growing up, humor was always a friend to our family. Our parents often teased with each other and played practical jokes on each other. They did the same with us kids, while teaching us the importance of not taking life too seriously. Our lives seem easier when we enjoyed the lighter side of our dark days.

It is working out well for Clark to take Jeff to Mom's on Thursday mornings when he goes to do Dad's therapy, and then we either pick him up Friday night or Saturday morning. He not only gets a chance to be with Mom and Dad, he also visits with friends and family who live near their house. Since we live twenty-five miles away, it is difficult to ask people to come over and visit, though when someone offers, I try to take them up on it. The weekends are usually the days people come to our house, which frees me up to do something else with the girls and Clark.

There are only a few of Jeff's friends who he feels comfortable visiting with, such as his old roommates Dave and Yvonne, and his childhood friend, Frank. He especially enjoys it when his friends bring him his favorite dinner: hamburger and fries. It is nice for Jeff to have someone different to talk to and with whom he can share his life's experience. He looks forward to feeling emotionally comfortable enough to actually go out to dinner with them, without me tagging along. As for now, it remains a struggle since he still gets self-conscious and very anxious going with other people.

My two close friends, Brenda and Midge, have also been available to help at the spur of the moment. Brenda brings Jeff homemade cookies every week, which he absolutely loves. Midge is my "doctor partner," since she goes to all of Jeff's doctor appointments with me. She helps me get him in and out, and sits with him while I make all the follow up appointments. We typically go to lunch after his appointments, which gives Jeff something to look forward to.

Journal 6—My parents have been overwhelmed by the support they have received. My dad was never one to concern himself with other people's needs, thus he is completely in awe that people actually take time out of their day to even make a phone call to see how he is doing. Many race fans and his friends have donated money, which again has been a real blessing given his expensive medical bills. The only things my dad is comfortable receiving are prayers; everything else makes him feel somewhat guilty. Since his accident, he is much more open to talking about the power of prayer. He believes that his life is a miracle. He often shares, "My life flashed before me, and I feel so lucky to even be alive."

Dad has certainly listened to Jeff and me talk about Jesus, but that never really affected his personal beliefs until he met his fate in the fire. Now that he is experiencing blessings in his own life, he has become a real believer in the power of prayer and faith. He has no doubt that he is alive for a reason.

Sometimes when my dad speaks, I can't believe it is really my father. Dad was always a very determined, hardworking, self-reliant man. He enjoyed racing on weekends and had never allowed the danger of his sport to affect his decision to put his family's well-being at risk. He now admits he was selfish and believed that he could do whatever he wanted to do, without depending on others.

He is now feeling horrible at the thought that our family would have really suffered if this tragedy had occurred when we were growing up. He feels sad about the hardship this has caused not only my mother, but the rest of us as well. He was never one to consider the needs of others, unless it involved his racing. For example, my dad would have never visited a sick person, especially if they were in the hospital. Now he knows the power of someone's time and selflessness.

Though my dad was never a harsh man, he certainly was a man with the attitude that "life happens, and you just need to deal with it on your own." Now he realizes that sometimes we do need people, and that they can really change our lives. It is amazing to witness how my father has been transformed by fire.

CHAPTER 26

Burn Man and Blind Guy

VIBRANT ORANGE-AND-RED-TINTED TREES GREETED ME as I drove up the driveway to my parents' modest home. A lush center island divided up the cul-de-sac, alive with colors only midautumn could produce.

I opened my car door, breathing in a fragrant bouquet of fall air. I sat there for a second, relishing the moment. I let Rusty out before I walked around the back of the car. Jeff stepped out of the front passenger seat, shut the door, and waited motionlessly for my arm to guide him to the house.

"Wow, it's a gorgeous day. Just take a deep breath. Do you smell the leaves?"

"Yeah," he said. "I love the smell of fall. It feels nice out. Is it cloudy?"

"No. It looks like it's going to be a really nice day for you and Dad to take a walk."

We continued to the front door. Rusty jumped up and down, eager to get inside for some belly rubs from Dad. I led Jeff to the couch and then joined Mom in the kitchen. Dad was reclined in his chair, trying to stay awake. Mom and I were getting caught up while the TV chattered in the background. During a lull in conversation, I overheard Jeff and Dad talking.

"So, Dad, have you done your exercises yet?"

"No, not yet. I'll do 'em later."

"Well, if you do them now, and again later, just think how fast you'll improve," Jeff repeated, just as Dad used to tell him when he first came home from the hospital.

"You're probably right, but I'm not up to it just yet."

He could not see that Dad was half-asleep, but Jeff did not miss the annoyance in his response.

His smirk disappeared. "I'm just kidding with you. Tammy said it's nice out, so maybe we can go for a walk after lunch."

"Yeah. We'll see how I feel. I'm just going to take a little rest now."

Jeff quietly turned his attention to Rusty, nestled along his side as usual. He patted his leg, and Rusty wasted no time rolling onto his back. Jeff scratched his belly while cooing at him, a ritual that seemed to be soothing for both of them.

After a restful morning and a hearty lunch, "the boys" were ready for their daily walk around the island out front. Dad had a scarf wrapped tightly around his face to protect himself from the stinging pain cold air delivered to his raw, sensitive skin. A heavy flannel shirt and winter coat kept the rest of his body well protected from the elements.

"Come on, burn man. You ready to take this blind guy out for a walk?" Jeff said, amused at the new phrase he had just made up.

Dad laughed. "I'm coming." He placed his good arm in reach of Jeff's hand and guided him out the front door.

"We're at the stairs; be careful," Dad said as he stepped down the first step, and then he waited. Jeff's hand gripped Dad's tightly as he cautiously tapped the sole of his shoe against the step to locate the edge. He then proceeded down the first step, then the next.

Arm in arm they walked toward the end of the driveway, chatting about the news, family, and their health issues. Instead of looping around the island back toward the house, Dad guided Jeff to the right and down the road, away from the house.

Toward the middle of the block, Dad stopped for a brief rest. "Hey, I've been meaning to talk to you about something."

Jeff lifted his head, listening intently.

"I wanted to say I'm sorry for not understanding you as a kid, especially when you first got sick. I had good intentions; I just didn't know what to do, so I let Mom handle everything."

"It's OK. I don't really remember that stuff anyway."

"Being injured has made me realize how hard it is to motivate yourself to do things. I didn't realize until now just how hard I was on you."

"It's not your fault. Nobody can understand it until you've lived it. Besides, if I'm being honest, sometimes I milked being sick too, so I probably needed a kick in the butt."

"I guess." Dad stepped forward, still holding on to Jeff's arm. Jeff followed, a pleasant smile across his face. They slowed, both in conversation and speed, as they edged toward the end of the block.

"How you are doing?" Dad wheezed, muffled by the scarf.

"Pretty good. But I'm getting a bit winded. It feels like we've been walking forever."

"Well, I figured we were strong enough to make it to the corner, but now I don't think I can make it back," Dad said. His free arm grasped a fire hydrant, a scant block from the house.

"What? We aren't in the driveway?"

"Nah. I tried pushing the envelope and didn't want to stress you out. Think about how happy you would have been knowing we went to the corner and back."

"You're probably right." A bead of sweat rolled down Jeff's cheek.

"Here." Dad placed Jeff's hand on the fire hydrant. "Lean against this until I figure out what we're going to do."

"Does Mom know where we are?"

"Well, not exactly." Dad's voice was fatigued and apprehensive. "I wasn't planning on us going this far when we left, but…since I was feeling pretty good and enjoying our conversation, I kept on walking."

"So now what?"

"I might need you to walk home and get Mom to come pick me up."

Pointing where he thought home was, Jeff mock laughed. "You do know that I can't find my way back—I've never walked outside alone, remember?"

"I'm teasing. What? You can dish it, but you can't take it?"

"Ha ha." Jeff enunciated the words, sour faced. "Do you have a backup plan?"

"I'm sure Mom will come looking for us pretty quick."

Shaking his head back and forth, Jeff said, "I hope so, but you know she's gonna be ticked when she gets here."

"It won't be the first time. Let's just take it slow and see how far we can make it back before she finds us." He put his elbow in Jeff's hand, and they began the long walk back home.

"Uh oh. Here she comes," Dad said as Mom's red car approached.

"Where have you guys been?" Mom shouted through the open passenger window. "I was worried sick when I realized you were gone."

"Dad decided he was ready to run a marathon—he just forgot to clue me in on it."

"What were you thinking, Kenny?" Her eyebrows pinched together. "You're going to give one of us a heart attack if you keep pushing yourself so hard."

Dad shot her a halfhearted grin but was too weary to banter back. He crawled into the front seat of the car while Mom helped Jeff into the back. The drive home was short. After an hour of walking, they had only made it six houses away from home.

CHAPTER 27

The Holidays

IT WAS THE WEEK AFTER Halloween, the start of the Christmas season in our house. Clark was out picking up the girls and Christopher from school while I worked feverishly to get decorations up before they got home. A miniature Christmas village lit up the family room mantel, while snow babies in artificial snow covered the tables. Just a couple more decorations in their traditional spots, and it was all set.

Kendra was the first to push open the front door, and before the others could get inside, she squealed, "The house is decorated."

Christopher and Kendra reminisced about their memories from last Christmas as they excitedly inspected all the decorations. Chelsey swung the door shut, dropped her backpack on the floor, and surveyed the living room. "It looks great. But where are our stockings, and what about the lights for our rooms? Are they up yet?"

"I haven't put the stockings up yet because I couldn't find the stocking hangers." Their enthusiasm was infectious. "I'll help you put lights in your room after a while."

Jeff sat quietly, curled up in his favorite spot on the couch with Rusty lying next to him. Rusty's eyes were closed, his head resting on Jeff's lap, enjoying the paw rub he was receiving. Jeff always had a childlike excitement about Christmas, sometimes starting his shopping in July. His annual quest for the perfect gift brought him as much joy as it did to the recipient on Christmas Day, but today his silence was palpable. I waited for the kids to go upstairs before I said anything.

"You OK?"

"Yeah, why?" He remained completely focused on rubbing Rusty's paws.

"You just seem a bit down." I sat near him on the couch.

"I'm OK." He paused and sighed. "Just a little bummed that I can't see what the kids are so excited about. And I don't even remember how your house looked last Christmas. It just…reminds me how different things are now."

"Yeah, I bet." I squeezed his hand, unable to imagine being in his position. "It's gotta be hard for you. I know how much you love the holidays."

"It really sucks being blind…" A long pause. "I'll never see Christmas lights again. Even the thought of shopping seems like torture. It's taking all the joy out of the holidays." His eyes welled up.

I pulled a pillow close to me. Squeezing it tightly, I buried my face. Alarmed, Rusty sat up and scratched at my arm. I couldn't let go of the pillow for fear I would fall apart. Getting no response, he lifted Jeff's hand with his nose and repeatedly licked it. My intense anguish passed unnoticed by Jeff, just as I had hoped.

"I'm fine, boy," Jeff said, patting Rusty's head.

"That dog is half-human," I said.

Rusty immediately jumped on Jeff's lap to stretch his front paws over Jeff's shoulders in a bear hug and rubbed his nose against Jeff's face while Jeff rubbed his hands over Rusty's back.

"He sure is. You hate it when I'm sad, don't you, boy."

Jeff and Rusty sat there together, and I quietly watched the amazing bond between my brother and his best friend. The distraction settled our emotions, and in a minute Jeff moved on to another subject.

"So since I can't go out shopping, I'm going to need some ideas about what to get the girls."

"Well, they asked me to buy them a Walkman, but you can get it for them, if you want."

"Do they want it really bad? Because I'd like getting them something really special." His voice brightened. It became obvious to me that, even under all this, he was ready to help make Christmas special for the girls.

"Oh yeah. That would make you the Christmas hero for sure."

He smiled slightly. "That would be great."

Throughout the days following, we continued to discuss different gift ideas for our parents and other family members, but the more we talked, the more disconnected he seemed.

"This is still really hard for you to think about, isn't it?" I asked.

"Yeah. I've been trying to get excited about the holidays for a while now, but I'm just not able to get up for it."

"It's OK to be sad, Jeff. After all, look at all that's happened in the last nine months: cancer, surgery, blindness. You've been through a lot. Even though things are getting better, it's still gotta be hard." I waited in silence for a reply that didn't come.

"It's gonna be OK. You can focus on the fact that you have an assistant to go shopping for you."

"Yeah, that helps." He acknowledged my advice, but hopelessness filtered through his words. "I'll just have to get a better attitude about it. I'm…trying."

"Well, let me help you." My exaggerated enthusiasm startled both Jeff and Rusty. "We're going to get you that better attitude."

"Oh no. What are you thinking?"

"I'll be right back." I left the room and then returned with a pad of paper and a pen.

"OK, here's what we're gonna do. When I can't seem to get myself out of a funk, I write things down. First, all the things that are bugging me, and then all the things that are going well."

"Are you talking about journaling?" Sitting up a bit straighter, he seemed a little more hopeful.

"Yeah, sort of." I sat back, put a pillow on my lap, and then propped the pad on the pillow.

"What do you mean?" he asked.

"So I think that when we're done, you will see that there are plenty of things we can count as gifts this Christmas, even though you can't go shopping for them. But first I want you to be able to share the not-so-good stuff, 'cause it's good to get those feelings out. I think it'll help you feel better. What do you say?"

"I don't know. I guess it can't hurt. So are you gonna take notes, or am I just talking?"

"Yep, I am ready to write. OK, let's start by getting out the crappy stuff."

"Well, I'm still recovering from my surgery after nine months, and I still don't know if I'm actively dying, which makes everything worse. And now that I have Cushing's syndrome, I'm fat, moody, and achy. The hot flashes and skin rashes drive me crazy. Add to that not being able to see, which adds a totally different dimension to my illness."

"Hold on for a sec so I can get caught up." I turned the page and continued. "OK, one or two more things, and then we can move to the good things that have happened."

"I have lost so many desires, and my life is no longer pleasurable. I especially feel that now that the holidays are here. I used to like window shopping; I miss it. I loved going to the mall to find the perfect gift, but now I hate it because I feel like people are staring at me. I miss seeing the weather—the fall days, the green grass, and the sky. I miss driving. I miss the independence of life."

I exaggeratedly tapped the pen on the pad, finishing the sentence. "I think you've covered the crappy stuff. OK, now tell me about the good things happening in your life."

"Well, the flip side is that I pretty much have it made these days." His frown turned upward. "I mean, who else do you know that has a maid, chauffeur, chef, personal—"

"You're real funny."

"OK, OK, being serious now. I do tell myself that I may have lost my car, but at least I don't have a car payment anymore. Or I may not be able to take care of myself, but at least I have family to help me. I'm thankful that I don't have to stress about money anymore."

"That's good. What else?" I asked, shaking out the kink in my fingers from writing so fast.

He pondered my question for a few moments. "I think my depression and coping skills are better. I mean, I used to be depressed for days and weeks over stupid stuff, and now I can usually get out of my funk much faster. And," he continued, a bit more animated, "since I've been sick, I live one day at a time, and I try to be grateful for what I have left. I realize that I didn't use what God had given me, and I totally took everything I had for granted, including my health."

"Wow, that's amazing insight. Even though you can't enjoy buying the kind of gifts you used to give, you certainly can give us some wisdom and insight."

"Yeah, I'm learning a few things. I'm trying to figure out how I can use my illness to help others—to help them see what is really important in life and not wait until it's gone before they appreciate it." I could see his spirits lifting as he spoke.

"You inspire me. I'm getting to learn right alongside you." I wrapped my arm around his neck and gave him a kiss on the forehead. "Thank you for sharing your thoughts with me. It makes me wonder why most of us fail to notice the real purpose of our life until something tragic happens."

"Yeah."

"I've got to go check in on the girls now."

"OK, thank you for helping me. I do feel better." He smiled.

The week before Thanksgiving, we finalized details for a surprise Christmas gift for Mom and Dad. I hired a photographer to take pictures of my three brothers and me, and their four grandchildren, Kendra, Chelsey, Kylie, and McKenna. We didn't know how long Jeff had to live, so it seemed like an opportune time to have some family photos. It was a very emotional realization that this could be the last photos of all of us kids together. We all had an awareness of that fact, which made the photo shoot a bit more intense. Jeff and the boys told plenty of jokes, attempting to keep the mood light. I knew this would be a treasured, but heartbreaking, gift for our parents and for us siblings as well.

The photographer took shots of Jeff alone, then Jeff with his favorite hat and jacket, Jeff with his four nieces, just the three boys, Jeff and me alone, and plenty of all of us. The photographer had the patience of a saint as she gave directions in between the bantering. After an hour, Jeff's smile diminished with each new pose, and his squirming increased. By the end of our two-hour session, Jeff was exhausted and ready to get home to his bed.

In the days that followed, the focus shifted to the next item on the holiday agenda: Thanksgiving dinner. Almost immediately Jeff began obsessing over every detail, rattling off his favorite foods, who would be coming, who would be making which foods, until I finally decided to have a planning session at Mom's house.

"I'll help make a list of all the food we need and who will bring what," Jeff excitedly informed Mom soon after we walked in the door.

Mom wrote while Jeff dictated. "Turkey, potatoes, stuffing, rolls. I like Terry's desserts, so have him bring the pies. Tammy should bring the sweet potatoes. Aunt Robin can bring her special appetizer…"

After about twenty minutes, and Mom reading the list to him several times, Jeff was satisfied and settled down to wait for Mom to tell everyone about their decisions.

Within an hour, he asked Mom, "Did you call and tell them what to bring?"

"Not yet, but don't worry about it. I'll get to it," Mom said.

Every hour, Jeff offered a subtle yet insistent reminder for Mom to call everyone about Thanksgiving. Mom finally made the calls, understanding that despite her reassurance, Jeff would continue to obsess until the calls were finally made.

Jeff's desire to have things done immediately could be overwhelming and frustrating at times, but we tried not to act frustrated. I appreciated his interest in making a food list and recognized that his anxiety still seeped out at times. I reminded myself that he was probably frustrated as well, especially since he had to rely on us to do simple things he used to do effortlessly for himself. I knew he was trying to help, trying to memorize phone numbers and the buttons on the phone so he could be more independent, but I also knew that it was a daunting task.

The holidays felt so much more significant knowing they might be Jeff's last and that we could have lost Dad too. We had always done the holidays up big, but this year we were planning an even bigger celebration.

When Thanksgiving Day finally arrived, Mom was up early to stuff the turkey, as had been the tradition as long as I could remember. Every Thanksgiving I would call first thing in the morning to hear about how big the turkey was and all the preparations she was doing as she awaited the arrival of family. It was the same on that Thanksgiving Day as well.

"Good morning, and happy Thanksgiving," I said when she answered the phone.

"Morning," she said, her voice wavering.

"Did you get your turkey in the oven?" I asked, unintentionally ignoring her mood.

"Not yet. We've had an emotional morning."

My stomach tightened. "What happened?"

She blew her nose and then answered. "Jeff was talking about how he used to enjoy chatting with me while I stuffed the turkey and prepared things. Then he started talking about how he missed being able to see, and I couldn't take it. I tried keeping it together, but I couldn't. I busted out crying, and then he did. We were a mess, but we're better now. I guess we just needed a good cry."

"I was worried it was gonna be a really hard day."

"Yeah. Some days harder than others."

"I'll hurry so I can get there and help."

"I'm fine. Just take your time, and I'll see you when you get here."

My stress kicked in as I got off the phone. I moved into high gear as I hurried the kids and Clark out of the house. We pulled into Mom's driveway just behind my Aunt Robin. As we approached the front door at the same time, I noticed she was carrying a tray covered with tinfoil. I held the door open for her and smiled, knowing everyone was in for a treat today.

She said, "Jeff, I have your favorite trailer-trash hors d'oeuvre."

"Oh yeah. Put it right here," he said, swiping his hand across the counter in front of him.

An ear-to-ear grin came across his face as he fumbled with the foil. He foraged through the delectable appetizers with his fingers looking for his favorite: lunch meat rolled up with a dill pickle and stuffed with cream cheese.

"Oh man, this is as good as I remember it," he said with a full mouth.

"Wait, wait," Aunt Robin shouted, grabbing Jeff's hand just before he crammed the other half into his mouth.

"You were about to bite into a toothpick."

"Well, that's a heck of a way to knock off a blind guy. I could've made the evening news: 'Blind man survives life-threatening cancer surgery only to choke to death on a toothpick.'"

Everyone in the room erupted in laughter.

"That's not funny, Jeff," Mom playfully scolded him.

"There, I've taken all the toothpicks out. You should be safe, but if you try to eat them all, I might just have to slip one back in," Aunt Robin said.

Thanksgiving Day proceeded much as it had begun: sorrow and then laughter, then more sadness and then more happiness. Despite the roller coaster of emotions, everyone seemed to cherish the time we were sharing. Jeff and Dad were constant reminders of all that we had to be thankful for, and both of them were openly expressive of their own gratitude for being alive. Instead of focusing on how bad this Thanksgiving could have been, we spent our time focusing on how good it was.

After Thanksgiving, there was a brief lull in holiday activities until Jeff's thirty-second birthday, December 20. We planned a birthday party for him, along with Chelsey and Kendra, who had December birthdays as well. Birthday shopping for Jeff proved to be a very difficult task, unlike past years. We used to buy him things for his collections—Drew Carey dolls, autographs of famous people, and statues of cartoon characters. He hoped to sell them someday as a way to get rich. He no longer had a desire for "things," leaving us to wonder what a blind, dying man would enjoy.

Mom and I went to the blind store in hopes of finding some unique yet useful gifts. We bought a plate that had dividers built in and a lip around the rim so food wouldn't fall off the edge of the plate. We also bought a cup alarm, which went off when the cup was full; otherwise he had to use his finger to know when the liquid was at the top of the cup. We also found him the Bible on tape and other books on tape. Our friend found a talking alarm clock and talking wristwatch. Jeff was pleased with his gifts, especially the Bible on tape. The girls were also happy with their birthday gifts, but they were even more excited for Christmas.

Jeff and Terry had always spent the night at our parents' house on Christmas Eve, and especially this year would not be different. Chelsey and Kendra were excited for Christmas morning; finally, there was something happy to focus on instead of all the sadness. They were relieved that Jeff was staying the night at Mom and Dad's house so they wouldn't have to witness the crying and emotion they anticipated. We were eager to fall into our normal routine—church on Christmas Eve, then home to open gifts with Clark's side of the family. Christmas Eve turned out better than I expected. It felt familiar and normal. Christmas morning was wonderful as well—gifts, smiles, and sheer joy filled the morning. The girls had been so tolerant and accepting throughout the year, and seeing them that excited was wonderful. I tried not to think about how Jeff and Mom were coping so I could relish their joy. I even tried to suppress my awareness that this could be Jeff's last Christmas, since we were already on borrowed time.

The drive to my parents' house was filled with anticipation. The chatter from the girls in the back seat got louder as we pulled into the packed driveway.

"Oh, good. Allison and Katie are already here," Kendra said as she flung off her seat belt.

Chelsey leaned over my seat. "Do we still get to open Uncle Jeff's present before dinner?"

"I'm sure it'll be fine. We can take Uncle Jeff in the bedroom where it won't be so loud, so he can hear your reaction. You guys are going to be so surprised."

"Did he get the same thing for Kylie and McKenna?" Kendra asked.

"Nope. He wanted to give you girls something extra special since you have sacrificed so much for him."

Clark barely had time to turn off the car before both kids bolted out their doors and ran into the house. We grabbed the bags of gifts and made our way into the festive home filled with my brothers, aunts, uncles, cousins, and friends. We were welcomed with shouts of "Merry Christmas" and offers of food. The chaos was exciting. Our family gatherings were loud and filled with lots of laughter; thankfully, this Christmas was no exception.

We had only been there for fifteen minutes when I felt a light tug on my arm. "Mom…" and again, more assertively, "Mom." Chelsey was standing next to me, impatiently waiting for my attention.

"Uncle Jeff said we can open his present when you're ready. Can we do it now? Pleeeeeease?"

"Chels, you're interrupting. Just give me a minute to get settled, and then we can do it."

A bit disappointed but no less excited, she skipped off to find Kendra. The two of them wasted no time in escorting Jeff, and his special gifts, to the bedroom for the grand unwrapping. About five minutes later, while giving Mom a hug, I felt a familiar tug on my arm. I looked down and saw Kendra's sheepish grin. "Uncle Jeff is waiting in the bedroom to give us his presents."

"Really? Did Chelsey put you up to this? Go back and tell her I need another minute, and then I'll be in there."

"OK." She then bounced back to the room.

"You should go do it now. Jeff has been as excited as the girls about their gifts," Mom said.

I turned and took a step in the direction of the bedroom.

"She's coming. She's coming." Chelsey's voice echoed toward me as she hightailed it back down the hall.

As I opened the door, Jeff and the girls were sitting in a circle in the middle of the room, with two nicely wrapped gifts sitting in the center. It reminded me of sitting around a campfire, mesmerized by the glow from the fire. Jeff, while he couldn't see the "glow" from his gifts, seemed no less enthralled.

"Jeff, are you ready for the girls to open their presents?" I asked.

"Yeah, but will you shut the door first? There's a lot of noise." He waited and then continued. "I want to tell you girls that I got you something really special because I appreciate all the sacrifices you've made for me. I know it's not easy having me live with you, and it's hard having to share your mom with me…I just want to say thank you." He abruptly concluded, swiping his forearm across his watering eyes.

I gently squeezed his shoulder and then looked away so my quivering chin and misty eyes would not trigger a full-out blubber fest among all of us.

Chelsey intuitively sat next to him on the bed and patted his leg. "We love having you live with us, Uncle Jeff." Her hazel eyes blinked hard.

"Yeah, we wouldn't want you to live anywhere else." Kendra's tone reflected her smile.

"Thank you, girls." His face brightened. "Let's get this show on the road before we all fall apart."

"Don't mind if we do," Kendra said, grinning with relief.

Jeff reached over and slid the gifts in the girls' general direction. They looked at me for approval, and with my nod, the tearing of wrapping paper began. Both of their hands scratched at the ribbon and paper on their boxes.

Once the word "Walkman" was visible through the torn paper, they shot each other a glance and then in unison let out a squeal of exhilaration that reverberated through every room in the house.

"Yes. Yes." Followed by a few fist pumps in the air. "I wanted a Walkman so bad. Thank you so much, Uncle Jeff," Kendra said while hugging Jeff—a rare moment of uninhibited joy, given that she was usually quite emotionally reserved with anyone but me.

"This is what I really wanted for Christmas. And I was sort of disappointed when we didn't get them from Mom this morning," Chelsey said while hugging Jeff.

Jeff's smile widened upon hearing a high five between the girls, and his hand instinctively went up in the air to get into the action.

"I'm so glad you guys like them. You might want to put your name on them so you don't get them confused with each other."

"That's a great idea," I said as I backed out of the room on my way to the kitchen. "I need to go help Grandma now." I left the bedroom with the girls telling Jeff what a great uncle he was and how happy they were that he was staying at our house. Soon after Christmas dinner, the family gathered for our traditional gift exchange. Jeff sat in a recliner, his legs tucked to his side and his head tilted slightly upward, which he had been doing lately when he tried to listen intently. Rusty was sleeping soundly, snuggled next to him.

I placed a gift in Jeff's lap. "Here is a present for you. It's from Aunt Mel and Uncle Terry."

"Oh, thank you." He squeezed it with both hands and then ripped open the paper. Searching for clues, he unfolded the cotton item.

"It's a dark-blue T-shirt," I whispered.

He had a sinister smirk as he held up the shirt. "Yeah, you tell me it's a blue shirt, but for all I know, it could be a pink shirt with yellow polka dots—"

Laughter filled the room, interrupting his rant midstream.

"What brand is it?" he asked suspiciously.

"Nike," I said, trying to keep the smile out of my voice.

"That's good," he said, relieved. Then, without missing a beat, as if it were a shtick he had worked several times before, he continued. "You guys could dress me in anything and make me look like a real dork if you wanted to, and I'd never even know."

Cracking up himself, he paused to regain his composure, but it was impossible. Everyone in the room was in hysterics at this point. My stomach was cramping, and I almost doubled over at the foot of my chair.

Then Jeff lowered his voice a notch. "Sad truth is, I probably would've found it funny to do that to someone else."

"You better be nice, or I might just dress you up real pretty," I said.

Quips from all sides of the room kept the hysteria rolling until Mom regained control and refocused us back on the gift exchange.

At that moment, it hit me. There wasn't a greater gift amid the pile of beautifully wrapped presents than the one we had just witnessed: Jeff's ability to laugh at his circumstances—a gift from Jesus that had appeared on the day following his surgery. He had developed a special way of using his humor to set those around him at ease.

The drive home was unusually quiet. I sat in the back seat sandwiched between Chelsey and Kendra, who were distracted by the music blasting through their new Walkman headsets. Jeff rested peacefully in the passenger seat.

Clark seldom talked while driving, so I was left to sit still with my thoughts about the day. It was late by the time we arrived home, so my first task was to help Jeff to bed.

"The day went pretty well, don't you think?" I asked while handing him his plaid pajama top.

"Yeah, it was OK, but it was hard not being able to see. I hate it. I can't enjoy things like I used to, and it just sucks." Seemingly out of nowhere, without warning, he started to weep.

Startled by this pent-up emotion, I was speechless for a second. Confused, in fact. I thought he had enjoyed the day. I mustered a few words. "I'm so sorry. I can't even imagine."

"I worked hard to hold it together so I wouldn't ruin the day for everyone, but it was too overwhelming. You know how I used to love Christmas and the whole gift thing. Now it's like torture. Nothing is the same anymore. I guess it will just take time," he said.

As our heads rested on each other's shoulders, our anguished souls welcomed the silence. As much as Jeff tried to use his humor to make light of the situation, there were still gaping wounds not yet healed.

Tamura Arthun

CHAPTER 28

Let's Go Swimming

ONE OF MY NEW YEAR'S goals was to help Jeff regain some of his strength. Over the past year, he had recovered enough to make his way around my house and also to have energy for short excursions. But he still had a long way to go. He got too winded to participate in any organized group-type exercise programs, and his blindness made that an unrealistic option anyway. But he needed to do something, or simply leaving the house would have continued to be exhausting. "So, Jeff, you know how we talked about getting more exercise, and maybe even starting swimming? I think we should go down to the pool today to check it out," I said as we finished our breakfast.

"Sounds good to me, unless you think my body will scare all the people out of the pool." Jeff laughed.

"I don't think anyone will say anything, but they might stare at you in passing. I would."

"I plan on telling anyone who asks that I was attacked by a shark," he said. "That ought to really surprise them, don't you think?"

"Oh yeah. They'll most certainly buy that story," I said, humoring him.

Jeff knew the jagged dull-pink scar looked more like something that had ripped open than the result of a talented surgeon's skillful hands. Despite not being able to see the facial reaction of some family members who had seen it, he was still a bit self-conscious.

We talked about the fact that many people using the pool were there for some sort of exercise or physical therapy. Some were recuperating from a stroke, heart surgery, or shoulder injuries, while others were trying to control obesity. I assured him that people might look at him, but they would not judge him. That was the last time we had that discussion.

We arrived at the community pool anticipating yet another interesting experience to add to our journey. The smell of chlorine hit us as we opened the glass door to the pool. I felt the pressure of Jeff's grip increase amid the pitter-patter of our steps against the wet cement deck. There were people in the pool, some just playing, others taking classes.

I approached an official-looking middle-aged woman wearing a blue swimsuit, shorts, and a red buoy over her shoulder. As we come alongside her, she grabbed the stainless-steel whistle hanging around her neck and let out a piercing pitch. She did not have to say a word; she just moved her finger side to side at the raucous boys in the pool. She glared at them for a moment longer and then turned her attention to us.

"How can I help you?" she asked sternly.

"I have some questions about your pool programs and whether they would work for my brother and me."

"Well…" She paused a moment and looked us over. "We mainly offer swim lessons and water aerobics classes." She paused again and concentrated on Jeff, who was silently standing arm in arm next to me. "I don't know if either of those would work for you."

"Well, maybe it would help if I tell you a little about my brother. This is Jeff, and he had cancer surgery on February fourteenth of last year. The surgery damaged his lung, so he gets short of breath easily. His overall strength is also compromised because of his illness, so we think the water will make it a bit easier for him to exercise."

Her eyes scanned the pool while I continued to talk to the side of her head.

"The surgery also caused my brother to go blind—he sees nothing."

With that her head whipped around, and her eyes focused on Jeff's blank stare.

"I plan on swimming next to him and helping him in and out of the pool," I said.

Her military demeanor fell away, and she seemed more intrigued. I continued. "I just don't know how your pool typically deals with people who have special needs—like which dressing room do we use, and such."

"Let me get another lifeguard to watch the pool, and I'll be happy to show you guys around," she said while motioning her coworker to come out from the office.

She explained that since Jeff was blind and the facility did not have a "special needs" dressing room, we could use the women's dressing room. I just needed to inform anyone else using the dressing room that Jeff was blind so they would not be worried about their privacy being invaded. It was uncommon for the pool to have people with disabilities as severe as Jeff's, even though there were a lot of people who came to the pool for rehabilitation. He would be just fine in the pool.

We finally left and headed out to lunch. "So when do we start going?" Jeff asked.

"Well, we can go in the morning after I get the girls off to school. We'll try to go three times a week. How does that sound?"

"I think it'll be fun once I get past the initial fear," he said.

Tomorrow came with much anticipation by both of us. Jeff anxiously waited for me to return from dropping the girls off at school so I could take him on his new adventure. He was wearing the swim trunks I had bought him last night and was eager to get on our way. I was a bit apprehensive as to how it was going to go, but it would at least fill Jeff's day with something different.

I parked the car, grabbed the bag with our clothes and towels, and guided Jeff down the short cement parking lot into the pool lobby. I confidently entered the women's dressing room as though I had done this many times before.

I felt a little embarrassed as the women around us paused to look at me and Jeff. There was one naked woman in the shower area, which had no curtains, and another drying herself off near the lockers. Their eyes met mine as if they were searching for an explanation as to why I was leading a man into the "wrong" area. I used my free hand to cover my eyes in a nonverbal attempt to let them know he could not see, hoping to relieve their concern. I quickly moved us through the locker area and into the dressing closet, which had a curtain across the front.

"Are people looking at us?" Jeff whispered.

"Yeah. They look a bit curious, but no one seems alarmed."

We showered and briskly walked out to the pool. Jeff held on tight as we gingerly strolled along the deck. The lifeguard offered help getting Jeff into the pool and cautiously guided him down the stairs into the water.

"This is so weird. You wouldn't think the water would feel that different just because you can't see it, but it does," Jeff said. He had a big grin on his face as he moved about in the pool. He appeared apprehensive yet excited.

I pulled him by the hands to familiarize him with our lane. "OK, there is a lane divider on one side, and the pool side is on the other. You can move around anywhere, since we're the only ones in this lane. If someone else comes in our lane, I'll swim right next to you. We're not going into the deep end just yet. I want you to get comfortable first."

"OK. I feel so good."

In amazement, I watched him get around the pool despite his blindness. It was hard to not guide him, but he clearly was learning on his own. As I looked around the pool, my eyes caught those of the curious onlookers. Surprisingly, most everyone was looking at him—sometimes staring, sometimes scanning back and forth appearing to be disinterested. I understood their curiosity, because I myself had looked at people who were different. But I was glad Jeff couldn't see their expressions, since he would probably feel uneasy.

Jeff's sense of direction had been impaired since the blindness; getting around the house or walking down the street were still challenges for him. As he attempted to move down the length of the pool, he tended to do circles instead.

"Jeff, go a little to the right," I said. "No, Jeff. The other right."

"I did go to the right," he hollered back as he ran into the lane divider.

It was obviously very difficult for him to go in a straight line, but I was certain that with some practice, he would improve. I quickly swam to retrieve him from the deep end before he got into trouble.

"You are really getting a good workout, aren't you?" I asked.

"Yes. I'm getting a bit tired, though. This really feels good. I'll hopefully improve a little each time we come. Are you ready to go?" he asked.

"Let's do one more lap, and then I'm ready if you are." I grabbed his hands, arms stretched out in front of him, feet kicking as we did one last lap, down and back. There were more women in the dressing room this time, and once again their inquisitive eyes met mine. This time I quickly informed them that my brother was blind and could not see them. I waited patiently, with Jeff on my arm, for the private shower to become available.

His embarrassment was masked by his nervous laugh. "Should we tell them I'm faking it and that I really saw all of them naked?" he whispered in my ear.

"You're real funny, but you're not the one who would have to deal with them when they freak out," I said.

As we left the pool, Jeff was already focused on our next activity. "Where do you want to go for lunch?" he asked.

"Maybe we can have Midge meet us at our teriyaki place?" I said.

"Works for me."

We arrived at Teriyaki Bistro at the same time as Midge. I settled Jeff into a chair and joined Midge in line. I ordered Jeff's favorite, chicken teriyaki, with extra salad and extra garlic sauce. Jeff chattered excitedly, telling Midge about the swimming trip. Although it was good to give Jeff something to look forward to, I didn't have the same level of excitement. I feared the major time commitment it was going to take on my part. It was not a question of how I would squeeze it in, but what I was going to have to sacrifice in order to do it.

After three weeks, we developed a routine and got to know the regular swimmers. The swimming pool became a real source of joy for Jeff and—contrary to my initial concern—to me as well. We also received permission to use the staff bathroom, as some women did complain that they were uncomfortable with Jeff's presence, even if he couldn't see them. Most days we had a lane to ourselves, except the days the middle-school kids were there for PE class.

Jeff was doing well moving down the lane by himself. I swam next to him so I could make sure he wouldn't run into anyone.

"Bummer, Jeff. The kids are here for class today," I said, seeing the kids walking in a single line along the pool deck.

"I heard them coming out of the locker room. Oh well. I'm ready to get out anyway."

As I rested in the shallow end, watching Jeff make his way down the pool, I heard a boy say, "Look at the freak," as he pointed his finger at Jeff.

Immediately my teeth clenched, jaw muscles tightening, and a wave of adrenaline rushed through my body. I quickly jumped out of the pool and faced the insensitive punk.

"What did you just say about my brother?" I asked, just before I was about to say something I would likely regret.

"Uh, I was talking about his tattoo," he nervously replied.

Then I heard Jeff holler from across the pool, "Tammy, he's talking about the Freakazoid tattoo on my shoulder."

The boy quickly said, "It looks cool." Completely embarrassed, I apologized to the boy and sheepishly returned to the pool.

Jeff was laughing hysterically as he held on to the edge of the pool.

"Who the heck is Freakazoid?" I asked.

Jeff proceeded to educate me about the name of the red cartoon character etched in his shoulder. I felt sort of stupid. I guess that maybe I was oversensitive to the fact that people were staring at Jeff after all.

On the way home, Jeff and I reminisced about how many fights I used to get in at school because I hated seeing kids get picked on. I always advocated for the underdog, and today was no exception. However, in my moment of anger, I forgot that I was no longer a kid and could have actually gotten into some trouble. Anyway, Jeff had a good laugh, and everything worked out well. And I was reminded that I needed to think before I snapped at people staring at Jeff.

After a couple of months, Dad was doing well enough that he and Mom started to pick Jeff up on the days I worked and take him swimming so we could keep the routine. They did not get in the pool with him, but Dad was able to take him into the men's room to help him get showered and dressed. Jeff was pretty committed to swimming two or three times a week. He certainly began getting stronger, and his endurance improved steadily.

CHAPTER 29

Transitions

LIFE REMAINED VERY HECTIC AS we approached the two-year anniversary of Jeff's surgery. Dad was completely independent, and his burns were still very painful, but they had healed. Mom was happy to finally be taking care of only one sick person.

Jeff continued to battle health issues but still had no sign of cancer. He was able to do most things for himself, except cooking. Most of the time I didn't mind cooking his every meal. However, there were those days when he would ask for chicken alfredo for lunch, and I would think, "What the heck happened to a peanut butter and jelly sandwich?" I would usually feel a wave of irritation, especially since I seldom ate lunch myself. But a second later, I would feel humbled, realizing that he couldn't make it for himself.

I continued my work in the emergency room, counseling people who were grappling with the most fundamental issues of human existence—life and death. I found them, and their caretakers, to be emotionally raw and honest. During the past year, I developed an extra sensitivity toward caretakers and the silent pressure they endured. When I introduced myself to other caretakers, I let them know that I was a caretaker for my brother, which often led to a sudden bond. We shared how being a caretaker was like having a full-time job, on top of other full-time commitments such as work or our roles as moms and wives.

Though all of us shared many similarities, I noticed that caretakers often interpreted responsibilities differently. Some believed they had no choice but to care for their loved one, so they treated caretaking as a burden; others believed they had a choice and that providing care was a gift to both their loved one and themselves. Most people I encountered, including myself, vacillated between both.

When I felt overwhelmed with my caretaking duties, I was quick to remember that someday I might not have a little brother to care for and allowed myself to slow down and enjoy my time with him.

The girls developed their own unique relationship with Jeff. Chelsey was very sensitive and enjoyed talking to Jeff about her woes. She and Jeff shared their struggle with anxiety, and he felt as if he could help her. She liked that Jeff was always available to talk and was such a good listener.

Kendra and Jeff enjoyed harassing each other and collecting pickup lines such as, "Girl, are you tired? Because you have been running through my mind all day long." They thought they were pretty funny, and I loved listening to them laugh.

Clark helped transport Jeff and prepared his meals when I was gone. Most of all, he supported me in having Jeff live with us, which was worth more to me than anything.

I missed many aspects of my old life, mostly the ability to be spontaneous. Yet there was something intense and powerful about the path we were walking. It seemed so real and significant. I could not waste a moment of time. Everything felt crucial and momentous, even going to ice cream with the girls. Given that we couldn't whimsically choose to do anything, that event itself became so deliberate and memorable. There was so much more that I would have liked to do, especially with my girls and Clark, yet I did my best to live in every moment, without wishing to change it.

Jeff was also learning to live in the moment, especially since his physical symptoms vacillated weekly. After receiving a hand-held tape recorder for his birthday, he decided to start journaling about his life again. I taught him how to use it, and I put rubber markers on it so he would know which buttons to push. He needed a lot of practice to get used to it, but one night I heard him recording into it for the first time.

Jeff's Recorded Journal—December 2001

I am two months from the two-year anniversary of my surgery and blindness. So far, so good. I have a real sexy body, if you are a person who is into guys who have bellies that look like butts. I'm getting more and more used to being blind, but I still have my days that are not fun. There are times that it feels darker in my head than others; I can hear, but everything comes at me all at once. I no longer remember what some people and things look like. I'm usually not sad, but I do get frustrated. Sometimes so frustrated that I imagine bashing in a car, or blowing up a building just to let the frustration out.

It is not easy at times, but I'm overall doing well. I give credit to God for my coping skills. I am using my white cane more, trying to get the hang of that. I can do almost everything for myself, but I can't cook for myself yet. I am really a good, safe driver; I do that really well. I think that after the New Year is up, I'm gonna apply for a cab license or school bus driver. If that doesn't work out, then I've always had a longtime goal of being an envelope stuffer, so I might be able to do that. Mom is still struggling with my blindness, and she wants to see me be more active. I need to work on that so I don't feel so gimpy. My spiritual walk is the most important. I am learning to pray more, listening to my Bible on tape, and other books on tape. I would like to be a mentor to people and help them through what they think is a difficult situation. Like if they have small dilemma that they think is a big one, I can be an example of a big dilemma. This is the lesson I've had to learn firsthand.

CHAPTER 30

Blind School

TWO YEARS HAD PASSED SINCE we were told that Jeff had only six weeks to live. Even though we knew the cancer was still coursing through his body, we still struggled with the question, is he better today or worse? Every ache was viewed with suspicion—has the cancer come back, or is it something new? Our anxiety kept us on an emotional roller coaster until lab results either confirmed or allayed our fears. Relief momentarily accompanied each negative result, quickly followed by the uncertainty of what would come next.

When we weren't focused on immediate health dangers, our attention shifted to helping Jeff become more independent. Unfortunately, we knew very little about how to help a blind and terminally ill man become self-reliant. Besides, it seemed that he would be safer if I took care of him.

While I finished my upstairs chores, Jeff typically waited patiently for me to come down and prepare breakfast. One day, though, as I made my way down the stairs, I heard an unfamiliar noise in the kitchen. I turned the corner and was surprised to see Jeff fumbling around in the refrigerator. I paused and curiously watched his fingers slide down a plastic gallon container, then move to the container next to it.

"Are there two jugs of milk, or is one of these juice?" he asked himself, his frustration audible.

"What are you doing, Jeff?"

"I'm trying to fix my own breakfast," he grumbled. "I'm looking for the milk. Could you help me out here?"

"You got it; the first one is the milk. The one to the left is apple juice."

"I hate this—I hate being blind." He slammed the fridge door. "We need to have certain spots for things so I can find it. I could have put apple juice on my cereal."

"I know, but it's been a bit since you got into the fridge, so it's easy for us to forget to keep it organized. We'll have to come up with a better plan so you can keep practicing," I said.

It only took moments for me to set my laundry basket down, guide him to his chair, and pour the milk over his cornflakes. I sat across from him at the table, watching him carefully eat.

"Sorry for snapping at you," he said quietly, head bent over his bowl.

"It's OK. I know this has to be so frustrating for you."

"I want to be more independent, you know. I feel like a little kid—everything is so much more difficult right now."

"I get it. Don't worry, though. We'll figure out how to make it easier for you. Maybe only your stuff will go on the middle shelf, and we can find a way to label it so you know what it is."

After a few minutes of chatting, I picked up my laundry basket and proceeded to the laundry room. With the door shut, I felt free to make my usual morning call to my mom.

"Good morning," Mom said.

"Hi."

She must have heard something in my voice, because she cut me off before another word left my lips. "What's wrong?"

"Nothing bad. It's just been a tough morning for Jeff. He got pretty frustrated this morning when he couldn't find the milk. We really need to come up with a plan to push him along."

"Yeah, I know we do."

"I've been talking to him about trying to get things for himself, like his breakfast and snacks. We both need to encourage him so we can get his confidence back."

Mom sighed. "I know I have to do better with that too, but sometimes…" Her words stuck. "It's so much easier to get his stuff myself. Watching him struggle just getting to the kitchen kills me."

"I do it too. But we're not helping him in the long run. I think I'll call the coordinator at the state school for the blind and see if I can get the rehabilitation people to come back out, or maybe we can look into their day program," I said.

"I agree. You know Jeff, though—we're gonna have to push him to get him out of his comfort zone."

Her words caused me unintended angst. "I know he's not interested in any of this, but if he isn't going to die anytime soon, then we'd better help him learn how to live in the dark."

"You're doing the right thing. Call me after you talk to them." I appreciated her unsolicited approval.

I came back inside to see Jeff sitting on the couch, Rusty snuggled close to his side. His face was somber, eyes shut, as he fumbled with the TV remote in search of his favorite show, *Judge Judy*.

"Hey, I have some calls to make, so I'll be upstairs for a bit. Do you need anything?"

He turned the volume down. "No, I'm good. Thank you. And sorry again for snapping at you."

"No worries—I totally understand." I gave him a long hug, reassuring both of us, before heading upstairs. I thought about his remorse for a moment. Why was he sorry? He was not usually sorry, mostly oblivious. But maybe he had put himself in my shoes, heard what I'd heard and felt what I'd felt. Perhaps my pain was too much for him to handle at this point in his life. A wave of nausea jolted through me as I tried to brush aside my feelings of helplessness. I took a deep breath and focused on the benefits of calling the school for the blind. A pleasant man, the coordinator for the school, listened patiently as I spent the first part of the call explaining Jeff's medical history and current disabilities.

I told him that Jeff couldn't prepare meals for himself nor, for that matter, could he even pour himself a glass of milk without difficulty. Though he refused to use a white cane most of the time, he could still move around inside the house fairly well, but he would be totally lost outside. He also had difficulty walking for long distances, due to complications from terminal cancer.

"OK," the coordinator said. "Does he see the value in getting some rehabilitation?"

"He says he hates the idea. I think it's because he gets frustrated trying to complete simple tasks. I think he'd much rather keep things in the current routine than face the loss of his sight. Jeff usually asks one of us to get him a drink, snack, or even make a meal, and we're mostly glad to do it."

"And what do you think of that approach?" he asked.

"Admittedly, it's harder on me to watch him struggle doing the most basic things, though I know I'm not really helping him by doing everything for him. Until now his physical health issues were our priority, but now that he appears stable, we understand that we need to help him adapt to his blindness."

The coordinator listened, validated the struggles we had gone through, and then encouraged us to visit the school. He told us he would have to meet with Jeff personally to further evaluate how his physical limitations would affect his school participation. Trusting I could persuade Jeff to agree, I scheduled a meeting for the following week.

Later that afternoon, I talked to both Jeff and Mom about my discussion with the coordinator. Jeff hesitantly agreed to check the program out, with the caveat that he was not agreeing to sign up for the program just yet. We all understood we would just be gathering information on how they could help Jeff become more independent and help us understand how to set up our homes in a way that would better support him.

A week later, Mom, Jeff, and I met with the coordinator of the program and several of the rehabilitation staff. As the coordinator told us about the program, Mom and I got excited about so many of the things he could learn. Jeff, on the other hand, wrenched his hands together after every word the guy uttered. The program was usually six to nine months long, and their goal was to teach each student how to successfully live independently.

The students varied greatly in degrees of blindness; most had gradually lost their vision over a period of time. Jeff was the only person in the program who saw absolutely nothing. In fact, they reiterated several times how rare his circumstances were, both in degree of blindness and the suddenness of having to adapt. Jeff was likely never going to live on his own because of his health issues; however, I became hopeful that he could learn to become more independent.

The coordinator and staff asked many questions about Jeff's breathing issues because several of their classes were at their other campus, about three blocks away. The students had to walk from the main campus down a steep hill and across a very busy four-lane street, then back up to the main campus after their classes. We explained that Jeff got very short of breath when he walked long distances; therefore, he would not be able to go between their two campuses. Their other main concern was that Jeff had to use the bathroom frequently because of a diuretic pill he took, and since he couldn't get around without a guide at that time, a staff member would have to accompany him. We suggested that we could hold the pill until the afternoon to try to minimize the number of times he needed to use the bathroom.

I became more discouraged with each obstacle they presented, while Jeff seem relieved that he might not qualify for the program. Mom and I did much of the talking and provided options to influence their consideration. We left the meeting with a plan to give the school a ten-day trial, and then we would reevaluate to determine whether it was working for them and for Jeff.

Resting comfortably in the front passenger seat of my black Lexus, Jeff expelled a sigh of relief as we began to drive away from the school.

From the back seat, Mom asked, "Well, Jeff, how do you feel about the program?"

"It sounds sort of hard, but I'll give it a fair chance." He paused. "I'm really nervous about the whole thing. You know me—I get anxious whenever I have to make a change."

"Just think"—her voice elevated with encouragement—"you'll learn new things, and you might even make some friends who understand what you're going through."

Gazing quietly at the red light, I tried to imagine what it might be like to be in his shoes. The more I thought about it, the more anxious I got.

"You're so quiet...what do you think?" Jeff asked.

"Well, I'm anxious about it too, but I think it's the right thing to do. We just have to give it a try, and if it doesn't work out, we'll at least know we tried."

"Yep, that's all we can do. I'm sure it'll work out just fine," Mom said.

Over the weekend Jeff shared with me how frightened he was to be away from me and out of his comfort zone. He talked about all the different medical issues that could happen and how vulnerable he already felt. I was scared too but did my best to reassure him—and myself. I reminded him that we just had to take it one day at a time.

Dread and hope kept me tossing and turning all night. I sipped my coffee, prayed, and gathered my thoughts before waking Jeff up for his first day of school.

"Good morning. How did you sleep?" I asked while getting his clothes ready.

"Oh, super good…I bet I got a whole hour," he said with a slight grin.

"I was afraid of that. I was awake a fair amount myself."

I helped him get dressed, combed his hair, and packed his backpack. "I'm sure it'll be fine. Let's just give it ten days, and if it isn't for you, then you don't have to go back." I patted his back as he stood next to me. "I'm sure you'll at least learn some helpful tools."

"I know." A smirk crept across his face. "I was just thinking that with my luck, they'll forget me in the bathroom, and I won't find my way out."

"That would be terrible." I laughed with him.

Despite my brave face, his humor did little to ease my upset stomach or erase the unwanted worry cluttering my mind. My thoughts were already spinning on the possibility of them losing him, or him falling. I had not felt such a fear since sending my little girls to kindergarten. But leaving Jeff felt even worse; at least my girls had been excited to make the normal next step in life. No part of this felt exciting or normal. I wondered how he would emotionally handle being away from me or Mom. Realizing that I couldn't protect him since I wouldn't be there only added to my anxiety. I began to wonder if we were doing the right thing.

"You OK?" Jeff's voice cut into my thoughts. "You got so quiet. What are you thinking about?"

"Oh, nothing. I'm fine. Are you ready?" I swung his backpack over my shoulder.

"Yep, let's do it," he said with uncharacteristic confidence as he stood up from the bed.

I handed him his long white-and-red cane as we got ready to leave. "Oh yeah, we can't forget this," he begrudgingly mumbled, grabbing the handle of the cane.

"Correct. You're supposed to start using it from now on," I said, closing the door behind us, and then we walked to the car.

We talked about insignificant things on the drive to the school, located near downtown Seattle. The area surrounding the school was predominantly low income. There was a lot of crime in the area, and it was not somewhere we felt safe. Growing up, it was an area we typically avoided, which made me feel even more scared about leaving my blind and vulnerable brother in the hands of strangers.

We got out of the car, his right hand clinging to my left arm, and we walked toward the entrance.

"You sure I'll be OK here?" His voice quivered.

"You're in good hands. They deal with this type of stuff every day," I said, distrusting my own words.

We entered the building, and I saw an older woman sitting at the front desk. She looked up and smiled as we approached.

"Good morning. Can I help you?"

"Yes. My name is Jeff, and I'm scheduled to start today."

She located his name on her admission sheet. "Oh yes, here you are. Mr. Jones will be with you in a moment. Feel free to take a seat. It's to your left about four steps." Her verbal directions were comforting; perhaps they did know how to deal with blind people. After about five minutes, a tall, balding man with a white-and-red cane tapped his way down the hall. He somehow knew exactly where to stop, and he turned toward where we sat.

"Hello, Jeff. My name is Jim."

"Hello."

"Is your sister still here?"

"Yes, I'm here," I said.

Jim extended his hand in my direction; I stood up and grasped it. "My name is Tammy."

"Nice to meet you, Tammy."

"I wanted to wait with Jeff to make sure he connected with the right person," I nervously explained. "You do know that he's not cane trained, right?"

"No problem. You don't need to worry; I'll help him find his way around." He turned toward Jeff. "Welcome to the program, Jeff. Are you ready to get started?"

"Yes, I guess so," Jeff said, rising to his feet while maintaining a firm grip on my arm.

Jim's left elbow extended away from his side. "Jeff, would you like to grab my left elbow, and I will lead you." Jeff reached out his right hand, and I guided it to Jim's elbow.

"Tammy, do you have any questions before we go on our way?"

"Umm, no." I hesitated. "I'll be right here at three o'clock. Have a good day, Jeff."

"OK…" Skepticism permeated his voice. "Bye."

I waited for a moment to observe what happened next. Jim led Jeff down the hall, and the sound of plastic hitting the wooden floor echoed back at me, getting fainter the farther they walked. Jim stopped in front of the elevator and ran his finger across some bumps on the wall to find the down button, then into the elevator they went.

I paused for a few more moments, just to see if the door would reopen with them still standing there. It did not, so I turned around, pushed the glass doors open, and filled my lungs with fresh air, hoping to relieve the nausea I felt. I wondered what it must be like to not only be blind but to be in a strange place with no familiar people. Panic engulfed me as I racked my brain for any rational reason why I had just left my brother in such a situation.

My car still in park, eyes too blurry to drive, I dialed my mom. "I hate this."

"I know. It's all so hard. Just think of how good it will be for him if it works out."

Unable to keep my emotions contained, I quickly ended our conversation. I blubbered loudly in my now fogged-up car. Not feeling any relief, I begged God, "Lord, please keep Jeff safe, and let him feel encouraged by others who understand his situation. Give him the strength and the energy to make it through the day. Help me, Lord. Help me get through this. Amen."

While the defroster was on blast to clear the windows, I wiped my swollen eyes and pulled out of the parking lot. I avoided making eye contact with other drivers who might have noticed my lips moving and my hands gesturing while I drove down the street. Talking to myself when I was alone had become more comfortable than I cared to admit.

I knew this was going to be good for him, especially if he learned to be more independent. I wanted for him to be able to be left home alone—not only for his dignity, but for our benefit as well. The girls needed me to be more available for them. I was sure he'd be OK, though; after all, this was a reputable school.

I headed toward my mom's house to wait for Jeff. She and I spent most of the day talking about how great it would be if he liked the program. We wanted Jeff to find some different ways to deal with his blindness. Since Jeff seldom complained and was not demanding, it was easy for us to continue caring for him. However, both of us agreed that he would eventually have to regain his independence. While at my mom's, I received a call from the special-service bus coordinator who was working on arranging future transportation for Jeff from home to school. We had considered using the bus program to help relieve some of our transportation difficulties. We scheduled a time for them to pick Jeff up from school the following Monday.

It sounded like a great program, and it certainly would save all of us some time transporting him from my house to school, and from there to my mom's house or back to mine. The coordinator told me it was not a problem as long as we scheduled a few days ahead of time. It would relieve some pressure and help with Jeff's sense of independence.

Three o'clock was fast approaching, so I left my mom's house to go pick up Jeff. When I got into the building, the friendly lady sitting at the front office directed me downstairs. I eagerly looked in the various workrooms—the kitchen, computer room, and last, the recreation room, where I found Jeff.

"Hey, how's it going?" I asked, tapping his shoulder.

"Oh, I'm doing good." His words were surprisingly filled with notes of joy. "My papers are somewhere around here."

The instructor, a tall, slender woman with brown hair, gathered the papers and handed them to me. "These will explain the activities Jeff will be working on in greater detail," she said. "Any reinforcement you can provide at home would help him a lot."

"Thank you. We will do what we can."

"Jeff can tell you all about what he learned today. Tomorrow we plan to work on independent living skills," she said.

"That should be helpful," I said.

"OK, then. I'll be here tomorrow," Jeff said.

"Thank you. See you tomorrow," I told her.

Jeff grabbed my elbow, and we headed toward the elevator.

"Hey, is that a new cane? It looks so much smaller than your other one."

"Yeah. They said that my other cane was way too long and that this one would be much better. It'll take some getting used to, though." Jeff spoke with new enthusiasm. "They had me learning braille today. I can read three letters, but it was super hard to learn how to get it right."

Relieved, I said, "Sounds like you had a good day."

"I did. They also taught me how to count my steps as a way to get around familiar places, like the elevator is twenty-five steps from the door. But that's going to take more time to master."

"Well, at least time is one thing you have."

I pushed the glass doors open to the outside; unlike this morning, a breath of fresh air didn't feel like a necessity. We had barely made our way to the car before my phone rang. It was Mom.

CHAPTER 31

Road to Independence

"Good morning, Jeff. It's time to get going. What do you want in your lunch today?" I asked, rushing to get him some breakfast.

"How about a tuna sandwich?" he said, still groggy and barely moving. "And maybe chips and a soda?"

"Sounds good. We have to move faster than normal today because I don't know what the traffic will be like this morning. We don't want to be late for you second day of school." Optimistic chatter filled the car as we made our way to school. Jeff held on to my elbow, extending his new white cane in front of him and swinging it side to side. I pushed open the glass doors to the school lobby with much more confidence than yesterday.

"I think the elevator is down here," Jeff said as he pulled my elbow to the left and then led me down the wide hallway. Tap…tap…tap…tap…and then he paused. "I think the elevator is right here, or somewhere nearby."

"You're right," I said as I pushed the call button on the wall, and we stepped inside.

With a pleasant ding, the elevator doors slid open to reveal another hallway. Jeff pulled me in the direction of a classroom to my left, and voices spilled out of it into the hall. Different activities were going on at each table; one student was using a computer, while another was placing domino-shaped blocks in some kind of order. A rotund woman in her early twenties was sitting in an electric wheelchair at the table closest to us. I stared at her fingers as they methodically skimmed across the blank white pages of her book. A raised voice from across the room acknowledged us.

"Good morning, Jeff. It's Mrs. Thompson."

"Good morning," he said, and then he confidently let go of my arm.

"Hello. Where shall I put his lunch?" I asked.

She pointed to the wood shelves near the door. "You can set it over there."

"OK. Have a good day, Jeff. I'll be back at three o'clock."

"I will," he said, standing awkwardly, waiting for direction from Mrs. Thompson.

I walked down the hall a little way, glanced back over my shoulder, and saw his teacher guiding him to a table. I felt slightly nervous, but nothing like the overwhelming fear I had experienced the day before.

Excited to hear about Jeff's day, I left early to pick him up. I arrived at two forty-five. Mrs. Thompson walked directly over to meet me.

"Jeff was a bit tired this afternoon," Mrs. Thompson said. "He said the walk to the apartment campus really wiped him out." My focus stuck on the words "the walk" as she continued talking. I instantly reflected back to our previous meeting when this was discussed, and I knew I had told them that Jeff didn't have the lung capacity or endurance to walk up the hill that separated the two campuses.

"Yeah, I bet he's tired. I'm surprised he even made it up that hill," I said, forcing a slight smile.

Jeff stood up from the table, his face stoic. "Will you grab my practice sheets?"

I was confused and tried to hold back my frustration as I politely collected Jeff's homework papers.

Unlike the day before, Jeff was silent as we walked slower than normal toward the elevator. He was holding his cane more like a support cane than a guide stick.

Buckled up and barely out of the parking lot, Jeff moaned. "I don't know if I can do this. It about killed me today."

"Uh, yeah. What the heck happened?" I took a deep breath through my nostrils and expelled a heavy sigh.

"Well, I was doing great working with the instructor in the kitchen. She was teaching me how to work the stovetop and microwave. She gave me some extra rubber dots to put on the stove at home so I would know where to find certain buttons. I was learning different ways to organize the refrigerator and cupboards so I can find what I need to make a meal. But then another instructor came in and said that there was an opportunity for me to go to the other campus down the street, and the cooking teacher encouraged me to go."

I interrupted. "Did you tell them that you weren't planning on doing that part?"

"No. I didn't want to make a fuss, so I figured I would just give it a try. The problem was the student who was my tour guide is not only legally blind, but she's in a motorized wheelchair. So I had to hold on to her wheelchair with one hand while holding my cane in the other."

I gasped. "She dragged you up and down the hill?"

"Well, sort of. I really had to push myself. I was scared."

"I don't believe it." I clenched my teeth as I imagined what he had gone through.

"I was already exhausted and afraid I was going to pass out. Then we came to a really busy street we had to cross. I could hear the cars humming by, and then the noise stopped. I heard a robotic voice say something like 'Walk sign is on.' Next thing I know, I felt the wheelchair jump ahead, and I had to run to keep my hand from slipping off the handle."

I felt as if I was going to throw up.

"The girl was nice and all, but she had no idea what was going on with me. We arrived at the campus, which turned out to be a single apartment, and I was having a hard time breathing. I couldn't even focus on what we were doing there because all I could think about was catching my breath and having to make the walk back to the school."

Furious, my hands clenched the steering wheel. "That's awful," I said while trying to control my rage. "I'm so sorry that happened to you."

I cleared my throat with a guttural cough. "I just can't believe they had you walk up that hill."

"It's OK," he said, obviously picking up that I was upset.

"So then what happened?"

"Well, we did some activities at the apartment for about an hour, and then it was time to head back. I was thinking that I might need to become real friendly with the girl so I could catch a ride back on her lap," he joked. "But I settled for holding on to her wheelchair with both hands and asking her to stop several times because of chest pain."

He paused, took a deep breath through his nose, and then grinned. "The last thing I wanted was to croak on my way back to the school."

His words passed unnoticed as terrible thoughts raced in and out of my mind.

"The poor girl had no idea how out of shape I am. I felt bad she had to wait for me. We finally made it back to the school, but I've been useless the rest of the day."

"Well, I'm sure glad you didn't croak," I said, trying to partake of his humor, "but I'm not happy they made you go through that. I guess I'll need to be a bit clearer with them about your physical limitations."

He stretched back in his seat. "Yeah, that's a good idea." He sighed. "I certainly don't want to have a day like today again."

"You don't have to worry; I'll make sure that doesn't happen again."

"I'm going to rest for a bit; do you mind?"

"No, just relax." The silence and slow traffic left plenty of time for my brain to stir, and I silently conversed as if I were talking to someone who cared to listen. "This is exactly why I don't leave him with anybody. People just don't listen. Don't they understand how sick he really is? He could die. I already have a hard time keeping his breathing issues under control; I don't need them making it worse. How am I supposed to take him back tomorrow and feel OK about leaving him? I mean really—it's only day two. I can't stand the thought of something bad happening to him—especially when I'm not there."

My silent rant continued. "It's scary enough that he was alone with just another student in such a bad part of town, but someone in a wheelchair. She couldn't have kept him safe if she wanted to. And that hill…of course he was having chest pains; it's steep even for a healthy person."

Then a rational thought came to mind, almost as if it were coming from someone else. "Maybe you're overreacting. He seems fine. He made it through, and nothing horrible happened. He was even able to joke about it." I argued with myself. "Yeah, nothing happened this time. But I'm trying to keep him from getting sicker, and this makes life harder on both of us." Spent and weary, I was relieved to pull into my driveway and put an end to the internal discussion.

Jeff slept from the time we got home until the next morning. He didn't feel well in the morning but reluctantly agreed to go to school after I assured him I would remind the staff about his special health needs. He didn't want to make a big deal about it, but he did ask me to make sure they knew that he wasn't being difficult or rude when he said he couldn't do something.

Upon our arrival, we met with Mr. Jones, the student coordinator, and shared our concerns. He was very apologetic and told us nothing like that would happen in the future. He also asked Jeff to let them know when he needed a break and to tell them how else they could help him.

I left the school slightly anxious but ready to go home and enjoy some long-overdue alone time. Mom was planning on picking Jeff up from school, since it was his weekend to stay at their house. We were trying a new plan by having him stay until Monday morning and then having the bus pick him up and take him to school. He said he was looking forward to trying the public transportation system as a way to relieve us from having to drive him back and forth. It was a bit scary for me, but surprisingly enough, he seemed eager to try something new. The morning sun reflected off the oversized white van idling in Mom's driveway. The double doors swing open, and a middle-aged bus driver stepped outside. He was casually dressed in tan pants and a brown shirt, his name monogrammed above the left pocket.

"Do you have everything in my bag?" Jeff asked Mom.

"Yes, everything's in there. Now, remember that the bus is taking you to Tammy's house after school. It's supposed to pick you up at three o'clock," she said, walking next to him as he walked toward the bus.

"Good morning," the driver happily said. "Looks like it's going to be a beautiful day."

"Good morning," Mom said. "So you're the lucky guy that gets to take my son on his first bus ride since he became blind."

Jeff's face turned red as he extended his hand toward the speechless driver. "Hello. I'm Jeff."

"Nice to meet you, Jeff." He shook his hand. "My name is Ted, and I'll take good care of you."

He nodded his head at Mom as he placed Jeff's hand on the handrail. "There are just two steps up."

"OK. Mom, wish me luck. I'll call you when I get to Tammy's house."

Ted helped Jeff into his seat and buckled him up before getting in the driver's seat. He pulled a lever to close the door and slowly drove down the driveway. Mom swayed her extended arm back and forth. Ted waved back.

Taking advantage of our new freedom, the girls and I treated ourselves to a special after-school outing. The warm sun radiated on us as we sat at a metal patio table outside the Sammamish Starbucks. Chelsey and Kendra slurped hot chocolate in between sharing the details of their school day. Enjoying the moment, I leaned back against the curved chair, took in a deep breath of spring air, and pointed my face toward the sun.

"I love it when we get to spend times like this together," I told them.

"Me too, Momma," Kendra blurted out as crumbs from the cookie du jour spilled over her chin.

"Now that Uncle Jeff is in school, do you think we're gonna be able to do this more often?" Chelsey asked.

"I sure hope so, but we have to wait and see how the school thing works out."

Kendra's brow furrowed, and her smile disappeared. "Do you think it will work out?"

I gently rubbed her back. "I can't tell yet, but if it doesn't, we'll figure something else out."

The slurping sound from Chelsey sucking the last drops of her drink paused. "What time will he be home today?"

I looked at my watch, and a bit of unexpected nervousness came over me. "He should be getting on the bus right now and be home in about an hour."

Kendra solemnly looked down at the table and then took another bite of her cookie. Chelsey continued to suck on her green straw, annoyingly moving it around the bottom of the empty cup.

"We better get going," I said. "I have to get a few things at the store before Jeff gets home."

While I was preparing dinner, my eyes obsessively drifted to and from the white clock hanging above the kitchen table. Chelsey was doing her homework, and Kendra was setting the table for dinner. I glanced out the front window anticipating Jeff's arrival any minute. I couldn't imagine why a thirty-minute drive had already taken over an hour. Thirty more minutes passed before my patience turned into panic.

I anxiously grabbed the phone and dialed the school.

"Hello. My brother Jeff was supposed to catch the bus today, and he's still not home."

I recognized the secretary's voice. "Oh yes. My records show he did get on the bus at three o'clock as scheduled."

"Well, he hasn't made it home, and I'm not sure what I'm supposed to do now."

"You should call the bus operator, who can connect you to the driver," she calmly suggested.

I quickly hung up, unsure if I said goodbye, and immediately dialed the bus company.

Watching me pace around, Chelsey asked, "What's wrong, Mom?"

I lowered the phone from my face. "I can't find Jeff," I said desperately.

A voice on the phone asked, "How can I help you?"

"I need to find out where my brother is. He was picked up at the blind school at three o'clock, and he still isn't home. This is his first time taking the bus home, and I'm worried something has happened to him."

"Ma'am," she said, "I'm sure we can sort this out. I can call the driver directly. What is your brother's name?"

"Jeff Longley." My voice quivered.

I tightly wrapped my arm around Chelsey as she clung to my side.

"I need to put you on hold for a moment."

I held the silent phone pressed tightly against my ear, and Chelsey stuck to my side as we paced around the kitchen. I looked up from the hardwood floor, and my eyes met Kendra's. She sat quietly at the table, reserving her reaction as she often did.

"Ma'am, it sounds like your brother is on his way to his mother's house. He's doing fine, and they should be arriving around five o'clock."

"Whew." I sighed heavily. "Someone really messed up, because he was supposed to be coming to Issaquah."

"I'm sorry, ma'am. Would you like to talk to a supervisor?"

I softened my sharp tone. "No, thanks. I'll handle it tomorrow. Thank you for your help."

"You're welcome. Goodbye now."

"Uncle Jeff's on his way to Grandma's." I let out a long breath while dialing my mom's number.

"Thank God," Chelsey shouted, finally letting go of my side.

Still silent, Kendra approached me and wrapped her arms around my waist while I explained to my mom that Jeff was on his way. My mom and I spent a few moments commiserating about how stressful the school was, as well as the transportation thing, before hanging up. The bus finally arrived in Mom's driveway around five o'clock, ending the two-hour faux pas. Jeff was now safe and resting comfortably on Mom's couch.

Mom tenderly rubbed his damp forehead. "I made spaghetti for dinner, if you're hungry."

"I can't eat just yet," he said. "The ride was long, and I knew something was wrong when the driver opened the bus doors and I heard the noise of traffic and people talking.

Then I said to the driver, 'Um, excuse me, sir. Where are we? It sounds really loud and busy around here.'

"The driver matter-of-factly said, 'We're in downtown Seattle. This is where you're supposed to catch your next bus.'

"'Uh, I think there's a mix-up.'" Jeff continued recounting the story with even more expression. "'Could you call my sister? Because I don't think I'm supposed to be in downtown Seattle. I don't even know how to get around out there, and I definitely wouldn't know how to catch another bus.'

"That's when the driver called his dispatcher and was told to come here."

"Thank God you didn't get off that bus. That would've been awful," Mom said.

"It wouldn't have been so bad going downtown." Jeff's lips turned up, and his eyes twinkled. "I could have sat on a corner with a cup and sang for some extra cash." He chuckled.

Mom offhandedly brushed the top of his head. "Jeffrey Michael…that's not funny."

The smirk on Jeff's rose-colored face elicited a few more disapproving comments from Mom as she got up to finish preparing dinner.

Even though Jeff was safe and seemed to be taking the whole thing in stride, an uneasy sense of vulnerability came over me as my mind spun on all the things that could have happened. And how could I have forgiven myself if something really bad had happened? How could I ever put him back on a bus again? What do I do about the school? How do I protect him?

All of this dampened my enthusiasm for the blind school and my commitment to finish the ten-day trial. Nonetheless, we continued the trial uneventfully, and Jeff was proud that he kept his commitment. But no one was surprised when the school called with their decision that Jeff was not a good candidate for their program. But the lack of surprise didn't make telling the kids any easier.

CHAPTER 32

Telling the Girls

I PICKED THE GIRLS UP from school the day I got the call. I was apprehensive about how they would react to the news, so I waited until we got home to tell them. As soon as we walked in the door, I called them into the upstairs rec room.

They plopped on the couch next to me and waited for me to talk. "So I got the call from Jeff's school this morning, and they told me he wasn't a good fit."

"What did they say? Was it because he couldn't walk that hill?" Chelsey asked.

"Well. A lot of things contributed to it, I'm sure. But the main reason is your uncle is too sick to participate in many of their activities."

Chelsey seemed slightly disappointed but handled the news easily. Kendra said nothing, then turned on the TV. I felt her disappointment. A part of me could even relate to it.

"I feel bad for Uncle Jeff," Chelsey said. "He must feel terrible."

"Well, he's sad he can't continue, but he's glad he had a chance to go for ten days. He learned a lot of good things."

"Is he really getting sicker? Like is he dying?" Kendra asked, somewhat annoyed.

"I didn't say he was dying. I said he was too sick to go to that school. As far as when he will die, I have no idea. Nobody does. Remember, they told us he only had six weeks to live. And here we are, two years later, and he's going to school."

"No, he's not," Kendra snapped.

"Rude," Chelsey said.

"OK, Kendra, what's going on?"

"Nothing," she sharply said, turning toward the window.

"It's not his fault, Kendra. He can't help being sick." Chelsey glared at her sister.

I gave Chelsey a disapproving look. She didn't have as difficult time as Kendra did with Jeff living with us.

"I know you are disappointed, and I don't blame you. I'm disappointed too."

Kendra continued to avoid eye contact, but the dampness on her sleeve from wiping her eyes validated that she was hurting.

"Please, will you tell me what you are thinking right now?"

"I just want our family to get back to normal." She buried her face in her lap.

A wave of nausea shot through my gut, nearly dropping me to my knees. My chin quivered as I said, "I know this is all so hard. I promise that I will try to find a way for us to spend more time together. We'll figure something out."

Chelsey's eyes surveyed mine as she patted my leg. "It's OK, Momma, and we know you're doing your best."

"I wasn't blaming her," Kendra snapped, suddenly remorseful.

"I know you weren't blaming me. You know I cry when one of you is sad too. It'll all be fine," I said, trying to convince myself. Clark entered the room and saw me sandwiched between the girls.

"What's going on?"

"Nothing...we're just having a moment," I said.

"I'm going to watch TV downstairs, then. Tell me when you guys are done." He shook his head as he walked away. I wished he were able to be a better support at times like that, but I knew emotional talks were not his thing.

"I want to explain something to you both, even though you may already think you know what I'm going to say." I looked over and saw the girls glance at each other.

"In your life, you will have many relationships with many people. Some of those relationships will be stronger than others. Some will be based on love, and some will be based on fear, but none will be exactly the same as the others. My relationship with your father is different from my relationship with you, but not just because he's my husband and you are my children. It's more than that. Are you with me?"

They were both sitting up now and fully attentive. It had been long time since we had had enough alone time for one of our special talks.

"Yeah," they said in unison.

"Well, my relationship with Jeff is different from my relationship with either of you, and that's partly because of who he is and partly because of who I am. When he was born, I was only four years old, and I loved him unconditionally, just as I love you unconditionally. And when he was your age, we were best of friends, just like you two are." They wrinkled their noses and smirked at each other. "I protected him just like I protect you and will always protect you. Do you know what I mean?"

Again, they echoed back in unison, "Yeah."

"Well, as Jeff got older, I was always there to help him with his problems, and he came to rely on me to keep protecting him. I made a promise to him that I would always care for him, just like I've made a promise to always care for you—forever. That's what you want, isn't it—for me to be there for you, for me to protect you forever?"

They both nodded assertively.

"Yes, Momma, we get it," Kendra said. Her demeanor switched from frustration to sadness.

Chelsey leaned in and hugged me, her gentle voice cracking slightly. "It's OK, Momma. We understand."

My body quivered as I tried to restrain my pent-up emotion. I subconsciously held my breath and tightly squeezed my eyes shut a few times. I took a deep breath and continued. "I want to remind you both"—I sniffled—"that you aren't bad for not wanting Jeff here and for wishing things could be back to normal. It's OK. It doesn't mean you don't care."

My breathing became easier, and my words flowed smoother as I continued. "I want you to always tell me how you're feeling—even if it's hard to say out loud. Jeff isn't the only one who matters in our family."

They wiped their eyes and nodded.

"And another thing. Just as you two are different in what you like to do and what you like to wear, it's OK that you handle Jeff being here differently as well. So, Chels, I don't want you to make Kendra feel bad that she feels different than you might about Jeff. And same goes for you, Kendra. OK?"

They both nodded.

"Now, let's go get some ice cream, and tell Dad it's safe to come back in." I kissed each of their foreheads before they bolted off to the kitchen. I buried my face in my hands, feeling torn as I grappled with doing the right thing for my family or doing the right thing for Jeff. Rarely were they the same.

CHAPTER 33

Sunday Service

ONE PART OF THE BLIND school Jeff really missed was being able to talk to other blind people about their experience, as well as his own. He agreed that it might be helpful to call a therapist the school recommended. Her name was Jenny, and she had been going blind since the age of eight. Jeff thought he might benefit from talking to her, since she knew firsthand what it was like to go blind after being able to see.

Jenny, along with her guide dog, met Jeff and me at the library, where she used a study room as her office. She was a middle-aged woman wearing dark glasses. She was very soft spoken and pleasant. Jenny shared with us that she felt less vulnerable meeting with clients in public places as opposed to a private office.

"Jeff, we can go into this room, and Tammy can wait out here for us."

"OK," Jeff said.

I guided him into the small room, where there were only two chairs and a desk. Once he sat down, I turned around, pulled the door shut, and peeked back in through the window in the door. I could see Jeff talking to Jenny as she listened intently.

After a while, the door reopened, and I heard them finalizing plans to meet again. Jeff and I walked down the library corridor, and I asked, "How'd it go?"

"Pretty well. This session was mostly about my surgery. She says we'll get into other stuff as time goes on."

I was glad he had found someone who could help him with his grief over losing his sight. And perhaps he could learn how to cope with it differently. If nothing else, he could add another person to his network of supporters.

"Did Jenny ask you what you hope to get out of therapy?"

"Yeah, but I didn't really have a good answer. I told her maybe to learn more about myself."

"What part of you?"

"I don't mean anything about my cancer or my blindness…more about how I feel about my life."

"How you feel about your life?" I asked.

He pondered for a moment. "Yeah…" Another pause. "Because I used to have bad feelings about myself, and I understand how that affected me. But now my feelings are changing so much that I don't know how they will impact my new life."

"I get it," I said. "I know that if you feel good about yourself, about your life, you will likely feel better physically and emotionally."

"I understand, but I don't know if I totally get how to figure that out for myself," he said.

"That's what you learn in therapy," I said. "She'll help you sort out your feelings."

"I did tell her that one thing I know for sure is that I want to give back. I want to walk out my faith, especially since I didn't do that so well before I got sick."

"I think you're on the right track, and I'm really proud of you."

Church had always been a regular part of my family routine, and more than ever it had become a much-needed time of reflection. The sermon the following week rallied us to become servants to those in need, to let Jesus use us wherever we were in our lives.

After the service, Chelsey and Kendra planned on going with the youth group to feed the homeless in downtown Seattle. I was excited to spend the time with my girls and to help the leadership team. Clark and Jeff made plans to stop for breakfast before heading home.

The downtown streets were quiet on a Sunday Seattle afternoon. Few cars passed by as we made our way out of the van. Most of the kids came from middle-class homes and had little awareness of what the word "poor" or "needy" really meant. They gathered in a small group with their designated leaders and prepared to share God's love with the homeless by handing out lunches made early in the morning.

"OK, kids, listen up. I want you to stick with your partner, and don't go out of the park," I instructed my group.

"Mom, will you walk with me and Lindsey?" Kendra asked as she lifted a white plastic bag filled with lunches.

"Of course. Let's go."

There were homeless men and women sitting on benches spread around the park. As the residents of the park realized that a meal was being served, they started approaching the kids, asking for a lunch.

A middle-aged, scruffy-looking man said, "Hey, I would like a lunch."

"Here you go," Jason said as he passed the brown paper bag to the man. It was filled with a ham-and-cheese sandwich, a bag of chips, a Coke, and a cookie.

The man opened the bag, seemed pleased, and said, "God bless you, young man." Then he turned, looked for a place to sit, and walked toward a large tree shading the park.

As we walked farther, we heard the rustling of someone coming up behind us. "Stay away from drugs so you don't end up here," an older man told Kendra as she turned to place a sack in his outstretched hand. She paused for an instant, connecting to his words before she moved on.

"Go to school and listen to your mom and dad," a disheveled lady advised Christopher.

As we headed to the cars, I encouraged the kids to glance back at the people eating their lunches. I highlighted how it had taken all of fifteen minutes to give out 110 lunches, a small sacrifice of time that made such huge difference. Just then, a middle-aged woman ran down the cracked concrete sidewalk, her greasy brown hair sticking out from a blue stocking cap, her heavy coat shifting with the effort of each frantic step.

"Can I have a lunch? I want a lunch," she pleaded.

Looking squarely into the woman's eyes, Chelsey said, "I'm so, so sorry. We just ran out."

"I always miss out on getting a lunch," the woman hollered to no one in particular as she turned. Head hanging down, she walked slowly up the hill from where she had come.

"Mom, we have to do something. Give her some money or something," Chelsey begged tearfully.

Watching Chelsey's excitement turn into disillusionment was hard, but I knew that if we gave to that woman, there would be another one just like her to follow. An endless stream of need was hard to comprehend, especially for a child.

"It'll be OK. I'm sure there will be some other groups coming down soon to bring more food."

Blond hair framing her pale face, her watery eyes looked into mine. "I feel so sorry for that lady."

"I know it's hard. But come on; we have to go now." As we entered the freeway ramp, heading back toward our middle-class neighborhoods, the van was filled with chatter as the kids shared their thoughts about the people they had just served.

We arrived home, and Chelsey promptly burst through the front door and headed to the rec room, where she anticipated Uncle Jeff was resting on the green sofa. Jeff heard her words before he felt her plop on the couch next to him.

"You wouldn't believe how sad it was…" The torment in her voice increased. "We didn't even have enough lunches for everyone."

She slapped her hand against the couch and continued. "There was this lady who got really upset and started yelling because we didn't have a lunch for her. And Mom wouldn't even give her money."

"Really? That sounds awful."

"Mom said that other people were bringing lunches too, but it doesn't matter."

"Were there a lot of people who got lunches?" Jeff asked.

"Yeah, there were so many." The distress in her face softened. "It took like only fifteen minutes to give away one hundred and ten lunches."

"Well, that's good, isn't it?"

"I guess, but I can't stop thinking about that poor lady." Her voice quieted. "It makes my stomach hurt just thinking about her."

"I'm sure she'll be OK, Chels. Just try to focus on those that you did help."

"OK, I'll try. I'm gonna go upstairs now. I'll be back down later."

Later in the week, while sitting at the kitchen table in our typical morning routine, Jeff was quieter than usual. I sat down, hoping that he would offer an explanation for his somber mood.

"Hey, you know how my therapist has been encouraging me to think about what I could do with my life?" He sighed deeply. "Well, after hearing that sermon last week, it left me wondering how God can use a dying blind guy like me."

"Hmm. What have you come up with so far?" I asked, relieved that his silence was not because he was feeling sick.

"Well, I was thinking that maybe we could make lunches, and I could go with you guys to feed the homeless again. The way I look at it is that Jesus has provided for me with food, shelter, and a family who loves me. I have so much more than a homeless person, and I still have an opportunity to make a difference in the world."

"Sounds like someone has been figuring things out," I said.

"I've been thinking that we could go more often. Just think of how many more people we could feed," he said.

"Yeah, that sounds like a great idea."

He continued energetically. "I've given food to some homeless people on the side of the road here and there, but now I'm thinking that maybe this is something I could do on a regular basis, and it will really make a difference in the world."

"I think you ought to follow your heart. I'll do what I can to help."

"It seems strange how differently I think about life now versus when I was healthy. Maybe by serving the homeless, they will see me and count their blessings. They might think, 'Wow, sucks to be that guy.' And if I can inspire just one person to look at his life differently, then my mission will be a success."

"Why do you think you're so different?" I asked.

"I realize now that I could have had it all if I would have prioritized my life right. Isn't that the point of all of this—it's a choice? It's a matter of how we choose to live our life and where we place our priorities. I had to lose everything before I learned to appreciate what I had. Now I want to help people learn the lessons I've learned, learn to appreciate what they have, learn to laugh at life. But don't get me wrong. I'm not saying I would choose to have cancer or blindness; I'm just saying I'm going to choose how I live with them."

"Wow. It's a gift to have that kind of attitude," I said.

"Yeah." He smiled. "A gift from God. I didn't make a conscious choice to have a good attitude about all this, but I do have to make the choice to keep it."

"Do you ever think of the cancer and blindness as a gift?"

"I don't know." He paused to think. "Maybe from the devil. I'm kidding. I don't know if it's a gift, or maybe just that shit happens. I only know that I'm trying to make the best of the cards I've been dealt, and every time I start feeling sorry for myself, I realize that it can get worse."

"And what do you think God has in mind now?"

"I think I'm supposed to make a difference in the lives of others during the time I have left." Wow. Jeff was changing. He had never had such insight and selfless goals, and he had never viewed things that way before. He saw it. I saw it. And it was apparent to those around him. Friends began spending hours talking with him and telling him how inspiring he was.

It seemed as if there was an old Jeff, and now there was a new Jeff emerging. The old Jeff had had everything he wanted, yet most of the time he was an anxious, depressed, miserable soul. He didn't treat people as a priority, could not sustain deep relationships, and was a pessimist most of the time. He was self-absorbed and stubborn in so many ways.

The new Jeff had lost everything—not only his material things, but his negative attitudes as well. And he wanted to share what little he had with people he didn't even know. He seemed to feel good about himself, was not depressed much anymore, and laughed more than ever. It was becoming evident that God had a different idea about the purpose of Jeff's new life.

CHAPTER 34
First Sack Lunch Sunday

THE MONTH FOLLOWING JEFF'S EPIPHANY was spent planning and organizing a homeless event. Jeff's goal to make a difference was finally coming to fruition. With help from everyone, Jeff was busy finalizing his new homeless project. He talked extensively about the homeless project, which focused his mind on something other than his poor health. He was almost obsessive about organizing every detail: the date of delivery, the type of sandwiches we would make, what snacks and drinks would be included, and so on.

Mom made it her job to help him send out e-mails to family and friends. She would type as Jeff told her what to say. His efforts were inspiring, and it seemed that people were eager to help when they got a request from a blind, sick guy to donate food, money, socks, or other miscellaneous items.

He even inspired all the neighborhood kids who regularly visited our house to gather used backpacks so he could deliver them along with the lunches. Chelsey and Kendra eagerly joined his cause by encouraging their classmates to donate. The word was spreading, and his project seemed to be gaining momentum.

"Uncle Jeff. Uncle Jeff," Kendra said, running into the house ahead of Chelsey, "you won't believe how many backpacks my class donated." Breathing heavy and fast, she struggled to get the words out through her excitement. "We collected twenty-eight."

"Wow. That's awesome."

She bounced up and down, words rapidly tumbling out. "And Chelsey's class collected nineteen…"

"Hey, I was gonna tell him," Chelsey said.

Undaunted, Kendra continued. "That means we have forty-seven from school, bringing our total to a hundred and five, counting the ones at Grandma's." She finally paused and took a deep breath, ignoring Chelsey's glare.

"I can't wait to see the homeless people's reaction when we make our delivery on Sunday," Jeff said.

Still giddy, Kendra bounced her bottom on the couch. "They're gonna be so happy."

"We are so blessed by all these donations and people who are willing to help," Jeff said. "I think we should officially call the ministry Sack Lunch Sunday."

"Yeah, that sounds good," Chelsey said.

The last Sunday of June 2002, about nine friends and family met at my house to help Jeff make lunches. He was excited that we had collected enough donations to make a record-breaking 450 lunches. It took about four hours to put all the lunches together.

After the large green garbage bags were filled with lunches, backpacks, and other things, we squeezed them into designated cars. The drivers barely had room to fit in themselves. When all the cars were loaded, we pulled out of the driveway, convoy style. As we approached Pioneer Square, I was encouraged to see that there were homeless people hanging out in the park.

"Wow, Jeff. There are so many people at the park today."

"That's great. Let's get it done."

I pulled into the parking lot and found a spot up front. The other cars in the convoy followed me in and found their own spots. We all got out of our cars about the same time, and everyone eagerly grabbed a bag of lunches to give to the approaching residents of the park.

Jeff stood by the side of the car, waiting for me to finish pulling the bags from the trunk. With his eyes mostly closed, he lifted his ears toward the voices that were coming from all directions. "You weren't kidding when you said there were a lot of people here. Do you think it's safe?"

"Oh yeah, we're good." Chelsey and Kendra led the other kids as if they were old pros at this gig. They confidently approached the strangers, offered them a sack lunch, and then rushed off to the next person. Each girl had a few friends hustling behind her as they raced to be the first to empty their big green bag. Mom and Dad split up to keep a watch on the kids as they ran from one end of the park to the other.

"Whatever you do, don't leave my side," Jeff said, clinging to my arm.

"Of course I won't. Are you nervous?"

"Yeah, a little. It's weird to hear all these noises and not be able to see what's going on."

"Let me describe it for you. Maybe that will help put you at ease."

"That might help."

"Don't you have any memories of Pioneer Square?" I asked.

"Only from when Aunt Betty took us when we were young. Isn't it the small park where all the drunks hang out?"

I smiled, remembering how our aunt Betty used to take us kids for late-night drives through the city to watch the crazy people out and about. It was cheap entertainment that usually concluded with a stop to the ice cream shop.

"Yeah, this is the one. But it isn't so bad during the day. There are about twenty wood benches around the square park. I see about forty people walking around. Some of them are just passing through." I continued to talk as we strolled toward an area that was away from the others in our group.

"There are a few people coming toward us," I whispered.

"Will you hand me a couple lunches to give them?" Jeff extended his arm as footsteps of a disheveled man approached us. "Would you like a lunch?"

The scruffy faced man carefully stared at Jeff and then passed right by us. I turned to watch him and saw that he took a lunch from one of the kids instead.

Jeff again offered another park resident a lunch, and that person too silently walked past us and accepted a lunch from one of the others.

"Hello, would you like a lunch?" I asked an elderly man lying on a bench with his heavily soiled coat draped over his head and shoulders.

"Thank you, and God bless you," he muttered as he took the brown bag from my hand.

"God bless you," Jeff said.

Jeff held my arm tightly as we carefully sauntered around the tattered cobblestone path that bordered the small park. It seemed as though people had a hard time accepting a lunch from him. More times than not, if he was the one holding out the lunch, people would pass by. If I was giving it away, they readily accepted it.

"I was hoping that I could talk to more people," Jeff said as we headed back toward our car.

"Don't get discouraged. I just think they're uncomfortable taking a lunch from a blind guy."

"Yeah, I guess. I would've liked to hear their story and maybe encourage them. Maybe remind them that Jesus loves them."

The kids and other volunteers gathered around and excitedly shared with Jeff, and one another, how amazed they were that it had taken only thirty minutes to hand out all 450 lunches. Jeff's smile broadened as he listened.

On the ride home, Jeff spoke loudly so the people in the rear seat could hear too. "Thank you all for your help. This little ministry is turning out really well. I certainly couldn't do it without you guys. It has been incredible to watch how God has moved people to give. I'm excited to get even more people involved so we can provide lunches more than just once a month."

Acknowledging utterances filtered back to him.

He continued. "This isn't just about feeding the homeless; it's about impacting the people who help as well. I hope this project stirs something up in everyone."

CHAPTER 35

Lake Sammamish, June 2002

It was a beautiful, sunny day, and the lake called to us. The girls were excited to go play, especially after such a busy weekend doing the homeless project. Eager to go ride the Jet Ski, they gathered their swim suits, towels, and accessories.

Midge, my faithful sidekick, arrived just in time to help me as I hurried around the house, gathering my own things as well as packing up Jeff. For the first time ever, we took Jeff to the lake with us. The previous year he had been too fragile, but now, since he was stronger and used to swimming, we figured he might enjoy it.

"Chrissy and I get to go on the Jet Ski first," Chelsey said, grinning wickedly at Kendra.

"That's not fair," said Kendra, glaring back at her and her bubbly friend Chrissy.

"Girls, we'll be there for most of the day. Chelsey called it first, but you both will get as much time as you want," I said.

Midge and I packed up everyone and headed off to Lake Sammamish. Once we were settled on the beach, I took Chelsey and Chrissy out for a ride on the Jet Ski. When we returned, I tried talking Jeff into going for a ride. He was pretty reluctant, given my reputation for being a crazy driver.

Having never ridden on a Jet Ski, Jeff shook his head side to side.

"Look, I'll make you a deal. If I get crazy, then I'll let you drive. That way you can have revenge for anything I do."

He finally agreed, with much trepidation, and I helped him into a lifejacket. Once Chelsey and Kendra had their turns, Midge helped me lead Jeff to the Jet Ski. Getting him on was a challenge in itself, since he didn't have enough upper-body strength to be of much help—not to mention he was extremely uncoordinated. It took both of us to stabilize him onto the ski.

Although it was my idea, I wasn't entirely certain taking him out on the water was the best plan.

Once he was mounted in place, I looked at him perched on top of the Jet Ski and shook my head. "This is crazy. What was I thinking?" I teased.

Jeff quickly replied, "Don't chicken out on me now." A devilish grin spread across his face as he pretended to rev the engine, twisting his hand on the grip as if he were on a motorcycle.

"I'm not chickening out. You really sure you're ready for this ride? It's not too late."

"Oh yeah. Let's go."

Midge helped me push the Jet Ski off the shore. As I climbed on and sat in front of Jeff, Midge hollered, "Don't go crazy, now. Remember, he isn't exactly well."

"Of course I will." I smiled and then waved at her and the girls, who cheered from the shore.

"OK, Jeff, just hold on tight. I'll go slow, but don't lean too far on either side, or we'll tip over. And we definitely don't want to tip over, because it'll be nearly impossible to get you back on the Jet Ski. This thing is really stable unless you tilt it way over to one side," I said.

He reached his arms around me and held tightly on to the straps of my lifejacket. As we accelerated away from the beach, I felt him pull harder. We scooted across the calm lake, increasing in speed as we drove. In my rearview mirror, I saw Jeff smile widely as the wind blew against his face. My smile matched his.

As we hit the wave of a passing boat, Jeff abruptly tugged my life vest, screaming "Whoa!"

I slowed down. "You're OK. We just hit a little wave." We sat idle for a moment. "Are you having fun?"

"Oh yeah. But it's really weird riding blind."

"Do you want to drive?"

"What? Are you serious?"

"Of course I am. You always say how much you miss driving, so now's your chance. I can help you. Besides, what's the worst that can happen? We fall in."

"OK. Sounds like fun, I guess," he said, a little nervous but mostly excited.

With the Jet Ski stopped on the lake, I stood up on the ledge, pulled my leg over the seat, carefully leaning so I wouldn't land in the water. I stretched one leg over Jeff's, and then the other. I sat behind him as he scooted toward the front.

"OK, here's the throttle for the gas." I placed his finger on the trigger. "The harder you squeeze it, the faster we go. There are no brakes, so when you want to slow down, you just have to let go of the throttle. The only thing you can do wrong is turn sharp when we are going fast. If you do, then you'll dump us off. Got it?"

His face beaming, he nodded. "I got it."

"OK, we're out in the middle of the lake, and there's nothing around us. We are perfectly safe. You can take off in any direction, and if I see any waves, I'll tell you which way to go, because we don't want to hit a wave sideways. OK?"

He nodded again.

"Now, just squeeze the throttle—slowly at first," I said.

He hesitantly squeezed the throttle, and we surged forward. Startled, he stopped, and we slowed suddenly.

"It's OK. You're doing great. Take it easy, and just remember, no fast turns."

He started squeezing the throttle a bit tighter. Our speed slowly increased, along with his comfort. We hit about forty miles an hour as we glided over the placid, greenish-blue lake. What a strange feeling it must be to drive blind, I thought. I closed my eyes briefly, attempting to experience the sensation for myself.

Jeff was grinning from ear to ear. "This is awesome," he shouted.

"You're going almost forty miles an hour now. Remember, no fast turns." I spoke directly in his ear, loud enough for him to hear over the engine noise.

He turned slightly to the left.

"OK, be careful. Go straight now," I said.

Suddenly he tightened his grip on the throttle and sharply turned right, overcorrecting. The rapid acceleration as he turned immediately launched us off the seat like a missile, and we landed about twenty yards from the Jet Ski.

When I came up from the water, I heard Jeff hollering, "Am I alive?"

I grabbed the strap of his lifejacket and pulled him near me. "Yeah, you survived," I said, my words barely able to break through my laughter. With my hands holding his, Jeff caught my contagious laughter. Everyone on the lake probably heard us.

"Are you OK?" I asked, still cracking up.

"I'm not sure, but I think so." He cautiously moved his head side to side as if he were making sure it was still attached.

"What were you thinking?" I asked, my side cramping as I tried to regain my composure.

"I think I panicked," he said, happier than I had ever seen him. Even before the surgery, I had never seen him laugh this much. "I didn't mean to dump us. Honest."

"This is too funny. How am I going to get you back on the Jet Ski? It's about a hundred feet from us. Do you think you can swim over there?"

"I can try, but I'm pretty tired already." Jeff started to look a bit worried. "Do you think you can pull me?"

"Don't worry; I'll get us out of here. It's not too far."

As I was tugging my two-hundred-pound brother back to the Jet Ski, I wondered how I had gotten into this mess. I realized that I should not have been surprised, since the odds were definitely in favor of a crash when letting a blind man drive.

"We're about halfway there, but I think it'll be faster if I just swim back myself and ride the Jet Ski toward you," I said.

"Great idea, but don't leave me here too long. With my luck, I've survived everything I've been through just to be killed by a crazy boat driver who doesn't see me in the water."

"You're gonna be fine. There aren't any boats in the area," I said. But my words were probably not that reassuring, since I had started laughing again.

I swam away and rode the Jet Ski back to where Jeff was bobbing with his arm dramatically flailing in the air. I jumped back in the water to help him on.

"Here's what you need to do. Put your hands right here…" I placed his hands on the seat handle. "And while you pull, I'll push."

"OK, but I don't know if I'm strong enough to pull myself up."

"I'll help you. Don't worry."

He adjusted his hands around the handle. "OK, I'm ready."

"On the count of three: one, two, and three—*pull*."

I was pressed underwater as I tried to push his butt up. We both let go, dissolving into hysterics. After a few more failed attempts, I finally got the bright idea to pull him up while I was on the Jet Ski and not in the water. That worked better, and after a few tries, he was on. We sat for a minute, both exhausted, but not as much from the effort as the hysterical laughing. It was a memory neither of us would ever forget.

The girls excitedly jumped up and down as the Jet Ski hit the sandy beach. "Was it fun, Uncle Jeff? Was it?" Kendra asked.

"Oh yeah." Jeff beamed.

Midge stood behind them, shaking her head side to side. "How did Jeff's hair get so wet?" she hollered. "Did you try to throw him in?"

"You betcha. It was just too good to pass up." I roared with laughter.

"But I got her right back." Jeff yelled back, grinning widely. "I'm sure she flew farther than I did." We pushed the Jet Ski onto the shore, and Midge helped me slide Jeff off. We gingerly guided him to a blanket in the shade, where he quickly fell asleep, allowing me to spend more time riding the Jet Ski with the girls and visiting with Midge. It was a joyful day, a day we all cherished.

CHAPTER 36

Blind Bowling

THE WEEK FOLLOWING OUR GREAT adventure, I was dropping Jeff off for his regularly scheduled stay at Mom's house. He could hardly wait to tell each and every visitor how he had catapulted me off the Jet Ski. I was sure that Mom had already told everyone, but he would recount it.

Our cousin Allison was at the house when we arrived. She usually tried to stop by for a visit with Jeff, since she lived near Mom's house.

"Well, there's the crazy couple," she said, holding open the screen door as we walked in.

"See, Jeff? I told you everyone already heard about it," I said.

He grinned.

I guided him to his favorite overstuffed blue recliner and then put his bag in his bedroom. I chatted with Mom and Allison for a bit before rushing off to get back home.

After lunch, Jeff returned to his cozy chair. One leg curled up under the knee of the other, Jeff was deeply engaged in a conversation with Allison, giving Mom a chance to get some chores done.

The phone rang, interrupting Mom's chores. She answered. "Hello?"

A wide grin spread across Mom's face. "Hey, Jeff, Cindy's on the phone. She wants to know if you're up for another adventure." Her words mixed with amusement. "She wants to know if you and Allison want to go bowling."

Allison pressed her hand across her mouth and looked away from Mom.

The corner of Jeff's mouth moved upward. "Well, that ought to make for an entertaining outing." His belly began to bounce. "I could barely bowl when I could see."

Unable to hold back, Allison snorted, followed by a high-pitched laugh.

"You comin' along, Allison?"

Imagining Jeff bowling, Allison said, "How could I say no? This should be quite the show."

"Well, looks like you have two takers," Mom reported back to Cindy, our cousin's wife who visited Jeff from time to time at Mom's house.

Mom helped Jeff get ready for what was likely going to be an interesting afternoon. Driving away, Allison's wide smile and twinkly light-blue eyes reflected back at Mom, who was happily waving goodbye.

The worn-out bowling alley had been around since our parents were young and was only a short distance from their house. We went there many times when we were young, mostly because it was cheap entertainment for four kids. Allison pulled open the door, the smell of sweaty shoes and disinfectant hitting them in the face as she guided Jeff to the lobby. "Well, here we go. I'm sure you'll make quite an impression," she said. Spotting Allison, Cindy and her two young boys waved as they eagerly waited at the shoe counter.

"I've already got us a lane. It's right over there." Cindy pointed. "What size shoes do you guys need?"

"I wear a size ten and a half," Jeff said, a smile stretched across his face.

"And I'm size eight," Allison said.

Allison led Jeff down the dreary carpeted corridor toward the well-polished wooden lane.

"It smells like nachos. I don't remember bowling places smelling like nachos before," Jeff said.

"Yeah, we're just passing the little concession stand. They serve hamburgers and hot dogs too," Allison said.

The loud clang of scattering pins and people hooting and shouting echoed throughout the place.

Cindy and the boys arrived with all the ugly bowling shoes. Cindy helped Jeff put his shoes, and then walked him to the rack of balls. "OK, Jeff, let's try to find a ball that fits just right."

She placed his hand on one of the smooth marble-colored balls. He put his two fingers and a thumb in the tight holes.

"Nope, this is way too small." He pulled his hand away just as a returned ball smacked against the others.

"Here, try this one," Cindy said, placing a larger but lighter ball in his open hands.

He slid his fingers in the holes and lifted the ball in front of his chest. "Yep, this one should work. Let's give it a try."

Cindy grabbed his shoulders from behind and gently nudged him toward the white line. "OK, you're at the line, and we have the bumpers up, so you should do fine. You just need to throw it straight ahead."

She stepped back. Allison and the boys were shouting words of encouragement in the background. Jeff swung the ball back, then forward before releasing it only a few feet in front of him. A loud bang from the ball slamming against the wooden lane reverberated back to him.

"How many did I get?"

"Hold on; it's slowly making its way to the pins."

"Hey, anytime it rolls down the lane, I count it as success," he said.

"Good job. You got two—not bad for your first try," Cindy said.

Jeff went again and knocked down only one pin. After everyone else took their turns, Allison again guided Jeff to the line. He confidently lifted his head high and pulled his shoulders back, his ball cradled waist high in front of him. He dropped his voice a few octaves deeper than normal, and in a loud announcer-type rhythm, he said, "Ladies and gentlemen, watch closely as the blind man scores a strike."

His feet spread apart, knees slightly bent, he placed his hands around the ball and then swung it back and forth several times through his legs, granny style. With building momentum, he finally flung the ball down the lane. He released the ball so quickly that it bounced over to the next lane.

The intense bowler whose lane Jeff's ball was rolling down passionately threw his arms into the air. "Hey, dude," he shouted as he shot an evil glare toward Jeff.

Oblivious to the fact that the man was talking to him, Jeff said loudly, "Well, how did I do? Did I get my strike?"

Doubled over, Cindy and the boys exchanged looks with Allison. Her hand covering her mouth, Allison looked away from the irate man, who was still glaring at Jeff.

"Guys?"

Allison whispered in Jeff's ear as she guided him to his seat, "You screwed up the guy next to you." She held her breath, trying to compose herself. "Your ball bounced into his lane. I don't think he's so happy with you."

Amid his nervous laughter, Jeff said, loud enough for the man to hear, "Sorry about that. I couldn't see where I was tossing the ball; I'm blind."

The man's furrowed brow lifted slightly as he curiously stared at Jeff's eyes. After a few seconds, the guy muttered, "It's fine," and stomped off to his lane.

"I take it I didn't get him a strike."

Holding her side, Cindy said, "A strike, no. But you sure landed a fine-looking gutter ball."

After a few random bursts of laughter, Jeff and the others finally contained their silliness, and from then on everything went smoothly—so smoothly, in fact, that Jeff's name appeared above Allison's at the bottom of the scorecard.

Extremely pleased, he bantered with Allison as he strutted back to the car, saying, "Oh yeah, I'm the bowling king." Cindy and her boys trailed behind, cheering him on as if it were true.

CHAPTER 37

Fall 2002

THE SUMMER FUN CONCLUDED, GIVING way to the much-anticipated predictable routine of fall. Even though the summer activities pulled Jeff out of his routine, causing him some anxiety, he enjoyed doing things and spending time with the girls and me. Nonetheless, we were all looking forward to settling into a regular schedule.

Despite the many distractions of being an active mom, I worked hard to keep Jeff's schedule somewhat consistent, as did our mom when he was with her. We understood that routine to Jeff meant order, consistency, and predictability. The more Mom and I kept things in order, the fewer things Jeff had to ask for. When he did not need to ask for help, he felt more independent and had a more positive attitude. And we had plenty of practice figuring out how to help him. We knew the best way to set the table, then how to place food on his plate so he knew the location of each item. In the bathroom, we put his shampoo and shaving lotion precisely where he knew to find it. In the evenings, we set out his clothes so he did not have to ask for help with dressing. Most importantly, we had developed a system for his medications so he did not take the wrong ones. Keeping to routine became a win-win situation for everyone.

Unfortunately, nothing about that fall turned out to be either normal or predictable. It brought unwanted changes for Jeff as his health began to slowly deteriorate. Increased worry accompanied new symptoms: muscle aches, nausea, and shortness of breath. He was tired more and was less talkative. At times, he was preoccupied with his physical aches and pains, which also made him feel depressed. It became difficult to separate what was physical from the psychological, especially since they often went hand in hand.

The abnormal fall not only left Jeff feeling unsettled; the girls' lives were also up in the air. The teachers in our local school district went on strike. Chelsey was going into the eighth grade and dreading the day school resumed. She was very content idling her days away on the couch, watching television and looking through magazines. Kendra was going into the seventh grade, and she, on the other hand, was excited to return to school. She liked being active and hated spending days in front of the TV, so with each passing day, her boredom increased. She could hardly wait to get out of the house and spend time with her friends.

The girls spent most of their time upstairs so they could horse around and watch "their shows" instead of having to compromise with Jeff over the shows he wanted. Often he would happily invite them to watch their shows downstairs with him, but they usually preferred to go upstairs. I noticed them withdrawing from him every time his health changed for the worse, and I avoided putting the responsibility on them to visit with him. It was hard for them to be around Jeff when he was not chatty and happy.

I felt guilty that they had been displaced by Jeff—the downstairs rec room used to be their usual hangout spot in the house. They used to like being near me as I buzzed around in the kitchen. As I had often done over the past two years, I was torn between wanting to be upstairs with the kids and wanting to stay downstairs with Jeff so he would not feel alone. Jeff seemed oblivious to the unfolding family dynamic and was content to pass his days away listening to his favorite TV shows, eating, sleeping, and loving on Rusty.

The start of school had already been delayed by two weeks, and no new negotiations were anticipated for at least several days. The extended summer break was becoming frustrating for all of us, even for Chelsey. I did my best to juggle the kids' boredom, my job, the house, and Jeff.

"Mom, when do you think school is going to start? I'm so bored," Kendra whined, following me from room to room as I straightened up the house.

"I don't know, Ken. Why don't you see if Christopher wants to come over and play?" It was the third time that day she had complained of boredom, and I was running out of ideas.

"There's nothing to do here. Pretty please, can you take us somewhere?" she asked.

"Where do you guys want to go?"

Her whole face instantly morphed into a smile. "I don't know. I'll call Christopher," she said as she ran for the phone. Christopher was her go-to friend. He was always happy and was willing to do almost anything with either one of the girls.

With Christopher waiting on the other end of the phone, Kendra shouted across the room, "Can you take us to the movies, please—please?"

"OK—"

"Did you get your chores done?" Jeff hollered from the rec room somewhat jokingly, but clearly hoping for a reaction from Kendra.

"Yes, Daddy Jeff," Kendra said in a snotty tone, rolling her eyes and scowling. Not that Jeff could tell.

Pleased, Jeff snickered, but before he could come up with a retort, I intervened. "OK, knock it off, you two." It was tiring hearing Jeff and Kendra bicker. He loved getting a reaction from her, and she was feisty enough to challenge his every remark. Their relationship could be loving and playful one minute and turn contentious the next. It was difficult to tell when they were serious or just playing with each other. Regardless, it was annoying for me to listen to them.

"But we have to hurry, Mom. The movie's gonna start in like fifteen minutes."

"OK. Let's go, then." I slipped on my shoes. "Jeff, I'll be right back. I'm gonna run Kendra and Christopher down to the movies."

"Would you mind if I go along for the ride?" he asked.

Kendra shook her head side to side, glaring at me before I even had a chance to respond. I instantly felt the pressure of wanting to please them both. It was very difficult for me to tell Jeff no, because he had no option to get out of the house unless I took him. And I knew that Kendra enjoyed any minute alone she could get with me; she was like that even before Jeff was around.

"Sure, let me get your shoes," I said. We had fifteen minutes, and the movie theater was only a five-minute drive. We could get there on time.

Kendra again glared at me and aggressively pointed to her watch before scurrying upstairs. I followed her.

"Why didn't you just tell him no so we can get going? It takes so long to get him ready." Her tone clearly reflected her frustration.

I felt torn—either way I was going to disappoint one of them. Having to choose which one to hurt this time was like having to choose between hitting my right hand or my left one with a hammer. I felt so responsible for everyone's happiness. This time I chose to disappoint Kendra.

I explained, "You know Uncle Jeff hasn't wanted to go out for the past few days because he's been feeling so miserable. The fact that he wants to go with me now is a good sign. I agree that it can be a hassle taking him along, but he can't help that he can't get out on his own."

My explanation did little to ease her frustration. "I know, but he's being super rude to me today," she said.

"OK, but it seems like you both are being rude to each other. I'll talk to him, because I've noticed that he's been picking on you more lately. But I want you to start being more respectful toward him as well. I know this is hard on you, and I'm sorry, but I don't know what else to do. Jeff can't help that he's in this situation."

She turned her back and rummaged for her coat in the closet. "Yes, Mom. I know. I'm just frustrated. I want to be on time."

"Don't worry; I'll get you there on time."

I got Jeff out the door, and we arrived at the movie theater just in time. The kids eagerly leaped out of the car and ran to the movie line.

"Do you want to stop and get a latte?" Jeff asked as we pulled away.

"Sure. That sounds like a great idea."

It was unusually slow in the coffee shop, allowing us the opportunity to relax and chat while we drank our coffee. When we were halfway done with our drinks, I cautiously approached the subject of his and Kendra's relationship.

"I want to talk to you about Kendra. I need you to deal with her differently, because she's getting frustrated."

His brow furrowed, and his expression shifted from lighthearted to serious.

I forced myself to continue, despite worrying that I was making him feel bad. "I know she can get sassy with you, and she can be rude at times, but she's having a much harder time dealing with all this than Chelsey."

"I understand. I've been thinking about it and trying to tone it down, but sometimes it's hard. Mostly I'm just joking around, but then she flips it back on me, and that's what keeps me going," he said.

"I've already talked to her, but I want you to take the lead to make things better in terms of how you guys treat each other." I gingerly pushed. "I explained to her that you haven't been feeling well, but I still want you to try."

His chin quivered, almost hitting his chest as he slumped back in his chair. "I struggle when she's standing in the kitchen. I ask her to get something for me, and she gives me some attitude. It's hard to take sometimes."

"I get it. I don't think it's that stuff as much as when you're monitoring her behavior, like whether she's done her chores and stuff. The little things I understand, but she doesn't like when you play a parental role."

"OK...that makes sense. I'll work on it. I'm not trying to be mean."

I reached across the table and put my hand on his. The churning in my stomach increased as a somber frown spread across his face.

"I'm not mad at you. I just want everyone to get along. And I hope you know that Kendra loves you. She's just having a hard time sharing her momma."

He sat up a bit straighter, took a sip of his drink, and mustered a slight smile. "I know. It's gotta be hard on both girls."

"Yeah, but they understand."

He cleared his throat. "Thank you for taking care of me. I know it's hard on you to be there for everyone."

I gently squeezed his hand. "I wouldn't want it any other way. We're a team—or at least I thought we were until you threw me off the Jet Ski." I giggled. His face lit up, as it always did when we recalled that memory.

Our discussion ended well, but it still hurt me to confront him because I knew it made him feel bad. But I strongly felt the need to protect Kendra; she was also a victim since Jeff's illness was taking so much of my time and energy away from her. Jeff's needs weren't more important than hers or vice versa; they were just different. I knew Jeff hated feeling like a burden, and Kendra had a hard time demonstrating much compassion when she felt so sad. The whole situation was difficult for everyone to navigate. I kept doing the best I could, and I only hoped it was enough.

CHAPTER 38

Where to Go from Here

Jeff was really starting to struggle with frustration and depression for the first time since the surgery. He was physically feeling worse and mentally seemed to be exhausted. He and Kendra continued to bicker, though each appeared to be trying to be more patient with the other.

"Hey, Tammy," he called from his bedroom, "do you know where I put my recorder? I think I'm going to try using it again."

"I saw it in the middle drawer of your nightstand a couple of days ago." I pulled open the drawer. "Here it is; do you need me to show you how to do it again?"

"Yeah. I can't remember which one is the Record button. Can you make sure I have the dots next to the Record button and the Stop button?"

We used felt dots to help him locate certain buttons on his remote control, clock, and other things. I put the recorder in his right hand, and then he ran his left index finger across it, stopping when he felt the first dot. "Is this the Record button?"

"No, that one is the Stop button. The Record is the one to the right."

He moved his finger to the right and pushed the button on and off.

"Looks like you got it. Are you all set? Do you need anything else before I go to bed?"

"No, I think I'm good. Have a good sleep."

"You too." I stepped out of the room. "Call me if you need anything." I shut the door and waited, listening through the door. Within moments I could hear him speaking quietly.

"It's been a while since I've recorded, but I feel the need to get my thoughts out of my head."

I exhaled and tiptoed off to bed. As I lay down, I heard Jeff's words through the baby monitor on my nightstand. Still journaling into his recorder, his hopelessness only added to the worry I was already experiencing.

"I am lying in my bed thinking about my life, and I just had a rush of emotion. I feel lost; I feel like I don't belong. I feel like a square peg trying to fit in a round hole. These feelings are so strange. I feel like a pet of some sort. I am just here, not really making an impact.

"I want to focus on living a more normal life. Well, not necessarily normal, but productive. What was once normal is gone, and I know it will never come back. I have to force myself to do more things for myself so I won't feel like such an invalid. I know that it isn't an easy life for my family either, having to take care of a sick person.

"I pray a lot, yet I'm tired of feeling alone, despite having everyone around. Sometimes the loneliness just eats away at me. Most of my friends are gone; it is like that part of my life is gone forever. I watch TV shows—rather, listen to them—and see relationships, and know I will never have a normal girlfriend relationship. I guess that's not so bad, since my wiener doesn't work now anyway. My body is all scarred up, I'm blind, feel sick most of the time, and I would have to take extra pills to even try to make it work. Not much of a catch for any woman. I'm a mess. I do thank God for taking away my sexual desires, even though it also takes away a part of my manhood, but better than the alternative. Sometimes that is hard to accept, but it's my reality.

"My fears are like those of a little kid in that I'm scared of anyone else outside my family unit. I love my routine, and I don't like it when we get out of it. I try not to look into the future. I do hope that God has some good plans, and I hope he doesn't want to keep me around a whole lot longer. I get scared that I will be stuck here forever, knowing it could take years and years to really adjust. When my mission is done, I guess that's when it will be done. I can say I don't want to be here forever, even though some days are OK. Days like this are tough. It's not easy, it's not fun, but it's doable.

"I don't know what it takes to finally accept the blindness. It is just so hard being in the dark, it's no fun. I don't think it was meant to be fun. The blindness makes it hard for me to do some things for myself. I keep trying to find new ways to do things which is difficult because I liked the way I used to do things. I hate having to plan everything and go through a bunch of loopholes. I miss being able to get in my car to go get a burger, or to just go anywhere. I don't usually feel angry—mostly just frustrated.

"It takes me forever to get up in the morning, and I can't wait to go to bed at night. I don't know if this is depression or just being totally dissatisfied with life. It's not that I'm unhappy—I'm just ready for it all to be over. I get nervous about all of the physical symptoms, and I don't know how to deal with all of the changes because it brings me back to a time when things were really bad. It feels like it was so long ago, but in reality, it wasn't.

"I don't know if it is helpful to talk about it, or just make jokes to keep my mind off the discomfort. Sometimes just talking in the recorder relieves my brain. There is no nice way to put 'my life sucks.' I just have to try to get through it. I don't like to tell others about how I feel because I want to be an encouragement to them. I especially want the homeless people to see me on the days I don't feel like this. I want them to have hope. I guess I can't have good days all the time. I am anxious to keep the homeless project going so I can be a witness to others.

"If I can keep my eyes focused on other people's problems and needs, then I can shove my stuff aside and work in helping with other people's stuff. I need a purpose. I am tired now, and I am going to bed."

I dozed off, and six o'clock in the morning came too soon. The sun was just peeking through the living room window as Clark and I enjoyed our favorite tradition. Clark sat in his brown leather chair, and I curled up on the couch with my well-worn pink bathrobe draped across my lap, and we sipped on our coffee peacefully.

"Looks like it's going to be a nice day," I said.

"It's supposed to be nice the next few days," Clark said. He was the weatherman for our family, and the girls relied on him to tell them how many layers of clothes they might need on any given morning.

"What are you guys doing today?" he asked after a moment of silence.

"Not much. I'm going to do some chores. Jeff's still feeling pretty miserable." I frowned. "It's been almost two weeks, and he's getting worse."

Clark nodded, and I continued. "I thought about calling the doctor, but he couldn't care less about Jeff's symptoms. He was having sharp pains in his stomach last night, and he's still feeling achy. It's like he's fine one hour, then sick the next. I really just never know."

"Well, it probably wouldn't hurt to call, just to see."

"What's the point?" I threw my hands up in the air. "The doctor never has explained this whole thing anyhow. Remember how he said Jeff had cancer in his brain—they were obviously wrong, and they've still never acknowledged it."

My recollection spurred more frustration; I paused and took another sip of coffee. "They don't care if he's nauseated or hurting. They always just assume it's his cancer coming back. But what if he has gallstones or something? Or if it's part of the Cushing's? They just expect him to be sick."

Clark listened patiently to my rant, having heard it many times before.

"They aren't the ones who have to watch him suffer every day." I took a deep breath. "I just don't know what I can do. His symptoms just come and go, and the tests haven't helped us so far, other than to tell us he doesn't have any new tumors."

"I guess we just have to keep an eye on him and do the best we can," Clark said, always practical. "Maybe you can bring him in for more tests if he's still getting worse in a couple weeks."

I sighed. "I guess so. I should be thankful that he still feels OK to go out sometimes. I'll call if the pain gets unbearable; otherwise, I'll keep using his nausea medicine and the heating pad. They help some."

Our momentary silence was broken by the girls shouting downstairs for Clark's weather report. I jumped up, remembering that the school district had finally finished negotiations, and they were headed back to school this morning.

CHAPTER 39

Back to School

THE START OF S HOOL WAS a relief on one hand and an added stress on the other. I could finally return to my normal routine, but every year Chelsey had panic attacks for the first week or two of school. At nine years old, she was diagnosed with a generalized anxiety disorder, and going to school was her worst trigger. She usually adjusted after the first few weeks, but getting her there was painful for all of us. She sobbed uncontrollably and could not eat because of her anxiety.

"Mom, my stomach hurts so bad. Please, can I stay home?" she asked, doubled over, holding her stomach. Past years had taught me that if I waited until her stomachache was gone, she would never go.

"Chels, I know it hurts, but it isn't going to get any better. You know you just have to get through these first couple of weeks. Come on and get in the car," I said.

We had been fighting about her going to school for the past two days, and I was at the end of my emotional reserve. Watching her in so much emotional pain gave me an anxious stomach. I felt so helpless and out of control. A part of me also felt guilty as I forced her off to school.

Chelsey finally got into the car. Her eyes were red and puffy, and she was still breathing erratically. It was difficult for her to regain her composure. Kendra and Christopher sat silently in the back seat, knowing all too well what was happening. Chelsey took deep breaths trying to contain her anxiety during our one-mile drive to her school.

As I pulled into the parking lot, she begged, "Wait just one minute. Please. Let me catch my breath. I don't want anyone to see me crying."

Kendra leaned over the seat, kissed my cheek, and hopped out of the car. Christopher followed right behind, waving.

Chelsey took another deep breath, wiped the last couple of tears off her cheeks, and straightened a bit. She finally got out of the car with a frown on her pale face.

"Try to have a good day, Chels," I said. Though I knew I was doing the right thing, it felt awful to send her to school in such disarray.

She walked off a few feet and stopped to give me one last look in hopes I would let her back in the car. Then she turned away and walked down the path to her classroom. As I left the school driveway, I wept the entire way home.

"Are you OK?" Jeff asked as soon as he heard the door shut. He had heard me pleading with Chelsey.

Jeff was helpful with Chelsey because he had lived with anxiety all his life. He understood what it was like to panic at seemingly normal things, and he was now at a place where he could share his experiences.

"I'm OK. It's just hard to see her go through all that, and I don't know what to do—she has to go to school; there's no other option. But forcing her through it feels so awful." I sat down next to him and put my head in my hands.

"I know, but trust me. You're doing the right thing. If you give in, she'll never learn to confront her fears. I've been there. It'll be better soon. I can try talking to her when she gets home, if you want. Maybe a different perspective would help?"

"I don't know if she'll feel like talking, but you can try. I'll take all the help I can get."

I felt a little hopeful, especially thinking of how much Jeff had changed. Maybe he could help her get better too.

After school, Jeff spent the better part of an hour talking to Chelsey about her anxiety. I could hear them from the kitchen.

"I know there isn't anything anyone can say to make your anxiety go away, Chels. It just takes time. I used to get stomachaches whenever I would have to miss a day of work, or whenever I went out of my routine. I forced myself to do things even though I felt anxious, and it usually worked out."

Chelsey was quiet, soaking in his advice.

"I even started getting a little better. Sometimes it helps to keep your mind busy, like focusing on your dance or spending time with your girlfriends."

"I know you're right, but it's so hard when I'm in the middle of it. You know, when my stomach is hurting and I feel like I'm going to puke. I just can't stop worrying about what happens if the teacher is mean or gets mad 'cause I don't know an answer, or if I can't do the work, or if some of the girls aren't nice…" Her voice faded.

"I understand, Chels. It's going to get better. I'm sorry you have to go through this."

"I'm happy that Chrissy is in some of my classes. She knows about my anxiety, and she checked in on me throughout the day." Chelsey smiled a little.

"That's great. I wish I had had a friend like that when I was in school. That makes it so much easier."

"Yeah." She briefly glanced at the TV and saw her show was about to start. "Thanks for listening, Uncle Jeff. It really helps that you understand how it feels. Not very many people know what it's like. Do you wanna watch this with me?"

I smiled as I continued washing dishes, happy to hear that Jeff had been able to help my little girl. It was great to see that he wanted to help her and that she was willing to let him.

CHAPTER 40

The Fair

OUR ANNUAL TRIP TO THE Puyallup County Fair typically confirmed that fall was officially under way. The days were getting shorter, the weather was cooler, and the leaves on the trees were changing color. That year, the fair was particularly special because my mom had entered the art contest, and one of her pieces won the blue ribbon. Mom and I were excited to see her art on display—validation that she was indeed talented. Jeff and Chelsey were eager to come along for the good food and to see the animals. In high spirits, we all packed into the car for the forty-five-minute drive. We were barely inside the fair doors when Mom noticed that Jeff looked a little pale.

"What's wrong, Jeff?" Mom asked.

"I don't think I'm going to be able to walk too far. My breathing is really off. Do you think we can get a wheelchair for me?"

I didn't hesitate. "I'll get one. You guys stay here." We sometimes pushed Jeff in a wheelchair simply because it was faster, but the fact that he asked for one was cause for worry.

Chelsey didn't mind pushing Jeff around while Mom and I looked through the art gallery. Mom's face lit up when she saw the ribbon hanging on her painting and again when she heard people's compliments as they strolled by.

We left the gallery and met up with Jeff and Chelsey, then we all wandered off to see the horse and cow barns, stopping for a funnel cake along the way.

"You want a funnel cake, Uncle Jeff?" Chelsey hollered as she rushed to the end of the line.

"No thanks," he said.

"You love those things. Why don't you want one?" Mom asked, her eyebrows lowering as she looked toward me. I met her eyes and shrugged.

"I'm just not feeling good. I'm a bit nauseated."

Jeff's health had constantly fluctuated between bad and worse in the past month, but there was so little I could do. We knew something was wrong. His medication wasn't enough to hold off the pain anymore. We left the fair much quicker than expected so Jeff could get home and rest. It was typical of how our days so often went—unpredictable and constantly changing. We lived just one day at a time, a cycle of uncertainty. Some days were a blur, and I was tired of trying to figure it all out.

I could see Jeff fading as I looked at him sitting in his favorite position on the couch: legs bent to the side as he leaned back, remote in his hand, and his loyal dog nestled at his feet. His eyelids no longer opened, hiding the window to his soul. His ashen skin covered his puffy cheeks. He was constantly maneuvering for a comfortable position. I watched him from the kitchen doorway as he flipped through the channels, searching for something that would take his mind off his discomfort. Once again, I wavered between hoping his suffering would end soon and wanting to keep my brother with me for as long as possible.

Finally, I interrupted him. "Do you need anything? Can I get you a glass of water or a snack?"

"I don't know. I don't think I need anything. It's just one of those days. I can't get comfortable, everything hurts, and there's nothing good on."

"What about your books on tape? Want to listen to a devotional?"

When there was nothing of interest on TV, Jeff often liked to listen to different books. It was a part of his search for salvation and guidance on how he should live his last few years.

"Nah. I've heard most of them so many times." He sighed. "I could probably give a sermon on all of them."

"Well, if you can't keep your thoughts away from the cancer, want to tell me what's going on? Maybe talking would help."

"Well, sure, I guess."

"It's OK if you aren't up to it. We can always do it another time. I don't want to pressure you," I said.

"No, no, it's OK. Getting out of my head would probably help. Besides, this is part of the journey—the bad days. I want to share this stuff so I can help you and anyone else."

Jeff sounded much more invested after thinking for a moment. He always wanted to share the painful parts of his cancer as well as the good days. Someday maybe it would help other patients accept that having negative thoughts was OK.

"Great. I'll go grab your recorder. Be back in a minute."

Hearing me plop into the chair, he asked, "Are you ready?"

"Yep, let me have it. Tell me what it feels like to be you right now." I clicked the Record button on and sat back in the chair, listening intently.

"OK, here it goes." He took a breath and then started talking. "My body is going through some changes that make me nervous and scared because I can't remember how much of this I had the first time I was diagnosed with the cancer. I feel achier every day. I feel short of breath, and my heart rate has been in the one hundred and twenties. My knees to my feet are so achy, it feels like I am wearing a pair of shoes that are too small. My right side is really hurting. It hurts when I move or breathe in. It feels like a bruise almost, like I have been slugged in the gut. I am starting to have hot flashes now, which are very uncomfortable."

He paused for a minute and wiped his sweaty forehead with his sleeve. I waited quietly for him to continue.

"I wake up every hour or two during the night, even though I take medicine. My urine smells strongly, and Tammy is worried I have an infection. I get sick and tired of being sick and tired. I am tired of playing the game, and I am ready for the end. I plan to put my No CPR bracelets back on in case I am getting ready to croak."

"Yeah, that makes sense. I thought about getting you a necklace that says Do Not Resuscitate as well," I said.

"Good. I don't want anyone thumping on my chest. I don't trust doctors too much. When they told me I had another five years of significant life, I took their word for it. Evidently, their idea of quality life and mine are very different. But the old adage 'shit happens' best fits my situation." He snickered. "My only choice is to either dig my way out of it or wallow in it. I don't want to wallow in it, so I have to find a way to dig my way out. I don't know how long my mission here will be, but I am trying to make the best of it."

He paused again, then dozed off for a moment.

"Do you want to keep going?" I asked.

"No. I'm done for now." He laid his head against the back of the couch and fell asleep.

Several days later, Jeff went to Mom's house, and I went to work. Though I could have used some rest, there were always too many things to be done. Running a few minutes late, I sat in traffic with my windows down and the radio blaring. I was singing along, whether I knew the words or not, just to keep my mind distracted. Just as the chorus was about to erupt, my phone rang. I reluctantly turned the volume down.

"Hello?"

"Hi, Tammy," my mom said.

"Morning. How's everything? Is Jeff OK?" I asked, slightly worried by her flat voice.

"Well, nothing happened, but I wouldn't say he's fine. He just seems so much worse. I knew something was wrong at the fair, but he hasn't cracked a single joke, and he's just not himself." Her voice quivered. "I just don't know where we're headed."

"I don't know either. I suspect the cancer is back, but we won't know for sure until we do some tests. I'll call the doctor's office today on my break and see what they think. I know it's hard not knowing what's happening, but I'll do my best to figure it out," I said.

"It's just so hard seeing him suffer. I wish there was more I could do," Mom said.

We talked about our various theories on how long Jeff had to live or what we might have to do to manage his care. We also shared our feelings about how hard it was to feel this helpless, and about the guilt we felt about wishing his suffering was over.

"Well, I better go. Jeff is waiting for me to go over the final details of the homeless project for Sunday. At least he's still excited to hand out the pizzas. If I have to go over how many pizzas and sodas we have one more time, though, I think I'm gonna go crazy," Mom joked.

"It's a good distraction for him, and maybe you too," I said. "I'll call you after I talk to the doctor's office. We'll get this figured out."

CHAPTER 41

Sick and Tired of Being Sick and Tired

A FEW WEEKS AFTER THE fair, Jeff's symptoms escalated drastically. His body, particularly his side, constantly ached, and jabs of sharp pain intermittently tormented him. He was too uncomfortable to focus on TV, sleep, or his books on tape. Nothing seemed to help, though the pain medication did reduce his discomfort for a bit.

I had not slept well for several days because of the pain I knew Jeff was trying to hide. During the day, he sat quietly toughing it out, but at night the monitor next to my bed revealed his real agony.

Lights on the monitor fluctuated up and down depending on how loud Jeff moaned. I lay in bed, listening to the inhale and exhale of his labored breathing, hoping he would fall into a deep sleep. I heard his covers rustle and then a soft voice.

"Tammy, I can't find my pain pills."

I jumped out of bed, quickly descended the fourteen stairs that separated our floors, opened his bedroom door, turned on the lights, and saw him sitting at the bedside.

"I don't know where I put my pain pills," he said, tapping his fingers around a drawer.

I saw the pills on his nightstand, in plain sight, yet clearly difficult for him to find just by feel.

"Here they are. Do you want to take both of them?"

"Yes, because I can't get comfortable. My side is killing me," he whimpered. "I'm wondering if the pain is from a kidney stone. It's pulsating at about an eight out of ten. It feels like a wave of pain, and then it calms down. When it hits, it even makes me nauseated."

I suddenly felt overwhelmed by helplessness. As much as I wanted to, there was little I could do to fix his pain. The grimace on his face was all the evidence I needed to know that something bad was going on inside his body.

"Let me get the heating pad. Maybe that will help. First take another sip of water, and then once you find a comfortable position, I'll put the heating pad on you." I reached over and grabbed the heating pad off the nightstand. Jeff took his pills and rearranged himself until he was more comfortable.

"I'm so sorry to wake you up. I know you need your sleep, but I didn't know what else to do. I don't even know what time it is."

"Don't worry about me. It's two o'clock, so I'm just going to lie in here, and hopefully we will both fall asleep," I said.

Once I got everything set up, I crawled into the bed next to him in hopes of settling him, or at least bringing him some comfort.

After a few moments of silence, Jeff asked, "Do you think my cancer is back?"

"I don't know, but we will know as soon as the labs are in. What do you think?" I asked.

"I don't know either. I just hope that if it is, they're able to do something about this pain. I'd do almost anything to make it go away," he said, almost panicking.

Overwhelmed and extremely tired, I grabbed a tissue and dabbed my eyes. "I wish I could do more. I think once we get your blood work back, there will be more things we can do for the pain. I do know one thing, though. God has a plan. He's brought us this far, and he won't let us down now. But for now, try to get some sleep."

Clark quietly opened Jeff's door at five thirty in the morning and whispered, "Tammy, it's time to get up."

"What? Oh, yeah. Thanks." Once I was fully oriented, I gently scooted off the bed, making every effort not to disturb Jeff.

"Why were you sleeping in there? Is he OK?" Clark asked.

"He had a rough night. His side is hurting really bad; something's going on. I'm going to go to work, but I think I'll have Dad bring Jeff to my ER later. Can you still take him to Mom's house this morning?" I asked.

"Yeah, of course, but are you sure you don't want me to just take him to the ER?"

"No. I have to see which doctors are on and how busy it is first. Plus, I need my dad to take him back to their house, since I'm supposed to work the next two days." I started getting ready for work, thinking about which of the ER doctors I would want Jeff to see.

"OK. Just let me know." Clark gave me a quick hug before I hurried out the door, determined to find some relief for Jeff, and myself. I could not handle many more nights like the last one.

As soon as I arrived at work, I scanned the roster to see which doctors were on duty that day. Thankfully, Dr. Handley was one of them. Several of my doctor friends at work were well aware of Jeff's rare condition, and they seemed genuinely interested in the progression. Dr. Handley in particular seemed to understand my frustration with not knowing what was causing Jeff's symptoms.

"Dr. Handley, can I ask you something about my brother?" I asked, stopping him at the front desk.

"Sure." He smiled and gestured to my empty office. "Why don't we talk in there?"

"What's going on? How's Jeff doing?"

As I described Jeff's symptoms and recent x-ray and ultrasound results, I could not help noticing his eyes slightly drop and the tone of his voice shift. Though Dr. Handley was an emergency room doctor and not a cancer specialist, he was familiar with the symptoms of tumors.

"It sounds to me like his cancer is probably out of remission. I suggest you get him in here today, and I'll do a CAT scan. It will likely give us a better picture of what's going on and how we can help him," he said.

I immediately called my dad and gave him the go-ahead to bring Jeff to the ER. I knew it would be about an hour until they could get here, so I went back to work, trying to focus on my cases. But I was too worried about Jeff to give my full attention to the patients I needed to help. I only hoped they wouldn't notice my inner turmoil.

"Tammy, please come to triage," I finally heard via an overhead page.

I quickly finished my conversation with a patient who was being discharged and hurried to the front of the ER. I opened the door to the waiting room and motioned for my dad and Jeff to come into the back. We were greeted by a friend of mine, a talkative and experienced nurse named Leitha. With a wide smile, she escorted Jeff, my father, and me to a treatment room. As we passed through the hallways, many of my coworkers stared curiously, having only ever seen pictures of my father's horrific injuries. I heard whispers about how good my dad's scarred face looked. It was hard for me to hear, since I still grieved the loss of the bright expression in his eyes and his big smile every time he saw me.

Leitha got Jeff signed in, took his vitals, and started an IV so pain medicine could be administered immediately. I went to let Dr. Handley know Jeff had arrived. I found him in the staff lounge, and we quickly returned to the room.

"Hi, Jeff. I'm Dr. Handley. Your sister told me about everything that has been going on for the past few weeks. Sounds pretty awful. Can you show me where you're hurting right now?" Lying on the exam table, Jeff said, "It mostly hurts here," pointing to his stomach and side.

"OK, can you give me a pain level from one to ten, with ten being the highest?" Dr. Handley lightly pressed on Jeff's abdomen.

"It varies between an eight and a ten. It seems to come in waves." Jeff winced.

"OK. Are you experiencing any other changes?"

"What else have I been going through, Tammy?" Jeff paused, waiting for me to jump in.

"Well, you've been constipated. And remember, you said your urine stream has been different; it just stops midstream—"

"Oh yeah. And I'm really tired, but I can't get comfortable, so I wake up a lot."

"Anything else?" Dr. Handley asked, jotting notes in the chart.

"He's been complaining of chest pressure—not necessarily chest pain. And I know his blood pressure and heart rate have been higher than usual," I said.

Soon after Jeff and the doctor finished talking, the CAT scan technician arrived and wheeled Jeff down to the machine. My dad and I waited in the room, chatting about work and hoping that the test might reveal more answers than the previous exams. I anxiously watched the clock; thirty minutes passed, and still no sign of Jeff.

"It's so hard to see Jeff suffering like this," Dad said out of the blue. "Especially since I understand what real pain feels like."

"You probably would know better than any of us what it's like to suffer. At least they'll be able to manage his pain once we get a diagnosis," I said softly, glad he was confiding in me. Before the fire, it had been rare for my dad to talk about anything emotional. But since then, he was much more open.

"I know, but it's still so hard. I feel so helpless. It's much harder now that we're so much closer." Dad quickly wiped his eyes, trying to compose himself as Jeff was wheeled into the room. Dr. Handley pulled me aside as Leitha helped Jeff back to the exam table. He was holding a copy of the test results.

"I want you take a look at the results before I go back in to talk to Jeff. Do you see these three masses? I believe they're new tumors. Since I don't have any of his previous tests to compare to, I can't tell you for sure. You really ought to take him back to the UW and have an MRI done to compare with his tests from two years ago. These tumors are right in the area where his pain is located."

"OK, I understand," I said, my eyes blurry.

"I'm sorry, Tammy; I know this must be hard for you." He gently gave my shoulder a squeeze.

"I just don't know if I should tell him yet. I know he's so scared…we all are," I said, wiping my sleeve across my eyes. Everything was suddenly so real, making it nearly impossible to maintain my composure.

I continued. "We thought it was the cancer several times already, and each time it was something else." I shook my head, deep down believing this time it was really the cancer. "Will you just tell him there is something there, but we don't know if it was there before? And I don't think we should tell him it's likely the cancer until we know for sure. I'll make an appointment for an MRI as soon as I can get him in."

My chin quivered as I tried to regain my composure before going back into Jeff's room.

With a nod and another reassuring squeeze of my shoulder, Dr. Handley stepped back into the treatment room. It was always hard to deliver bad news to patients, especially when it was to someone familiar. Pausing only for a quick glance at my father, he sat on the rolling stool and scooted close to Jeff to gently share the results, omitting his fears as agreed. He prescribed some new pain medications to try at home, as a way to hold Jeff over until his MRI scan. Jeff's typical defense of denial and functional ignorance prevented him from asking too many questions, for once to my relief. Jeff and Dad left for home while I got an update from a nurse about a drunken patient waiting on me for an evaluation. With barely a deep breath between my last cry, I stepped back into my routine, one I knew by rote. I moved where I was needed, and the hospital swirled around me. Life just had a way of going on, whether I liked it or not—more patients, more paper work, more running.

At one point in my workday, I called my mom to explain. She immediately began to sob. I could barely hold myself together, but the lounge had other staff members meandering in and out, and I didn't want to draw attention to myself. We didn't know for certain it was the cancer, but all the same, we all felt the change, like an oncoming flood.

After work, I called Mom's house to chat with Jeff and to find out if the new pain medication Dr. Handley had given him was resolving his pain. My dad answered the phone and then quickly handed me over to Jeff.

"Hello?"

"Hey, how are you feeling?"

"A little better. Those pain meds are helping," he said. His voice sounded weak.

"So how are you feeling about the test results?" I asked, trying to keep some of the worry out of my voice.

"I don't care…really…'cept for the pain and what it does to you guys." He drawled through the receiver, tone numb. "It's pretty bad."

"Don't worry about us; we'll all get through whatever happens."

"I know, but I've been through all that stuff with Dad, so I know how it feels to be the worried one now." He paused, seconds ticking past. "It sucks," he said, finally.

"What sucks is that you have experienced both sides."

"I know, right…I'm the lucky one." He snickered and then turned serious. "I only hope that if I'm getting ready to check out, that I touched some lives through this whole thing. Hopefully my life served a purpose, and I don't die in vain."

A lump in my throat, I swallowed hard. "You definitely have touched many lives."

"Thanks, sis."

"Well, I gotta go, but you can call me if you need anything. Love you."

"Love you too. And thanks for having the doctor see me today. Even though it wasn't the best news, at least he gave me stronger pain meds."

Four days later, with the MRI complete, Jeff and I sat in Dr. Smith's office waiting to be told the results. Wanting to give us privacy, Midge waited outside, planning to go to lunch with us after our appointment. It was eerily similar to two years earlier, yet the fear was no longer about Jeff possibly dying, but rather how long he had to live and how sick he would become.

A sharp knock, and then Dr. Smith entered, holding a thick chart. "Hello, Jeff." He patted Jeff on the shoulder and then nodded at me.

"Hello," Jeff said.

"So tell me what's been going on and how you're feeling right now."

"I've been pretty miserable for the past month or so. The pain is about a five right now, and it's mostly in this area." He ran his hand from his belly button along his right side, and toward his back. As with Dr. Handley, Jeff asked me to add more details about his symptoms.

"OK..." Dr. Smith opened the chart toward the back. "Well, I have the results of your MRI from yesterday, and I compared them to the scans we did about two years ago." Sitting next to Jeff, I squeezed his hand as he took in a deep breath.

Dr. Smith continued. "We did see some tumors behind the vena cava, which is where the cancer was before. The tumors were not there on the last scan, so I'm pretty convinced your cancer is in fact back." He paused as he flipped through the chart.

Jeff squeezed my hand and expelled a heavy breath. I sat silently, waiting for Dr. Smith to continue his thought.

"We can do a biopsy and a cortisol urine test to confirm it for sure," Dr. Smith said.

"Would the biopsy require he stay in the hospital overnight?" I asked.

"It could, depending on how the procedure goes."

"If the urine test can confirm it, then I would rather do that. I really don't want any more procedures," Jeff said.

"I don't blame you. That's the path I would recommend. I'll get the urine test ordered. Do you need another prescription for pain meds?" Dr. Smith matter-of-factly asked.

"Yes, we do. The last one was just from the ER doctor," I said.

Dr. Smith wrote a few more notes, leaned toward Jeff, and put his hand on Jeff's knee. "I'm sorry. I know you've been through so much."

Taking a tissue from his pocket, Jeff wiped his runny nose. "It's OK. It's been a hard road, but at least I have my family to help me," Jeff said.

"Do you have any idea how long we have?" I asked, choking up.

"It is too difficult to know, but if I had to guess, I would say less than a year for sure." He stood up and headed toward the door. "I'll have the nurse bring in the urine containers, and I'll call Tammy with the results. If there's anything else I can do, don't hesitate to call me." His eyes met mine, and he gave me a slow nod before walking out. Though he had been wrong in his predictions before, I believed he was likely accurate this time.

Midge, Jeff, and I left the doctor's office and headed out for lunch, which was our tradition. Jeff chose an Italian restaurant, and Midge and I were happy to oblige him.

"Well, how did the appointment go?" Midge asked from the back seat.

"He said I'm going to die. So I plan on going out to eat at all my favorite restaurants before I croak," Jeff said.

"OK, then..." Midge smiled. "We certainly can make that happen."

"The doctor said he believes the cancer is back, and they'll do a urine test to confirm it," I said.

"Yeah, he said I likely have less than a year," Jeff added casually.

I looked through the rearview mirror, and my eyes met Midge's. She slowly nodded, silently acknowledging the seriousness of the situation. She then quickly returned to chattering with Jeff.

Jeff slid across the cushioned seat into our favorite booth. The aroma of garlic and other spices filtered through the bustling restaurant. A young, bubbly bus girl poured ice water into each of our glasses while making small talk.

"Hello. How's your day going so far?" she asked.

"Not bad for a blind dying guy." Jeff chuckled, unable to resist using his favorite line. Midge and I simultaneously shook our heads and smiled.

The confused bus girl stood speechless, immediately looking to Midge and me for some direction, as did most people when Jeff used that line.

"Just ignore him. He likes to get a reaction," I said.

She smiled awkwardly, placed a menu in front of each us, and then scurried off.

"Jeff, you're awful," I said jokingly. "It's so unfair that you can't see her expression. You made her wonder if she said something wrong."

He tried not to be serious, but he couldn't wipe the smirk off his face. "I'll apologize to her when she comes back." His smirk slowly dissipated. "We gotta laugh at this crazy ride; otherwise, we'll be crying."

"I get it," I said.

Midge and I looked over the menus, searching for the special of the day. Jeff lifted his menu too and intently stared at it.

Amused, Midge asked, "What looks good, Jeff?"

Before Jeff could answer, a waitress arrived to take our order. She looked puzzled, noticing that Jeff's menu was upside down and backward, but kept her composure.

"Hi. I'm Mary, and I'll be taking care of you folks this afternoon. Do you have any questions about the menu, or are you ready to order?"

With a straight face, Jeff tapped his pointer finger on the upside-down restaurant logo. "I would like this."

Mary scrunched her eyebrows as she stood speechless.

"You are hilarious, Jeff," I said, enjoying every minute of his humor. "Your menu is upside down, goofball." I grabbed the menu from his hands and gave it to Mary. "Don't mind him. He's blind and likes to tease with people."

Mary giggled with us. "I was wondering what he was doing."

"He'll have the spaghetti alfredo, and I'll have the Caesar salad."

"You always have a way of making us laugh," Midge said. "I'll have the Caesar salad too."

The waitress dropped off a plate of bread and olive oil with balsamic vinegar at our table a few minutes later. Jeff savored the warm bread, and then he washed it down with a gulp of water. "This is so good. Eating out is one of my simple pleasures." He dipped his bread in the oil. "I hope we get to do this more often before I get too sick."

"I agree. We need to make the best of every day we get," I said.

That evening, Jeff went to his room earlier than normal. I checked on him before going up to bed myself. He clicked his tape recorder off as I entered his room.

"You doing OK?" I asked.

"Yeah. Just journaling about the doctor stuff today," he said, his demeanor subdued.

"Are you feeling worried?" I asked as I sat on the edge of his bed. Rusty immediately considered it an opportunity to get a belly rub, and he rolled over onto my lap.

"Oh yeah, I won't lie." He scooted himself up. "I feel a little anxious, a bit spooked. When I stop and think about what's happening, I just wanna hide. It takes a lot of effort to not just curl up in a ball and never come out into the world again." He cleared his throat before he continued. "I feel like I'm lost. You know—just out there. It feels like everything is going on around me."

I listened intently, his words weighing heavy on my heart.

His thoughts continued to flow freely. "I'm pretty much prepared that the cancer is back, but it will help to know for sure."

"I feel the same way. At least we won't have to keep wondering what else it could be that's causing all your new symptoms."

"To be honest, I'm ready for death to take me home. I'm not real fond of my life right now. It's not like I despise it. I just don't wanna keep doing it…" His chin quivered, and he swallowed hard. "I feel sorry that all you guys have to experience this whole journey."

I pressed my quivering lips together and sighed heavily. "I'm sorry you have to experience so much pain. I understand why you're ready to go. I would be too." I squeezed his hand. "I believe there's a reason for all this, but sometimes it's still hard to endure it."

"I know. I'm thankful for all that I've learned so far, even though it's been rough much of the time."

Noticing the time, I said, "Let's try to get some sleep, and we can talk more tomorrow."

"OK," he said, pulling the covers over his chest.

I put his recorder in the drawer and set up his nightstand just as he liked it before heading to the door. Three days later I received a call from Dr. Smith's nurse with Jeff's urine cortisol results. She informed that the results confirmed that his cancer was in fact back. I asked her for a hospice referral, and she happily agreed. She gave me her condolences before ending the call.

I hung up the phone and sat silently on the side of my bed. A variety of emotions raced through me: sadness, relief, fear, uncertainty, and powerlessness. I took a few forced, heavy breaths as I tried to grasp the reality. I knew it was real, yet I didn't know which emotion most accurately represented how I felt about the fact my little brother was for sure going to die. I felt my heart beat deep in my gut as I thought about walking downstairs to tell Jeff.

He was resting on the couch listening to the TV. I grabbed the TV remote off the table and pushed the mute button, then sat next to him.

I struggled to get my words out without tears. "That was Dr. Smith's nurse who just called—"

"Let me guess. They confirmed it's back."

"Yeah. She said your cortisol is up and that the test confirmed that it's the cancer causing your symptoms." I reached for a tissue.

His lips pressed together tightly, and he took a deep breath in through his nose. "I don't know what to feel. It's like…" He exhaled and then started to cry.

His emotion made it even harder to maintain my composure.

He started to say a word, pausing as if waiting for his thought to become clearer. "It's like I've just been given a bus ticket, and I'm waiting to get on the bus." His lips turned up slightly, leaving me intrigued by his analogy, I silently waited for him to formulate the rest of his thought.

He continued. "So when we do another cortisol level next month, and if that's even higher, then it's time for me to get on the bus." He smiled. "Bet you're glad you won't be on that bus."

I couldn't muster even a snicker, but he seemed pleased with where his thoughts were taking him.

"So let's say we then recheck the stomach growth to see if it's growing. And if it is, then it's like the bus is leaving town, and how long it will take to get to my destination is unknown. I don't know what road it will take or what the ride will be like, but we do know where it will end. I can only hope it's a better road than the one I've been on so far."

CHAPTER 42

Cancer Update

I WAITED FOR A FEW hours before I called my family with the news. Mom cried, devastated by the results, as she quickly focused on what it would be like to lose her child. My dad cried too, but he focused on the fact that we needed to be thankful for every day Jeff was with us. Terry didn't share much emotion, but I could tell he was upset, because he only said a few words before hanging up the phone, not cracking a single joke.

Hospice quickly moved in new equipment, once again converting my house, as well as my mom's, into a mini-hospital designed to help Jeff be comfortable. They brought in oxygen tanks, a bedside commode, and different medications to help manage his sleep and pain. They also assigned a nurse to manage Jeff's pain and other symptoms that would most certainly arise.

Christine, the same social worker we had had the first time Jeff was on hospice, was eager to work with us again. She and I had kept in touch over the past two years and occasionally crossed paths at work. Christine planned on meeting with Jeff on a weekly basis to help him mentally process all that was happening to him physically. She also planned on meeting regularly with me and my parents, since it was her job to help not only the patient but also the family work through the emotional aspects of the dying process.

The next few days were difficult as my family struggled to accept the reality that Jeff's cancer had finally returned. While we didn't have a firm time frame of when the cancer would take him, we were certain that it eventually would happen.

The news of Jeff's cancer recurrence seemed to trigger a renewed interest in our lives. The outpouring of support from friends was overwhelming, in contrast to what we had experienced earlier. For several days, I received calls from friends whom I hadn't talked to in months. They asked about how I was feeling and what they could do to help. Some even offered to stay with Jeff so I could spend time with the girls. The support felt nice, but I couldn't be sure it would last.

During the month following Jeff's cancer diagnosis, our routine remained much the same. Jeff continued to swim, go out for lunch several times a week, and run his homeless ministry. I tried to include him in as many activities as possible, though it was becoming increasingly difficult to be spontaneous due to his ongoing pain issues. Jeff continued to experience changes in his body: itching, pain, nausea, and an overarching fatigue. But for the time being, the good days outnumbered the bad. The hospice nurse adjusted his medications on a weekly basis to keep up with the various symptoms, but the minute we got one thing under control, a different one popped up.

We tried to live life as normally as possible, despite the awareness that every moment felt as if it should be treasured. I still watched my step-grandson two days a week, along with my other step-grandkids as needed, which I found enjoyable despite the extra attention it required. I found myself running the girls to and fro so that their lives could remain somewhat normal. I planned to keep working for as long as I could, anticipating I would take a leave when Jeff got too sick to go to Mom's house. I knew Jeff preferred to die at home, in his big bed with Rusty at his side, and I was determined to be right there with him.

Jeff continued to meet weekly with John for Bible study. He and John spent hours discussing what the Bible said about salvation and life after death. Unlike the first time he had faced death, Jeff seemed much more at peace about where he believed he would go after he died. He wanted people to notice a change in his life from before he was sick to then—to witness how Christ had changed him.

In addition, Jeff threw himself enthusiastically into the homeless project; it seemed even more important to him than ever before. He talked about wanting to make a lasting impression on everyone around him, especially those who were down and out.

Though we went through the same motions as we had three years ago, there was finality in the air that made everything different. I would be relieved to know that Jeff was no longer suffering, yet I would miss him and the realness of the whole experience. Even though he was pleasant to care for, with his appreciative and inspiring attitude, it was still difficult to be responsible for someone else twenty-four hours a day. My anxiety spiked as I realized that I needed to continue my everyday life while caring for Jeff as he slowly deteriorated. As Jeff's health declined, there would be more pressure put on me as his primary caretaker, slowly squeezing out the little time I had made for my family and other responsibilities.

Despite the difficulty, Mom and I had a goal of making the time Jeff had left the best it could be and to keep him as comfortable as possible. I wondered how God would take him and how long we would have him—time would tell. It had been such a roller coaster ride, and I felt as if we were hanging upside down in one of the loops, especially because the doctors could not give us a time frame. Even though I trusted God's perfect timing, it did not always make it easier.

CHAPTER 43

Movie Time

WHILE SEVERAL FAMILY AND FRIENDS became more involved after Jeff's cancer returned, there were those who had been there all along and who continued to offer support. Jeff seemed to enjoy the variety of interactions that kept him from focusing entirely on his illness. The two neighbor boys, Patrick and Christopher, were the type of friends who had been there all along. They were at our house hanging out with the girls, as they did most days after school. They were more like family than friends and always made time to chat with Jeff.

"Hey, guys, are you going to that new thriller coming out?" Jeff asked, cozied up on the couch.

"Yeah, you wanna go?" Christopher asked nonchalantly.

"I would, but Tammy and the girls don't like those kinds of movies, so they won't go along."

"That's OK. We can handle taking you by ourselves," Patrick said.

I was surprised Jeff was willing to go without me or the girls, let alone that he would want to go to the movies as a blind man. Patrick and Christopher excitedly left to change clothes and get Patrick's car.

Wearing his black beret and blue jacket, Jeff eagerly waited for them to return.

"Do I look OK, Tammy?" he asked, posing as if he were a fashion icon. "I don't wanna look like a dork."

"Yep, you look snazzy. I love that hat on you."

"Did you put the money in my wallet?"

"Yep. There's a ten-dollar bill, which is folded in half lengthwise, and a five-dollar bill, which is folded the other way."

He zipped his wallet into his jacket pocket and stood by the front door, waiting for the boys to get back.

Upon Patrick and Christopher's return, I gave them a brief refresher on how to guide Jeff, since they had never been responsible for him outside our home.

About three hours later, I heard the car pull into the driveway. Moments later Christopher swung open the front door, Jeff clinging to his elbow. Patrick followed close behind.

"Tammy, you'll never guess what Jeff tried to do," Patrick excitedly shouted the moment he saw me. Patrick was a tall, handsome young man with an infectious laugh and a voice that carried throughout the house.

"Oh no. What did he do this time?" I asked.

"Hey, you told me I could tell the story," Jeff said, grinning broadly.

"Yeah, but no offense, Jeff, you couldn't see her face. It was priceless," Patrick said.

"OK, go ahead." Jeff waved his hand at Patrick to continue, half chuckling.

Christopher guided Jeff to the table chair and then eagerly sat in the chair next to him. Tucking one leg underneath him, Christopher bounced in his chair anticipating my reaction to Patrick's story.

Patrick was too giddy to sit, so he stood at the edge of the kitchen table. "So let me set the scene," he said dramatically, pausing his story as he collected himself. "So here we are standing in line to get our tickets." He started laughing again. "Everyone was looking at us sort of weird. Well, they were looking at Jeff."

I began giggling, as did Jeff and Christopher.

"Then we finally got to the ticket counter, and the girl working looked like she was maybe thirteen."

"I'm sure she was in high school, but it was probably her first job," Christopher said.

"Anyways, just as she was ringing us up, Jeff leaned up to the counter and with a totally straight face asked the girl if he could get a discount on his ticket." Patrick slapped his hand on the table, unable to continue, tears rolling down his cheeks.

"What?" Jeff asked sarcastically. "I just asked her if I could get my ticket for half-price since I could only hear the movie and not see it." His grin gave way to a snort.

"I could have died," said Christopher, who was definitely on the more sensitive side and feeling bad for the girl.

"You should have seen the girl's face." Patrick doubled over, his abundant laughter bouncing off the walls. "She had no idea what to do—she had this totally confused look on her face."

"So what did she say?" I asked, amused more by Patrick than by the story.

"'Well, sir, I'm, uh, not sure if I, uh, can do that…'" Patrick spoke in a high-pitched voice as he mimicked the girl. "'I'll need to check with the manager to see if they have any such discount.'"

"I told her to never mind, that maybe next time we would call and ask before we come down," Jeff said.

"I had to tell her that he was just having a little fun with her," Christopher said. "She seemed relieved, but I don't think she found us too funny."

"Well, I figured it was worth a shot," Jeff said innocently.

Patrick gently slapped Jeff on the back and said, "You were hilarious."

"You can't be trusted to behave yourself. But I must admit, that was a good one to try," I said.

"I was pretty happy that I was able to say it with such a straight face," Jeff said. "Well, I've had enough excitement for the day. I need to go lie down."

"OK, Jeff. Thanks for coming with us. That was great—haven't laughed that hard in a while." Patrick again slapped Jeff on the back, and then I walked him and Christopher to the door.

As they were putting on their shoes, I stopped them briefly. "I don't think you both understand how much it meant to Jeff for you to take him out. It made his day, and I'm sure he'll be repeating that story for weeks."

"It was nothing—we always like hanging with Uncle Jeff," Christopher said.

"Oh yeah. He won't be the only one telling the story for weeks. You bet all my friends will hear about it." Patrick grinned back.

As I shut the door, I thought how rare it was to have such great kids surrounding Jeff. I will forever be grateful for the sacrifice the boys made to spend time with him. Not every teenager has a blind neighbor they could take to the movies, and even if they did, very few would make the time. We were blessed to have them, and I trusted that they were blessed in return by Jeff.

CHAPTER 44

Brothers

THE MOVIE OUTING LEFT JEFF exhausted even into the next day. He rested much of the morning so he would be up for a visit with Terry. We all enjoyed it when Terry came over; his quick wit and wry commentary always lifted our spirits. The girls especially enjoyed every minute they could get with him. I informed Jeff and the girls that Terry's new boyfriend, Peter, would be joining us for dinner as well. We hadn't spent much time with him, so I wanted to remind all of them to be on their best behavior.

"Hey," Terry said as he swung open the front door, letting himself in.

"We're in here," I said.

"Wassup, y'all?" he hollered, arousing the house and probably the neighbors as well.

The girls busted out of their rooms and scrambled down the stairs, excited to see their favorite uncle.

"Hi, Uncle Terry. Hi, Peter." Kendra's excitement was palpable to all.

Chelsey paraded down the stairs, turned in a circle to give Terry a good look, and then landed in a model pose. Wasting no time on greetings, she asked, "Do you like my new jacket?"

He raised his eyebrows and gave her a flippant nod. "Oh my, it's lovely. Did you just get it from the thrift shop?"

"Nooo." She giggled and slapped his arm playfully. "I got it when Mom and I went shopping."

"And what did you get, little princess?" He reached out to mess Kendra's hair.

Kendra huffed and pushed his hand away. "Only people who don't touch my hair can know."

Terry opened his mouth to protest, but Kendra had already moved on, whispering to her sister and shooting him an exaggerated dismissive glance. He returned the expression in kind and half sat, half fell onto a chair next to Jeff.

"So, Jeff, how's that whole dying thang going?" he playfully drawled, sending us all into laughter. Except Peter—he just sent Terry a disapproving look, seemingly unsure of how else to respond.

"Don't worry, Peter. We're all used to his humor," I said. He nodded, still mildly bemused.

Still laughing, Jeff said, "Well, I haven't croaked yet, so I guess I'm doin' OK."

"And I reminded the kids to be on their best behavior," I said, shaking my head in mock disappointment.

Terry leaned in closer to Jeff and murmured, "Seriously, how have you been feeling?"

"Not too bad, I guess. The new pain patch seems to be helping, but it makes me itch a lot."

"Well, I guess it's better to be itching than in pain, huh?" Terry said.

"That's for sure."

We spent the rest of the evening chatting happily. The girls bantered back and forth with Terry about their favorite shows, music, and latest teen idol crushes. Peter, a soft-spoken, sophisticated man, asked the girls questions about school and their other interests. He too enjoyed Terry's humor but avoided joining the banter. Terry's visit didn't disappoint; it was a welcome distraction from the overarching illness that was increasingly robbing our home of such joy.

As I tucked Jeff into bed, he said, "I really enjoyed my visit. It was good to laugh. I'm so thankful Terry has been around through this whole ordeal."

"Yeah, he's the best. He makes everyone laugh. He should be a comedian," I said.

"It makes me wish we had a better relationship with Gary." His smile faded. "I'm sad that he's missing out on nights like these. I mean…" He cleared his throat. "I don't even really know him, ya know—like what he's really like. And he doesn't really know me."

"I get it. I just don't think there's really anything we can do about it. I've tried talking to him a million times, and so has Mom."

"I know, but maybe I should've tried harder." His guilt-ridden words pierced me.

"You haven't done anything wrong." I tried to keep the anger out of my voice. "Gary is the only one who should be feeling bad. You and Mom invited him down to visit so many times over the past three years. He just keeps avoiding it."

"I didn't mean to upset you."

"You didn't. I'm just frustrated because I know that you would like things to be different, and so would I. But we just can't make him care."

"I'm sure he cares—he's just avoiding it all because it's hard. I'm afraid I might have been the same way before I got sick. I still remember how selfish I was back then." Jeff's words reminded me of the wisdom he'd gained through this whole journey.

"I know. I've seen it before in other families I've helped." My tone softened. "Every family has someone who can't handle being around the sick person or is too busy to take time out to help."

A pensive expression gave way to his words. "I've been trying to focus on enjoying everyone in the family and being grateful for every one of them, even if I don't always like all of them. I'm trying to remember that they still have feelings and can get hurt. It's like God is telling me to just appreciate them for who they are, and if all they do is treat you nice, appreciate them for that." I went to bed thinking about Jeff's insights, but they didn't completely relieve the disappointment I felt about Gary. Despite the fact that we always felt like a close family, we felt abandoned by one of our own.

Gary just had not helped as much as we hoped. His continual avoidance created an additional sense of loss for our family. Mom and I tried in so many ways to include him. We understood that some people could not be directly involved, so we provided him opportunities to help in other ways.

I reflected on the on-again, off-again relationship Gary and I had growing up. I had thought ours was the kind of relationship in which he would be there when I needed him. I knew Terry and Jeff expected little of Gary; they had never been very close to him, primarily seeing him at family functions.

Lying there, I felt my anger stir up, remembering how his absence had felt after Dad's crash. Gary was the closest to Dad, both because of their shared interests and because he lived only three doors down. Mom expected more out of Gary than his occasional, unannounced, and very brief visits. At times, she was caring for two very sick men, and she needed more than the sporadic help he offered only when it was convenient for him. It almost seemed unforgivable that he abandoned my dad during his sickest days.

Needing to calm down and get some sleep, I rolled over and tried to see things through Jeff's eyes. I couldn't even do that. Jeff was blind. I sighed quietly. He was blind, and he was dying, and he was hurting, and no one, especially not Gary, understood what all that meant to him. The least he could do was show up. Say hello, kiss the girls, and bring a cake. It wasn't that difficult to be empathetic.

I sighed again. Empathetic? I guess I needed to be empathetic to Gary too, even if it was hard. I considered the thought for a moment, anger still bubbling up. I might have a chance to be empathetic to him when everyone else didn't need my help.

CHAPTER 45

Serving the Homeless

A RESTFUL SLEEP DID WONDERS for my attitude. My moment of anger with Gary had passed, and I was looking forward to helping Jeff prepare for the homeless project. It was Mom's weekend to have Jeff, so I gathered up his bag of clothes, recorder, and some supplies. Just as I came in from loading the last bag in the car, Jeff called for me from his room.

"Hey, did you happen to grab the stack of socks that were in the corner of my closet?" he asked, poking his cane around the closet floor.

"Yes, I already got them. All the stuff's in the car."

"OK. What about the backpacks the girls collected?"

"Yes, got them too," I said. "I have everything loaded."

"All right. I guess we're ready to go, then. Right?"

Feeling a bit annoyed, I took a deep breath before responding. "I have your medications, clothes, supplies, recorder, and homeless stuff. The only thing left is to get you in the car."

He reached for my elbow, and we walked toward the front door, where he stopped. "Wait, wait. What about the..." A mischievous grin crept across his face. "Just kidding. I trust you got it all."

"It's a good thing, since you really don't have a choice but to trust me. Besides, do you really think I would tell you if I forgot something? Your OCD would really kick up."

It was typical for Jeff to need reassurance that nothing was forgotten, especially stuff that he needed for the homeless project. Usually I had patience with Jeff's obsessive need to recheck my steps, but sometimes his questioning was frustrating. Worried I might hurt his feelings, I typically hid my feelings behind sarcasm or humor.

As I drove up the driveway, Mom stood on the front porch, waving her arm through the crisp fall air. Per our usual routine, she helped Jeff into the house before helping me haul in the other stuff.

"Wait till you see how much stuff the girls and their friends collected. You won't believe it," Jeff said.

"Well, you're gonna be surprised by the donations we got from the last e-mail we sent," Mom said as she set a stack of socks on the living room floor. We finished bringing in the socks, backpacks, and drinks, along with his usual bag of stuff.

"I can't wait to see what we got," Jeff said, sitting at the edge of his seat.

Mom knelt on the floor near him. "OK, so remember how in your last e-mail you asked for enough donations to make two hundred lunches?" She paused, building the suspense.

"Yeah, yeah," he said, his head bobbing up and down.

"Well, we collected enough tuna, bread, drinks, and snacks to make about two hundred and thirty lunches." Her voice filled with elation. "And that's not counting what you and Tammy just brought in."

Jeff pumped his fist into the air just as my and Mom's hands slapped together.

"That's so awesome. Praise God," he said. "So does that mean we also collected enough socks to go in each lunch?"

"Yep. We have enough of everything," she said. "It's all right here in these bags."

I lifted a full green bag onto his lap. "Check this out."

Jeff reached inside the bag, and his face glowed with pride. "Wow, that's a ton of stuff."

He leaned back in his chair, content to have Mom verbally identify each and every item as we emptied all the bags and boxes onto the floor. I helped her sort them into piles: socks, snacks, drinks, condiments, and miscellaneous—such as the backpacks. Jeff always enjoyed keeping track of exactly how many of each item we had. It was as if it was his way of keeping track of how big a difference he was making.

The following morning the girls and I arrived at Mom's to help make the lunches. Terry, Peter, and a few friends were there before us and had already started the preparations.

"'Bout time you made it," Terry teased.

Terry always picked the sandwich station, which was where the streamlined assembly line started. I was sure it was so he could be in charge of how fast things went and so he could finish his task first. After making lunches every month for over a year now, we had a pretty efficient process for putting the lunches together.

"Hi, guys," Jeff said, sitting cross-legged on the living room floor, folding a pair of socks from the pile that covered his lap.

"Hello," we said in unison as we dispersed to different stations.

I sat near the growing line of stuffed brown lunch bags to help Frank do a final check before they went into the delivery box. Chelsey moved to the snack station, the rectangular dining room table covered with cookies and chips. Kendra plopped herself in the kitchen, as close to Terry as she could get, to stuff the sandwiches in plastic bags. She loved listening to his wry commentary as he worked.

As was typical, the assembly process took us less than an hour. The time could vary slightly depending on how many lunches we were making and the number of volunteers. Mom and I shared the supervisor role, monitoring things to make sure each lunch was complete with a sandwich, snack, drink, and pair of socks. Occasionally we had extra of one thing or another, so we would put it aside for the next outing.

The city park was particularly full that day, a sad blessing in a way. We were eager to share the two-hundred-plus lunches we had made, and just as many hungry souls were excited to receive them. I walked with a bag of lunches in one hand and Jeff holding on to the other. He tapped his cane side to side over the crumbling brick path as I described the scenery ahead. The rest of the group split off in different directions, happy to share with those in need.

The rumble of city buses and the far-off wail of sirens faded in the background as a disheveled man pushed his rickety shopping cart toward us. I stopped, reached into the stuffed plastic bag, and pulled out a sack lunch. I handed it to Jeff so he could be the one to give it to the man.

"Hello?" Jeff said, looking in the direction of the rattling wheels.

"Well, hello to you, sir," the man said pleasantly. The stench of wet, musty clothes mixed with sour body odor increased with each approaching step.

"Would ya like a lunch?" Jeff asked, the brown bag dangling from his outstretched hand.

"That's mighty nice of ya." He grabbed the lunch and gently patted Jeff on the shoulder.

Jeff didn't flinch. Unusually at ease, he engaged the friendly older man. "So have you lived in the city long?"

"You might say it's been a while…" He paused, distracted as he riffled through the sack lunch. "What about you? What brings you to the park?"

Jeff tucked his cane by his side and lifted his head high, eager to answer. "Well, I just wanted to give back, since I've been so blessed." He paused, hearing the rustling of the paper bag.

"Uh-huh," the man uttered, peeling the plastic bag away from the sandwich and taking a bite.

"So anyways, I became blind as a result of surgery from terminal cancer, and I've been blessed to make it this far. I figure the least I can do to share a little hope is bring someone, someone like you, a lunch."

Staring at Jeff's closed eyelids, the man swallowed hard. "I'm really sorry to hear that." He placed his calloused, grimy hand over Jeff's. "I sure hope you'll be OK."

"Well, thank you." Jeff smiled, firmly shaking the man's hand. "God bless you, and I hope you enjoy that lunch."

"Thank you, sir, and God bless you too," the man said, lowering his damp, hollow eyes toward the ground.

He looked up and gave me a nod as he hid his lunch under a blanket near the front of his overstuffed cart, turned the cart in the same direction he had come from, and pushed it up the path with all his might. His sincerity left a lump in my throat.

"He got teary-eyed when you were talking," I told Jeff as I watched the man walk away.

"I wasn't sure if I shoulda kept talking, but I didn't want the guy feeling bad for me."

"You did just fine. He was ready to move on."

I pulled my arm slightly forward to lead Jeff down the path toward another park patron, a man who was sprawled out on a bench, huddled under a tattered blanket.

"This one's asleep, so I'm just gonna leave a lunch for him," I whispered in Jeff's ear, quietly setting a lunch near his worn duffel bag.

"I really like it when I can interact with the people," Jeff said as we continued to walk. He abruptly stopped. This time the sharp stomach pains that had recently plagued him left him momentarily breathless, and he nearly doubled over.

"You OK?"

"Yeah, it'll pass. Just let me catch my breath for a sec." He sucked air through his pursed lips as he forced himself upright.

I helplessly observed the grimace across his red face, waiting for signs that the jabbing pain was subsiding.

Jeff exhaled as relief relaxed his tense facial muscles. "Whew, that was a bad one," he said, gingerly walking forward.

"I'm sorry you have to go through so much pain. Hopefully, the nurse will be able to change up your meds again."

"I hope so too, 'cause I wanna keep doing this." His volume increased. "I wanna touch as many lives as we can, and maybe I'll even be able to lead somebody to Christ through this process—or at least give them hope, even if they don't realize it at the time."

"You already have impacted so many people, and I'm sure you'll continue," I said.

"I hope so. I wanna do this for as long as I can."

Just then Frank came running toward us and suddenly stopped a few feet ahead of us. "Keep walking," he said, looking through the lens of his video camera. "I wanna shoot some footage for our homeless video."

"Oh, good. I was hoping you were getting some good shots," Jeff said, smiling.

CHAPTER 46

A Grateful Heart

Preparations were already underway for the next sack lunch delivery. Jeff wasted no time in e-mailing people to ask for food, clothing, and volunteers. He was especially excited that the next outing would be to Tent City. There were usually about 120 residents at the well-organized homeless camp, and they were always appreciative of our donations.

Jeff and Frank were grateful to have received permission from the camp officials to take video footage of Jeff interacting with the residents. They planned on using it to complete a project they were working on. Frank met with Jeff weekly to help put together a video about Jeff's journey and his homeless ministry. They planned on finishing the video by the end of the month, leaving little time for Jeff to finalize his part, a monologue about his journey. We hoped to share the video with churches or other organizations as a way to inspire others to feed the homeless in Seattle.

I rushed through the last of my morning chores so I could keep my promise to help Jeff rehearse for his speech. We only had a half hour before Frank was scheduled to pick him up and take him to the beach. They figured the fall leaves and slapping waves would be the perfect backdrop for Jeff's interview, and it would also afford them some privacy.

Coffee cup in hand, I slid into the chair opposite from where Jeff sat deep in thought. His lips moved, but no words came out, as if he were in prayer or contemplation.

"OK, I'm all yours till Frank gets here," I said.

Aggressively picking at his fingernails, he lifted his head and sighed. "I don't know why I'm so nervous."

"I don't either. It's not like you can't do it over if you mess up."

"I know, but I just wanna make sure I say everything I've been wanting to share." He sat up straight, adjusting his back against the chair. "So I'm gonna do a practice run, OK?"

"Sounds good." I relaxed into the chair, sipping my coffee.

"I'm just gonna pretend like you're videoing me, and you can give me feedback after I'm all done," he said.

"I'm ready when you are, and I'll try not to interrupt you."

"OK, here it goes…" The kitchen was ghostly silent as he collected himself, eyes closed.

"I was born a po' black child…" Unable to keep his composure, he collapsed into giggles. I could barely keep from spewing coffee all over. For a few minutes, the house echoed as we laughed, first at Jeff's joke, then at each other. Finally forcing himself to calm down, he said, "OK, seriously, I'm gonna start."

Once he got started, his words flowed seamlessly as he recounted how he was diagnosed with a rare terminal cancer and endured a fourteen-hour surgery, only to wake up blind. He talked some about his life before he was diagnosed and how different it had been since his illness. Since I was intimately familiar with that part of his story, other thoughts momentarily captured my attention. It was only when he paused for several seconds that I snapped back into reality, forcing myself to listen intently to what he was saying. He still looked deep in thought, pausing and restarting as words and phrases seemed to fall into place.

"I want people to remember that there was this blind guy, dying of cancer, and he was still able to serve God. I want them to know that, despite their situation, they can make a difference in the world too. You can't help but feel good when you're helping others. We are called to serve the less fortunate, but I know some people have a hard time helping the 'bums' or people who seem to 'choose' that type of life. I don't always understand how they stay in that situation, but I imagine it is difficult for them emotionally and physically to be homeless."

He paused, and I silently waited. His chest expanded as he inhaled deeply, and I felt my own swell in response. He nodded, in agreement with his thoughts, and continued to speak. I listened, blurry eyed.

"I try to remember that we all have made mistakes, but some suffer more for theirs. Or perhaps they suffer from their parents' mistakes. It isn't our place to judge them—we don't know what their circumstances were that led them to get there. Regardless, it makes me sick to know that they have to eat out of trash cans, or eat leftovers from who knows where. That's why it feels so good to give them a warm meal and let them know that someone cares."

Licking his dry lips, he reached for his water bottle and then took a big swig. Staring blankly, brows furrowed, he finished his thought.

"I didn't always think this way—that's why I thank my Lord Jesus Christ for providing me with the desire, means, and helpers to make it possible for me to do the homeless project. I want the focus to stay on him and what he can do through us."

The doorbell startled us, abruptly ending Jeff's practice run. I wiped my eyes, awed at the transformation Jeff so eloquently articulated.

"That was amazing," I said, hurrying to let Frank in.

"Wow, you just missed Jeff's practice speech—or should I say sermon," I said exuberantly.

"So you thought it was OK?" Jeff humbly asked, rising to his feet.

"OK? No, it was great," I said.

"Well, guess I'll get to hear it in just a bit. I've got everything ready to go, and I think we have a good chance of finishing your part today," Frank said, giving Jeff a congratulatory pat on the back.

"Then we'll only have Tent City this weekend, and we'll have it all wrapped up," Jeff said, zipping his jacket and heading toward the door.

I waved goodbye, slammed the door shut, and thought about rejoicing. It seemed like the appropriate thing to do, since it had been years since I had had four hours to myself, alone in my house with no kids, no

Jeff, and not even my husband. Instead, I aimlessly puttered through the house, picking up as I went, reflecting on all that Jeff shared and all that was happening in our lives.

So many changes—some welcome, many not. It felt as if I should've planned something special to do, maybe meet Clark for lunch or make plans with a friend. Instead I felt sort of lost, empty of purpose outside the duties that had consumed me for the past two and a half years. Always a "deep thinker type," I had had lots of practice finding all sorts of things to lift my spirits when I felt heavy hearted. Playing with the grandkids was one of my favorites. But I wasn't able to shake it. Instead, I mindlessly fixated on cleaning the decaying leaves out of my pond, not really feeling sad, mostly just contemplative.

The phone had rung several times before I managed to get back inside to answer it, breathless. It was Leitha, calling to invite me to a football game the following weekend. The University of Washington was my alma mater, and I had always wanted to go to a game. After checking the calendar, I excitedly accepted. Immediately I felt a little lighter. The chance to hang out with one of my favorite people, while watching my favorite college team play—live no less—was just what I needed to lift me out of my funk.

I was surprised by how fast the time had passed—Jeff and Frank's return seemed sudden. I could hear them jubilantly chatting as they made their way onto the porch.

"How'd it go?" I asked.

"It turned out great," Frank said, his entire face lighting up.

"Yeah, I think you'll like it," Jeff said, making his way to the couch and then plopping down. "I'm pooped."

"We stopped by Tent City—"

"Don't forget, man," Jeff said, "you can't leave until we call my mom."

Ignoring Jeff's comment, Frank continued, his face lit up with a twinkle of mischief. "Jeff sorta—"

"We both did," Jeff said.

"OK, we kinda volunteered your mom to make soup for the camp on Friday night," he spurted.

Amused by their audacity, I couldn't refrain from dialing Mom's number. I placed the phone in Jeff's hand—but not before pushing the speaker button—and nestled next to him. "This oughta be good." I giggled.

Frank knelt on the floor near our feet, his hand covering his sheepish grin.

"Hello," Mom said.

"Hi, Mom...uhum..." Jeff tried acting nonchalant. "So Frank and I stopped off at Tent City after we finished filming, and, um..." His words slightly stuck as he began chewing on his knuckle. "Nobody's bringing them a meal on Friday, so we told 'em that we could bring 'em some homemade chicken-noodle soup."

"Well, that was really nice of you," she said, voice a bit too chipper.

Frank's eyebrows rose slightly, and he mouthed, "Uh-oh." He knew our mom well, having grown up in our neighborhood and being Jeff's close friend since kindergarten. He could read her sarcastic undertone as well as any of us.

"Yeah, they were totally excited," Jeff said. "I told them we could also bring them some rolls."

"Great idea, but where ya getting the soup?" she asked, feigning curiosity. "Is Frank's sister making it?"

"Well, we...um...didn't think you'd mind whipping up some soup and rolls for them," Jeff said.

"I see." A deep sigh echoed through the speaker. "How many people we talkin'?"

Jeff hesitated before answering. "They said only about a hundred."

Her shock reverberated through the phone. "How many?"

"I'll come over to help ya," Frank quickly said.

"You bet your butt you will. You both will," she said, reprimanding him halfheartedly.

When I realized the sizeable task ahead, my amusement suddenly turned to guilt. I felt bad that I would be working, leaving Mom to pull off two food deliveries without my help that weekend. I put a gentle hand on Jeff's shoulder and spoke into the receiver. "I think Jeff and Frank better get on the computer and send out an e-mail telling people what they volunteered to do and what kind of help they're gonna need."

"We better get at it," Frank said, resolving to help his friend out of another predicament.

"Do me a favor," Mom said. A small snicker softened her demand. "Next time you think to volunteer me, check with me first."

"OK. Thanks, Mom. We'll get some help to pull it off," Jeff said, slightly remorseful.

Normally Mom wouldn't have thought twice about whipping up some soup for a hundred hungry people, but since she was already working on Sunday's delivery of two hundred lunches, the request was a hefty one.

It was hard for Mom or me to get very frustrated with Jeff for volunteering his help to others, but his help also required our own. Having to be the ones to make it happen was definitely time consuming, and at times overwhelming. It required more shopping, more food preparation, more coordinating with people—more of the things that already taxed us—even more patience and empathy. However, it was a sacrifice both Mom and I were willing to make in order to help Jeff fulfill his passion, perhaps his life mission.

The hectic weekend behind, I tried to settle down for the night. Jeff's voice streamed through my bedside monitor, clearly relaying his gratitude as he spoke into his recorder. As he continued talking, I drifted in and out of sleep, his words warming the deepest part of my soul.

"It is Sunday night, November 2002, and the weekend was busy since we decided to do two homeless projects this week, one on Friday night and the other this morning. My mom, along with some friends, made homemade chicken noodle soup for Tent City. We even had rolls and cupcakes. I bought them candy bars as a special treat this week. We also collected some essentials for them, like batteries, tape, and other supplies. On Sunday, we made ham-and-cheese sandwiches for the downtown folks.

"I enjoyed talking to the people, hearing their stories and having a chance to share mine. There were several homeless people who came up and talked to me and even shook my hand. Some people even remembered my name. That's pretty special—that some homeless guy remembered my name from two months ago; it really touched my heart. Hopefully, I can learn something from them, and they can learn something from me.

"I always thought the people at Tent City were there until they could get back on their feet. I was surprised to learn that many of them are satisfied with living in the tents. Several are still using drugs and alcohol, even though they aren't allowed to use them in the camp itself. I guess I hoped that they would be trying to get away from all that stuff. However, it isn't my place to judge them; I let God do the judging. If they're hungry, it makes me happy to be giving them food for their bellies. Regardless of their life choices, they still need to eat. I think God did some wonderful things there today.

"I've been saving my money to buy a three-man tent for Tent City. I'm really excited to give it to them for Christmas. I love being able to help them; I only wish I had more money and access to more resources. It isn't easy for me, though, because I always have to rely on everyone else. I'm so grateful that I have so many people supporting me in this journey. I recognize that it's my mission, and perhaps the only reason others are involved is because they want to help me. It's especially true for the kids. I know that being a teenager and helping a homeless person isn't usually top on their list of things to do. But I trust that they are still benefiting.

"I realize that I am using my illness as a springboard to do this homeless project, which almost doesn't feel fair, since I probably wouldn't be doing it if I hadn't become ill. I am glad that my family and friends are helping, even though they aren't sick. It makes me feel good because I wish I would have done that before. If I knew the things I know now, back then, I would've been happier and more successful by far. I would've felt much better about myself.

"Frank and I finally finished the video. I think it turned out pretty good. We are going to continue to record so we can sort of keep a video journal of the different people we meet and the different projects we do. Tammy and I are going to take it to different churches and show it to as many people as we can, and maybe we can inspire others to serve the homeless.

"I just hope I can continue to do this for a long time. I know that once I get to heaven, I will be surprised to see the people that may have been touched by my life, and the homeless project."

CHAPTER 47

The Ups and Downs

CLARK GENTLY RUBBED HIS HAND over my back, waking me from a deep sleep. "It's time," he quietly said, apologetically. "I would've let you sleep, but I know you'd get upset with me if I let you miss our coffee time."

I rubbed my knuckles across my sleepy eyes, stretched my arms into the air, and mumbled, "Thanks. I'm glad you woke me up; I'll be right down."

"I'll go pour it now," he said, turning to leave the room.

"Make sure Jeff's door's shut; we were up again last night, and I want him to get some rest."

"OK," he whispered, gingerly stepping down the stairs.

My worn terry-cloth robe draped around me, I sat in my usual spot on the couch. Clark served me my coffee before sitting in his leather chair across from me.

Wrapping my hands around the hot cup, I savored my first sip of coffee.

Concerned, Clark said, "So what do you think is happening with Jeff?"

"I'm not really sure, but I know he's lost six pounds over the past week. It could be the cancer growing bigger, or maybe side effects from the pain meds..." I trailed off and took another sip. "I don't know if we'll ever really know for sure."

He nodded. "Well, I heard back from my boss. I'll be off on Saturday, so you can go to the game."

"That's awesome." A twinge of excitement raced through me. "Thank you for doing that. I'm really looking forward to it."

"You don't need to thank me—I'm your husband." He was uncomfortable whenever I gushed at him.

Our sacred coffee time concluded just as Jeff hollered for me. I swung his bedroom door open and saw his head between his knees; he was vomiting all over the floor. The retching caused Clark to rush in to help.

"Grab some towels," I nervously shouted.

"I'm sorry; I tried to grab the garbage can," Jeff said, his head still hanging.

Clark laid towels over the mess and handed me a wet washcloth to wipe Jeff's face.

"There's nothing to be sorry about." His hand rested gently on Jeff's back, steadying him. "You can't help that you're sick."

We hustled to get Jeff—and the floor—cleaned up and get him settled back in bed. Dreading another day of unexplained symptoms, I racked my brain for all possible explanations. Since the results from the urine test we had taken a few days ago showed that the cancer was only slightly progressing, we could comfortably rule it out as the main cause of Jeff's nausea, headaches, sore muscles, and stomach pains.

Clark returned to the room with a fresh cold rag and carefully placed it across Jeff's forehead. Worried about Jeff being home alone, even for a few minutes, he hung around longer than usual so he could drop the girls off at school for me.

I put a straw to Jeff's lips. "Here, take a sip. I have your nausea pill when you're ready."

"Thank you…" He sipped the water, grimacing as it passed through his raw throat. "I don't know what I'd ever do without you guys." His raspy words successfully conveyed his appreciation.

I fluffed his pillow and pulled his sheet across his bare chest. "We're in this together. Try to relax for a bit while I make you a piece of toast." I flipped the cloth over and replaced it before walking out, my head stuffed with worry.

The first part of the week continued much as it had started—Jeff feeling very sick and me trying to figure out how best to help him. By that Thursday we had discovered that some of Jeff's symptoms were related to the pain medications—the same pills that kept him from suffering. Relieved that he was feeling better and excited that the football game was only two days away, I embraced the day with a little more hope.

We spent the afternoon away from the house, enjoying lunch with Midge and going grocery shopping. Jeff always enjoyed tagging along on his good days, and I relished the fact that he was able to hang out with me.

Saturday-morning cartoons blared from the living room, a familiar reminder that the weekend had begun. The girls were snuggled up on opposite ends of the couch, floral fleece blankets stretched across their torsos.

"Morning, Momma," Kendra said sweetly, Chelsey hurrying to echo. Neither girl moved her eyes from the TV.

I deliberately strutted in front of the screen. "Morning, girls. Notice anything?" I slowly twirled in a small circle.

"You must be excited if you're already dressed for the game," Chelsey said.

"Oh yeah, oh yeah." I danced silly, jumping up and down.

"We're happy you get to go to the football game," Kendra said, straining her neck to see the TV. "You do realize it's not until this afternoon, though, don't you?"

I continued wiggling around, well aware that I was blocking the television from view.

"Mom." Four little eyes glared back at me.

"Will you please move away from the TV," Kendra demanded. I delivered one more quick celebratory dance before leaving the room.

Regardless of how often I looked at the clock, it seemed that time was passing slower than normal, or at least slower than I wanted. My excitement increased with each passing minute, especially after Leitha called to finalize our meeting plans. She had a way of building the anticipation, reminding me of our tickets close to the field on the fifty-yard line and the tailgate excitement I was sure to enjoy.

Appropriately garbed in my University of Washington gear, I covered a few last-minute details with Clark about Jeff's evening medications. It had been a long while since he had been responsible for helping Jeff with his nighttime routine.

"Hey, Tammy…" Jeff weakly called from the rec room.

"Yeah?" I said. A tiny worry shot through my stomach as I approached him.

"Do you think you could grab me one of those nausea pills before you leave..." His Adam's apple rose up, then went down. "I all of a sudden just got really queasy." He swallowed again. "Maybe it's just something I ate."

As I rushed to get his pill, my stomach felt hollow. I slipped it between his pale lips. "Here, take a sip of water."

He put his hand in front of his mouth, color quickly disappearing from his cheeks.

"You better get me a pan," he mumbled, his hand covering his mouth.

Clark was already on his way with a pan in one hand and a towel in the other. "It's OK. I can take care of him," Clark said firmly. "It won't be the first time I've cleaned up puke," he said matter-of-factly, calmly setting the pan on Jeff's lap.

"You gotta be kidding." I sat next to Jeff, rubbing his back. "I'm not leaving. There's no way I could go knowing he's getting sick again." I glared at Clark, confused as to how he could possibly think I would really go.

"It's up to you, but I'm certainly capable of taking care of him," he said.

Unable to hold it in any longer, Jeff threw up in the pan. My heartbeat intensified as he heaved harder. Helpless, I waited for the cycle of vomiting to cease. Clark stood over us, waiting to take away the soiled pan. I wiped Jeff's mouth, handed the pan to Clark, and brushed the tears from Jeff's cheek.

"I'm so sorry, sis. Are you sure you don't want to go?" he whimpered. "I know how much you were looking forward to the game."

Walking out of the room, Clark shook his head at me, disappointed I wouldn't leave. It wasn't the first time he had disapproved of my choices, nor was it likely to be the last. He knew that it wasn't that I didn't trust that he was capable of handling the situation. I didn't trust that he could check his gruff demeanor while doing so. Though my disappointment was palpable, it paled to the intense responsibility I felt for Jeff.

In between vomiting episodes, I took the phone upstairs, out of Jeff's earshot. Heavy with sadness, disappointment, and guilt, I dialed Leitha's number.

"Hey, are you almost here?" she whooped.

The words barely squeaked past my lips. "I'm so sorry, but Jeff just started throwing up—" Choking up, I paused.

She quickly said, "Hey, don't worry about it. It's me you're talkin' to here. I understand."

"I'll pay you for my ticket, even if you can find someone else last minute."

"Don't be ridiculous," she said empathetically. "We'll have another chance to go. Seriously, it's OK."

Feeling a moment of self-pity, I was incapable of being cheery. "I'd better get back to Jeff. I'm so sorry. I hope you guys have fun."

"It's OK. I'll just have to find some random soul to sit in these amazing seats with me," she said kiddingly.

I appreciated her efforts to make me feel better, but as bad I was feeling, I knew that my little brother felt even worse.

CHAPTER 48

God's Healing

It was frustrating that I had once again let my anticipation build, leaving me that much more disappointed when things didn't work out. I should have known better than to let the excitement carry me away, but clearly, I still did not know how to have *hope* while truly having to live one day at a time.

I knew one way to cope was to postpone making any future plans, especially ones that could leave me as sad as missing out on the game did. Instead, I focused on Jeff, figuring that the day would come soon enough when I would no longer have a little brother to care for, no longer have our cherished late-night talks, and I wasn't yet ready to embrace that reality.

Jeff and I spent many hours puzzling over what it was that God was teaching us through his constantly changing symptoms. Contemplating the purpose and plan for the lessons we were learning became a regular, and priceless, part of our relationship. In the years since his diagnosis, Jeff had become much more interested in exploring his faith. He spent a majority of his free time listening to the Bible and other Christian books and working through some of his questions with John during their weekly Bible study.

One night, Jeff and I got off on a tangent about the Bible story of how Jesus healed a blind man. A light-bulb moment led me to see the parallels of how Jesus used a blind man to perform a miracle and what God had done for Jeff's life. The man in the Bible was born blind and therefore destined to a life as a beggar, yet Jesus chose him to be his witness. When Jesus opened the eyes of the blind man, skeptics prevented a celebration from taking place because they doubted whether the newly sighted man was actually the blind beggar. Few believed what they witnessed, and many tried to dismiss the gift Jesus gave to the blind man. Nonetheless, the blind man followed Jesus even though he never knew why Jesus chose to let him see.

Jeff was born sighted yet lived a life blinded by depression and loneliness. He searched to find real happiness and joy, but he was never able to see beyond the challenges in his life, beyond the dark clouds. It wasn't until he became blind that he was able to *see* the blue skies and the many gifts he had been given. It was as if he received spiritual sight through his physical blindness. I realized that many people might have looked at Jeff's broken body and believed that God hadn't healed him, but I saw it differently. Jeff had experienced more joy, peace, and purpose over the past two years than he ever did in the previous thirty years. In fact, I believed we all saw more clearly since walking in Jeff's darkness. Just as God used the blind man in the Bible, I believed he was using Jeff as well. God was healing not only Jeff's spirit, but many of ours.

It was an epiphany for sure, but one that didn't wipe away the reality facing us: my brother was slowly fading away. Trusting that God had a purpose and a plan was comforting, but not enough to totally absolve me or Jeff of the grief the dying process caused.

Jeff appreciated my comparison and even agreed with my analysis that he was healed in many ways. Nonetheless, he still felt a little frightened by the process. It seemed to be the case with most of our discussions that his feelings and thoughts vacillated widely, sometimes moment by moment.

Our nightly discussions typically inspired him to journal his thoughts. After he got the recorder and I stopped transcribing for him, Jeff gave me an open invitation to listen in while he spoke into the little recorder. Many times I passed, but I felt certain that our rich discussion that night would lend itself to some interesting insights.

I listened as he expounded on his thoughts. "This whole process is still scary and takes all I can do not to cry because I don't want everyone to see me deteriorate. I recognize that my pain will likely be there forever, meaning I will have to take more and more pain medications, which is fine if it works. I don't want my family watching me go through this because it's not a pleasant sight—It can't be. It is so scary and doesn't seem fair that they have to witness it at all, yet I'm glad I don't have to go through it alone. I am so thankful my parents, my sister, brother-in-law, and nieces are here to help me. I pray and ask God to give them strong hearts.

"I pray that everybody who witnesses this remembers it, because I have learned that it can happen to anyone overnight. When you get that phone call telling you that it doesn't look good and that you need to make an appointment to see a specialist, then you go to the appointment where they tell you that you have cancer—that's the moment my spirit felt like it was just gone. It seems like after that, everything is just in a big fog—I don't know if it is denial or what.

"If I had my choice, I would be gone tomorrow—of course, after I say goodbye to my family and friends. On the other hand, I am fighting time because I want to leave a legacy. I have never been anything in my life; I have always been the underdog. I have been the guy that was last to be chosen for sports or other games. I want to leave this earth being the first chosen. I want to accomplish something and have those accomplishments be remembered when I am gone. I want to make a difference in the world.

"I am really training myself to live one day at a time. It isn't always fun. I am trying not to worry about other people's issues, but still be there for them as a friend. I remember how I used to be about all the small stuff, being upset over little things. My life was complicated by poor choices, divorce, and little irritations. I was a different person before I got cancer and went blind. I didn't like the person I was back then. I can't go back and change my past; I can only try to do better now. I make a conscious choice to focus on the good and not the bad. I can think of other people now, and I'm a better listener. I feel like I am less judgmental, more considerate, thoughtful, and more open minded. I want to give back and not be a taker.

"I remember what it was like to have my own home, job, car, and so forth, and now I lost all of that. I used to be able to wear my jeans and T-shirts, but now I am stuck having to wear sweatpants every day. I am grateful I have them, but sometimes I do miss wearing my old clothes. I miss driving to work and going wherever I want. Though I miss many things from my past, I try to focus on what I do have now. I remind myself that I took all that stuff for granted, and I don't want to take all the good I have now for granted.

"I want to be there for my nieces—Chelsey, Kendra, Kylie, and McKenna—to help them make wise choices. I want to teach them, and others, to be givers and not takers. I want them to value the family we have and to share their feelings and love just out of the blue, not only when something bad happens. I don't want anyone to forget that at any moment things can change. I would like to help them avoid my mistakes, or at least let them know that I care and want to listen.

"I may not have the same stresses now in my life, but I remember what it was like. Now, just living is stressful enough, such as just getting a glass of milk or making a sandwich. It's all relative, but we can choose to look at the glass as half-full. I still get irritated, like when the homeless project isn't going as smoothly as I would like; however, it is a waste of blood pressure and energy. I make myself think about the fact that it isn't such a big deal. When I let those types of things frustrate me, I am quickly reminded of my old ways.

"I am enjoying my new Bible study with John; we are doing a study on prayer. I want to be a witness to people and hopefully lead someone to Christ. I might not get to know whether I did or not while I am here on earth, but it'll be nice to know once I am in Heaven.

"God has made it very possible for me to be content. He has provided so much for me, which I never want to take for granted, like my home, family, the health I have left, and my new perspective. I want to incorporate more spirituality into my homeless ministry. I may just be a small fish in a big pond, but I want to make a difference. I want to be remembered."

CHAPTER 49

Video Debut

ONE DAY AT A TIME seemed to be our new motto. Jeff's health remained unpredictable from one day to the next, making planning for anything nearly impossible. After my letdown with the Huskies game, I certainly wasn't going to let myself get excited about anything in the near future.

The holidays were fast approaching. Frank was excited by how well the video turned out and finished editing in time for Jeff and me to pitch it to our pastor. He made several copies for us to give to the church, as well as to our friends and family.

I first watched the tape with Jeff, Clark, and the girls. Unjustifiably, I was amazed at how professional it looked. I had no idea Frank was so talented. It started out with Jeff sitting on a bench at Alki Beach, his old favorite haunt, telling the story of how he became blind, much as we had rehearsed. Frank then interjected scenes showing Jeff and all the helpers handing out lunches during the homeless ministry. Jeff talked about how God had worked in his life through his illness, and the video concluded with Jeff encouraging the viewers to appreciate what they had, because it could be lost in the blink of an eye.

The part that made me sob were the pictures of Jeff from the time he was a baby through his school days and up through his illness. I had forgotten that Frank had asked Mom and me for pictures; we had no idea he was planning on using them in the video. Frank wanted to let the audience get to know Jeff, in order to give his story a more personal impact. The music in the background added the dramatic effect that sent me over the edge. I could barely finish watching it without bawling. Even Clark cried, leaving Jeff quite proud.

Frank had done an amazing job not only showing the transformation Jeff had gone through, but chronicling the changes our entire family had gone through. My sadness compounded as I wondered what it must be like to view it from Jeff's perspective, to put something like this together never being able to see it. The video was such a reminder of how something like this could happen to just anyone.

The following Sunday, I gave Pastor Bill a copy of the video and asked him to watch it. Over the past few months, Jeff and I had mentioned it in passing, so he wasn't surprised by my request. Pastor Bill was the jovial type, and even though he was only in his thirties, he was well respected even by the older folks of our church. He assured us that he would view it and get back to us with his feedback.

Not expecting to hear back for at least a few days, perhaps even a week, I was quite shocked when Pastor Bill called that evening. He asked to meet with Jeff and me the following day, adding that he had a plan about what he wanted to do with the video.

"Jeff, Jeff," I whooped as I raced down the stairs.

"What's wrong?" he asked.

"Pastor Bill just called, and he wants to meet with us tomorrow at ten."

Lacking confidence, Jeff asked, "Did he watch the video?"

"Yes, and he said that he has an idea about how he wants to use it." My heart was beating as fast as I was talking.

As Jeff finally embraced my excitement, his puffy cheeks were lifted by his smile. Quiet for a moment, he abruptly sat up straight, and his nose wrinkled as he tried to keep a straight face. "Well, guess I gotta get myself ready for the big day. I better get my toothbrush out and find my deodorant. It is my big debut, after all."

We laughed and rejoiced. Jeff's dream of inspiring more than just a few volunteers at a time looked as if it was coming to fruition. We both had trouble getting to sleep that night and were up early the next day to get Jeff ready.

Excited but nervous, Jeff jabbered the entire drive to Pastor Bill's office. The office secretary warmly greeted us and invited us to have a seat while we waited for Pastor Bill to finish his other meeting. The lobby was as quiet as a library, with the exception of Jeff's foot tapping against the linoleum floor. I pressed my hand against his bobbing knee, but that only temporarily stopped the annoying sound.

Pastor Bill finally opened his office door, shook hands with the couple leaving, and then invited us to come in. "Hi, guys. Sorry to keep you waiting."

"It's OK. I don't have to be back to work right away," Jeff teased.

Pastor Bill chuckled, giving Jeff a friendly pat on the back as he passed through the door.

Jeff and I sat next to each other, across the large wooden desk from Pastor Bill. A five-by-seven family photo, a calendar, a small plant, and box of tissues were neatly placed near the corner closest to us.

Pastor Bill pulled himself up to the desk, his clasped hands resting on top of a black, worn Bible. "I appreciate you guys coming down on such short notice. I'm sure you have a pretty busy schedule."

"I'm grateful you took your time to meet with us," Jeff said.

"I'm mainly here for moral support," I said.

"And to make sure I didn't crash the car driving here," Jeff said.

Pastor Bill and I both laughed. Humor was Jeff's go-to when he felt the need to break the ice, especially when he was feeling stressed.

Still amused, Pastor Bill asked, "Were you always so quick-witted?"

"No, not really. I wanted to be, but my brother Terry got that gene, I guess."

I nodded in agreement.

Pastor Bill playfully slapped his hand on the desk. "Joking aside, I gotta tell ya that I was really moved by your video."

Jeff modestly grinned. "Thank you, but it was my friend Frank who did all the hard work."

"That may be true, but it's your story that I wanted to talk to you about today," he said. Jeff lifted his chin slightly, tilting his ear toward Pastor Bill, listening for him to continue. "So what I would like to do is show the video, and then have you come up on stage and share your testimony with the congregation." Pastor Bill sat back in his chair, giving Jeff a moment to digest the idea.

Hidden from view, I squeezed Jeff's knee, excited by the thought that he could share his story with the two hundred people who attended our church on any given Sunday.

"That'd be great..." Jeff hesitated. "But—I ain't gonna lie—the idea of being in front of that many people sort of freaks me out. I can't do it unless Tammy's up there with me."

"I'd be happy to be there with you. This is exactly what you've been praying about," I said.

"I'll go along with whatever makes you the most comfortable, Jeff," Pastor Bill said. "So are you available this Sunday? I thought it would a perfect message, since it's Thanksgiving time."

Jeff squirmed in his chair and looked in my direction. "Are we available?"

"I believe so, but even if something's on the calendar, I'll change it. I mean, this is your big break—the debut of your Sack Lunch Sunday mission," I said, my arm resting across his shoulders.

"Well, I better practice my Stevie Wonder impression." Jeff bobbed his head side to side. "I'll set up a tin can and see if I can collect some sympathy donations."

Pastor Bill burst out laughing.

"You are awful, Jeff," I admonished halfheartedly.

Jeff's tension appeared to have dissipated, and he seemed to grasp that it was time to get serious. "Sorry, I'll stop."

"It was funny, though," Pastor Bill said, gracefully shifting the subject. "I would sure like to hear your testimony, if I could."

Jeff sat up a little straighter and started his story from when he was ten years old, sharing about his health issues and how he and I used to pray together when we were teenagers. He recounted his experience helping with the youth program, as well as the times when he wasn't involved with church at all. Pastor Bill and I attentively listened as Jeff openly shared how he sometimes felt abandoned by God, as well as rescued by him.

Moved by Jeff's words, Pastor Bill wiped his moist eyes. "God is good, isn't he?" he stated with conviction.

"He is indeed," I said, sniffling.

Pastor Bill continued. "I'm excited for the congregation to hear you speak on Sunday, Jeff. Thank you for being so flexible and willing to do this on such short notice."

We stood up, and he shook hands with Pastor Bill. "See you on Sunday," Jeff said.

Unusually early for a Sunday, footsteps and drawers opening and closing interrupted my plans to sleep in. The robotic voice from Jeff's talking clock announced that it was four o'clock. I turned the volume down on my bedside monitor, hoping that Jeff would be able to go back to sleep. Unable to fall back to sleep myself, I went downstairs to check on him.

I opened Jeff's bedroom door and was surprised to see him digging through his shirt drawer. "Hey, you all right?"

"Yeah. I couldn't sleep, so I figured I'd straighten out my drawers."

"All right, then. Well, since it's only four thirty, I'm gonna go back and lie down for a while."

"OK. Sorry for waking you. I'll try to be quiet."

He never did go back to bed, and neither did I. We ended up spending the wee hours of the morning discussing his church presentation. I listened patiently as he wondered how many people would show up, how many donations we might collect, whether he would forget what it was he wanted to share, and whether or not he would have an impact on the people in the audience.

My parents joined Clark, the girls, and some of our friends in the front row of the church. The exchange of pleasantries, joyful squeals of children as they saw their friends, and rattling of metal chairs as the congregation got seated nearly drowned out the band playing in the background.

We met Pastor Bill in his office, and he said a quick prayer with Jeff and me before the service started. Jeff's sweaty hand gripped my arm as we walked up the aisle and up the four steps onto the stage and took our seats near the side of the pulpit. We were only minutes away from the answers to many of the questions Jeff had wondered about early in the morning.

Leaning into my shoulder, Jeff whispered, "Sounds like there's lots of people. Can you see Mom and Dad?"

"Yeah, they're sitting with everyone in the front row. They're at your two o'clock."

He looked slightly to the right, in their general direction, and smiled.

"They waved at us," I said.

The worship leader invited the congregation to rise to their feet and join him in singing a hymn.

"How many people are here?" Jeff whispered a little louder, his face pressed into my ear.

"The seats are full. Probably about two hundred and fifty, I bet."

He smiled and leaned back into his seat, tapping his foot to the music.

The music ended, and Pastor Bill moved to the pulpit. I saw people glance at Jeff and me and then whisper to one another as Pastor Bill gave a brief overview of Jeff's story. Several of my friends smiled and nodded. I felt nervous for Jeff but excited.

Pastor Bill gestured his hand in our direction. "I now would like you to meet this amazing man and hear his incredible testimony. Please welcome Jeff Longley."

Loud applause erupted as I led Jeff toward a pair of chairs at the front of the stage. The tech guy tapped on the wireless microphone before placing it in Jeff's hand.

Jeff held the microphone near his lips. "Thank you for coming today. For those of you who might not know, this is my sister, Tammy. She's my security blanket up here." He smiled nervously.

"I'd like to start by telling you a little about my life and my testimony, and then I guess we are going to see a video I made about my mission to feed the homeless of Seattle. After the service, we'll stick around in case you have any questions."

Jeff spent twenty minutes briefly talking about his childhood and then about his illness and blindness. As he shared, sniffles and occasional muffled chatter filtered through the otherwise quiet auditorium. He talked calmly and without much emotion, just matter-of-factly. Yet his words held the attention of most everyone listening.

"Pastor Bill asked me to share with you my Christian walk. As I said, I was first introduced to God by my sister, and it has been a rocky path, for sure." He paused, took a sip of water, and coughed a few times as it went down wrong. "Don't rush out; I'm not gonna croak up here." He cleared his throat. "Just choked on a little sip of water."

Laughter erupted amid a few sympathetic murmurs.

His smile dissipated as he squeezed his eyes shut, searching his thoughts, and then he continued confidently. "Well, I feel like I have two lives to compare to—before surgery and after surgery. Before, I wouldn't have thought about other people as much, except at holidays. I didn't take the time to make a phone call or just stop by for a visit. I saw some family only at Christmas or a funeral. It's the same with my Christian walk. I'd go to church, pray once in a while, and read my Bible occasionally. I'd drive right by the homeless people or just look the other way. I didn't think about my faith as an action."

He again paused and took a sip of water. Sitting up taller, projecting his voice a little louder, he spoke with humble conviction.

"I was pretty inconsiderate and selfish. I was always depressed and negative, for no real, valid reason. Actually, now I have real reason to feel depressed, but through Christ I don't struggle with that as much. I used to go crazy over little things like being cut off on the freeway, losing my wallet, or misplacing my keys. But now I know that frustration over that stuff is such a waste of energy. I never really liked myself before, and now I like myself a whole lot better."

He paused and took a deep breath. "In fact, I know that if I could see, I wouldn't do half of what I do now, and it certainly wouldn't have the impact. My strengths and attitude come from God. I wish I knew back then what I know now—that it feels much better to be kind, generous, and considerate, and that it's very special when people return the kindness. I have so many new friends and much closer relationships than before, probably because I never gave of myself before. Life is too short, and it doesn't need to be so complicated."

"Amen," a man said.

"Oh yeah—preach it," a woman shouted simultaneously.

A lump in my throat and fighting back tears, I avoided direct eye contact with my close friends, but out of the corner of my eye, I could see some of them, and others, dabbing their eyes with tissue.

Uninhibited, Jeff concluded. "My goal is to influence others to make changes in their lives without having to suffer like I have; I want my actions to be an example and a reminder that people can change. I would like to encourage others who might have a disability to think outside the box. I used to be constrained by my hopelessness and negative thoughts and was in my own little world, so I know what it's like. I just want to give others the joy I have now—not to mention the purpose. I mostly want to leave *you* with my faith…it's all I have that means anything. My faith in God has given me the ability to get through this journey with a smile and laughter. He has carried me through this entire challenging time. I give full credit to him for changing me, because I seldom have to work hard to have this attitude. It is clearly a gift from God—one available for everyone. God has truly opened my eyes."

Pastor Bill came up on stage; he stood next to Jeff and placed his hand on his shoulder. He asked the congregation to bow their heads as he said a prayer for Jeff. He finished, and loud applause filled the room as Jeff and I walked offstage.

We sat in the back while the video was being shown on the large screen. Jeff whispered, "This is going pretty good, don't ya think?"

"Yeah. You did great up there." I squeezed his hand.

Applause filled the room at the end of the video. Some people turned around and glanced toward Jeff, smiling warmly, while others were sniffling and drying their eyes. A few people eagerly left their chairs early to come shake Jeff's hand, and some even shared their own stories with us.

"That was beautiful," a lady in her sixties tearfully said, squeezing Jeff's hand. "My son has cancer, and it's been real hard for me to talk to him about it. You have really helped me see what God can do through this process."

"Well, thank you. That means a lot. Like I said earlier, I can't take the credit. If your son ever needs someone to talk with, I would be glad to meet up with him," Jeff said.

"Thank you. I will certainly share that with him." She moved on so the others in line could talk to Jeff.

A middle-aged man approached Jeff next. "Hello, Jeff. My name is Don…" His voice cracked. "I can't thank you enough for sharing your story. I really needed to hear your message."

"I appreciate that, Don."

"I especially liked what you said about not just giving the homeless people the leftover canned foods that you didn't like or wouldn't eat," Don said.

Jeff nodded. "Yeah, I'll never be that kind of giver again. If I don't eat it, they won't have to eat it either. That's why I really enjoy giving them food that I would miss if I were homeless, like pizza, cookies, and candy bars."

Don shook Jeff's hand, then mine. "I sure look forward to helping at the next Sack Lunch Sunday," he said just before walking away.

I enjoyed listening to Jeff talk with all the people who waited in line. It seemed, at least for that moment, that all his suffering was not in vain. He was making a difference, and I was proud of him. I was grateful to be able to watch it happen.

CHAPTER 50

Cherished Gifts

Jeff's testimony and video presentation were greatly successful, not only in terms of the money and food donations, but in the way people's lives were touched by his story. We received several calls from people who wanted Jeff to know how his testimony had impacted them. Others called to find out how they could help make and deliver the lunches to the homeless people.

Despite the positive impact Jeff was having on others, he was secretly falling into depression. This was his third Christmas since his diagnosis, and he believed it would be his last. Based on his symptoms, I agreed. But then again, I'd been making that kind of prediction for the last three years, so I guess I really didn't know what the next year held. I prayed for wisdom, feeling conflicted by the joy of making it special and the sorrow of its potential finality.

Jeff was resting on his bed while I was sorting through his clothes, making room for the new sweat pants and shirts I planned on giving him for his birthday and Christmas. He had gained about twenty pounds from the steroids and other medications, and his clothes were no longer comfortable.

"Thanks for helping me get organized," Jeff said sincerely.

"You're welcome."

Subdued, he said, "We can hand out the clothes that are still in good shape to the homeless people next Sunday. They would probably really appreciate having some warm sweats."

"Good plan. We have about two green garbage bags so far," I said.

"Hey, since you're in my closet, will you see if you can find my box of collectibles. I remember you said you put them up top somewhere."

I reached up to the top shelf and pulled down a brown medium-size box. "Yep, they're right here."

I set the full box on the foot of his bed as Jeff sat up, waiting for me to open the box. "What do you want in the box?" I asked, pulling out the crumpled newspapers covering his things.

"Well, I've been doing a lot of thinking lately, and I decided that I want to give away some of my collectibles at Christmas. I mean, I still want you to buy the gifts I put on my list, but these will be something a little special," he said.

A rush of sadness made it difficult for me to speak. "That sounds..." But my words died before I could finish. All I could do was sob, sitting next to him on the bed. He wrapped his arm around my shoulders, sniffling a little too, but he focused on just letting me be sad. I knew from my professional experiences that giving away personal items was one of the ways people found closure during their dying process. I was even more convinced that it really would be Jeff's last Christmas, the last time I would receive one of his well-chosen gifts.

He patted my shoulder as I slowly began regaining my composure. "Sorry 'bout that," I said, sniffling. "I wasn't expecting you to say that."

"It's OK. I know this is hard on you," he said, still lovingly patting my shoulder. "Especially since I've been so down the past few days."

"You can't help it. The holidays always seem to make grief feel worse."

"It sure has mine. I think being blind makes it even so much worse."

I sat upright and took in a deep breath. The sadness slightly dissipated, leaving me puffy-eyed but ready to help Jeff sort through his things, and maybe his thoughts.

He continued. "It frustrates me that I can't see all the decorations, lights, and presents under the tree. I remember how fun it was to go shopping for the perfect gift. It seems like my memories have been making me more depressed lately."

I reached into the box and unwrapped one thing at a time while he talked.

"I've even been missing seeing you guys. It seems like I'm having a harder time remembering what everyone looks like. It sort of makes me panic." He sighed. "I know I don't want to live like this, but then I feel guilty about complaining. It's hard, 'cause I have all my needs taken care of, yet it's hard for me to enjoy things. I've been trying to remind myself to be grateful that I don't have it worse. I mean, I could be a quadriplegic, and then I wouldn't be able to wipe my own butt or even scratch myself," he said seriously.

"It's normal to have sad days, and even days that you feel sorry for yourself. You don't have very many of them, so give yourself a break," I said as I took the last thing out of the box.

"I know." He tapped his hand across the bed, searching for his treasures. "So what all was in the box?"

"Let's see…there are nine collectible Ron Lee–Warner Brothers cartoon statues, a Darth Vader mask, a couple of key chains, three Disney statues, and a folder with your autograph collection."

I handed him one of the statues, and he rubbed his fingers around the character mounted on a small chunk of marble. "Let me guess…this is Scooby-Doo."

"Yep, you got it."

"I've been thinking a lot about who would get each statue, and I plan on giving Chelsey this one, since she worries a lot."

"That's perfect," I said, handing him another one.

His fingers methodically moved around the yellow sombrero. "This is Speedy Gonzales." He smiled confidently.

"Right again."

"This one is definitely for you." He snickered. "It reminds me of how you zip around everywhere."

"I can't argue with—"

"But you can't have it until Christmas."

Lightheartedly, I said, "That's what you say, but I might just sneak it and put it on the mantel. You'd never know."

Our moods a little brighter, Jeff rattled off who would be getting which of his prized possessions and why.

Dad would get Yosemite Sam, since he was a tough guy. Mom would get the Martian, since she liked outer-space stuff. Clark, the rooster, since he kept chickens in the backyard. Kendra would get the frog because she would sit patiently although not always quietly. He hadn't completely decided on who would get his other treasures, but contemplating it seemed to bring him a little joy.

Toward the end of the week, Jeff's depression lifted as he focused on the homeless project. He was excited to be handing out clothes along with the lunches. He even bought candy canes and chocolate bars to make things extra special. His attitude shifted from a feeling of hopelessness to one of excitement as he planned to buy gifts for a needy family, Tent City, and the Urban Rest Stop. He wanted to buy a tent for Tent City, gloves and rain ponchos for those at Pioneer Square, underclothes for the folks at Urban Rest Stop, walkie-talkies and a remote-control car for the kids he sponsored, and a day planner their mother wanted, adding in a coffee mug and gift certificate for Starbucks. He shared that he wished he could see their reactions as they opened their gifts, but regardless, he was so happy that he could bring a smile and some joy to someone else.

CHAPTER 51

Celebrations

THE THANKSGIVING HOMELESS PROJECT WAS a success, according to all of those who helped serve, as well as those who received. Our focus quickly shifted to finalizing plans for Jeff's thirty-fourth birthday, Christmas, then my and Clark's fifteenth anniversary.

Jeff chose to go out for a steak dinner with the family to celebrate what we all assumed would be his last birthday. Despite feeling achy, tired, and itchy from the steroids, he seemed to genuinely enjoy the day. He was especially happy that our parents had bought him the Bible on CD. He planned on listening to it from beginning to end.

One gift Jeff received on his birthday turned out to be from a "Secret Pal." The anonymous giver left a package on our parents' porch.

"Jeff." Mom's voice elevated with excitement. "I found a present on the front porch for you." Her words lingered as if in a song. She placed the blue-and-silver-wrapped box on his lap.

His eyebrows pinched together as he carefully ran his hands around the box, and then he shook it slightly. "Hmmm. I wonder what it is."

"I don't know. It just says it's from your secret pal. Hurry, open it."

"OK. OK."

He ripped the Christmas wrap off the package, opened the flaps of the small cardboard box, and then pulled out two jars.

"Whoever it is must know that you love strawberry jam," Mom said.

"That's awesome. I wonder who it was?"

Touched, she said, "I have no idea, but what a fun way to make someone feel special."

The next morning Dad opened the front door to get the newspaper. "Jeff, there's another package from your secret pal."

"Really? What is it?" Jeff asked, more puzzled than the day before.

Mom and Dad waited eagerly as Jeff opened a Christmas-themed bag. "Smells like chocolate-chip cookies," he guessed, lifting four stacks of cookies from the bag.

"I'm pretty sure your pal wants you to share those with us," Dad teased.

"Is your name on the tag?" Jeff said, biting into a cookie. "Just kidding—you can have one. Wow, this person sure knows how to bake," he said, cookie crumbs spilling out of his mouth.

Mom and I called around to family and friends, trying to get hints of who Jeff's secret pal might be. Our sly attempts to get a confession failed. We were in the dark, just like Jeff.

The next morning, there was a package on my front porch, this one a little bigger than the last two. I brought it in and set it on the table, resisting the temptation to open it before Jeff woke up.

Hearing a little rustle from Jeff's room, I excitedly flung open his door. "Finally. You're awake."

"Barely," he said, still groggy.

"You know me; I'm not so good at not peeking at presents," I said, holding the present over his bed. "Your secret pal left something for you."

"What? Really?" He sprang up, instantly fully awake. "They came all the way out here? Now I'm even more confused."

Playfully bouncing up and down on the bed like a little kid, I said, "Do you want me to help you open it?"

"I think I can do it." Purposely moving slowly to prolong my anticipation, he carefully unwrapped the round tub. "What is it?"

"Oh, bummer. Just some dog bones for Rusty."

"Really? Don't be lying—that's evil, and God will get even for me."

"OK, OK…" I twisted the lid. "Smell this…"

He took a big whiff. "Oh, yeah. I love me some peanut butter cups." Licking his lips, he grabbed a candy from the jar.

Baffled, I said, "One thing we know for sure is that they know what you like to eat."

"It has to be someone who's around a lot. I wonder if it's Midge? Or maybe Allison? It could even be Brenda."

Jeff rattled off several other names, as did I, trying to figure out who would not only know what he liked, but someone who would travel the thirty minutes between both houses.

The final gift from Jeff's secret pal was left on my front porch Christmas morning. The wrapped box had a sealed card tucked under a large red bow. I just knew that the secret pal had signed it this time, but Terry and Jeff had spent the night on Christmas Eve at Mom and Dad's house, as they did every year. Since I was hosting Christmas Day, I would have to wait for them to arrive before my curiosity would be satisfied.

"Let the Festivus begin," Terry playfully hollered as he flung open the front door.

Dad, Mom, and Jeff trailed behind, chanting, "Happy Festivus."

"Glad you finally made it." I took Jeff's coat. "I can hardly wait for you to open your gift and find out who's your secret pal."

"Me too," he said, rubbing his hands together. "But you'll have to wait, because I want you guys to open the gifts I bought before I open mine."

"Seriously? The suspense is killing me," I said.

The girls eagerly helped bring in the last of the presents from the car. We all gathered in the living room so we could open our gifts before the rest of the relatives arrived. We traditionally shared presents with our immediate families and then played a gift exchange game with everyone else.

Jeff leaned in close to me. "I'm really excited for you to open my gift. I really think you're gonna love it."

Mom handed me a flat, rectangular-shaped present with a tag indicating it was from Jeff.

"Nobody needs to tell me twice to open a present," I said. Everyone's eyes focused on me as I ripped the wrapping paper, revealing a framed picture.

My mouth fell open. "Did you paint this?"

Bobbing his head excitedly, Jeff said, "Yep. Mom helped me get set up, but I painted it by myself."

"Turn it around so we can see it," Chelsey said.

I held up the colorful wax painting. Wiping my eyes, I laid my hand across my heart.

Mom's tear-filled eyes connected with mine. "It's his first painting."

"Aw. Thanks, Jeff." I hugged him. "That really means a lot." I studied it carefully, surprised Jeff had not only been able to paint it, but also that he could keep a secret from me.

Smirking, Jeff said, "I hope you like it. I couldn't do art before, but at least now I can't be disappointed with it, since I can't see it."

Once everyone else opened their gifts, I passed out the "special gifts" Jeff had chosen to give each of them. He happily explained his reasoning behind who received which statue. Dad choked up as he opened his, which brought everyone to tears.

"Sorry, guys…I didn't mean to upset you." Jeff's lip curled upward. "I was just trying to get rid of my junk so you won't have to worry about it when I'm dead."

Without missing a beat, Terry said, "I'm sure I can sell mine for a small fortune. Maybe I'll even be able to retire early."

The sadness quickly dissipated amid the laughter, as so often was the case when things got too emotional.

Finally, it was time for Jeff to open the gift from his secret pal. Sitting next to him on the couch, Mom opened the card and read it out loud. "Merry Christmas, Jeff. I hope you enjoyed this little game as much as I did. You have brought so much joy and happiness to all of us, and I wanted to give you back just a little of that joy. You are loved, and I hope you have the best day ever. Love, Cindy."

"Wow. That's so nice." Jeff wiped his cheeks with his sweatshirt. "As busy as she is, I would never have guessed she could find the time. She is so wonderful." He opened the box and pulled out a cozy blanket.

Cindy had pulled a fast one over all of us. She would be over later in the day, so Jeff was happy he could share his gratitude in person.

"Oh, wait," Jeff said excitedly. "I think there's one more thing for Tammy outside."

Perplexed, I looked at Mom. She shrugged, grinning. "You better go see."

As I stood up, the girls jumped up and down, making it obvious that they knew about my surprise. Clark and Dad both shrugged and followed me out the door. Mom led Jeff out to the porch. Blankets covered a very large rectangular item lying on the driveway in front of the garage door. I had absolutely no idea what it could be.

"Open it, open it," Kendra yelled, still jumping up and down.

My heart was racing as I lifted a corner of the blanket and saw a printed picture on the box. I ripped the blankets completely off. Taking a step back, I stuttered, "No…no…way. Is…is…is this really what's in here?"

"It sure is," Jeff said joyfully. "Mom and Dad went in on it with me. We know how much you've always wanted one."

Jumping up and down, I couldn't help but throw a few fist pumps in the air. I loved playing air hockey, and now I had my very own table. It would take up a huge spot in the rec room, but I didn't care.

I cried happily and gratefully. "Thank you so much. I can't believe you got that for me. You know me so well. But two secrets, Jeff. How did you do it?" I gave him and my parents each a tight hug.

"What's hilarious is that you thought my painting was so great. It was meant to be a gag gift." Jeff laughed.

I begged my dad and Clark to set the hockey table up so I could play against everyone who was coming over for Christmas Day. They agreed, knowing full well that I wouldn't have settled for anything less. It was probably my best Christmas present ever, certainly the best since I was a little kid.

The Christmas festivities behind us, Clark and I looked forward to our anniversary getaway. I had some apprehension about being six hours away from Jeff, but my need to get a break from everything was greater than my worry. Jeff encouraged me to trust that he would be OK, yet I could tell he was a little nervous about my being so far away too. He reminded me several times to call and check in and to be really careful on the snowmobiles, especially since we had never been on them before.

While the girls were excited to be spending two nights with their friends, Clark was looking forward to time alone with me. Not usually one for weekend getaways, he genuinely seemed excited for our little adventure.

We drove to Winthrop, a small town in eastern Washington where the winter wonderland scenery was magical. Colorful Christmas lights adorned the doors and windows of all the little shops. Light poles wrapped with red and green lights and hooks holding wreaths sparkled from one end of town to the other. Sharp white mountains surrounded the little snow-covered town. Puffs of smoke drifted up from individual chimneys dotting the mountainside. We crept up the slick, windy road until we finally arrived at the quaint log lodge. The breathtaking view from the top of the mountain immediately relieved me of any and all stress. As we opened the door to our cabin, a waft of wood smoke drifted past us. By design the rustic room offered little in the way of electronic distractions, as it was sparsely furnished with a four-post log bed, two bedside tables, a cozy couch, and a coffee table. Beautiful river rock bordered the crackling wood fireplace, an inviting setting for sure.

"Wait—is there no TV?" Clark asked. His brow wrinkled.

"I thought I told you that." I covered my devilish grin with my hand.

"I don't think you did." He shook his head, fighting off disappointment. "So what are we supposed to do?"

"Well, I was hoping we could spend some time actually talking, relax by the fire, maybe take a walk. You know"—I playfully threw my hands in the air—"we can do whatever we want."

Peering out the window at the line of icicles hanging from the roof, he took a deep breath and then exhaled. "Well, it's gonna be different, if nothing else."

I gave him a hug; he forced a smile and hugged me back.

Clark's idea of relaxation typically included working in the yard and then kicking back in front of the television. Mine was to take hikes, talk by the fire, or maybe watch a football game. I never was a fan of watching much else on television, but I forced myself to so I could connect with Clark outside our coffee times.

It took a few hours for him to adjust his expectations. We enjoyed a nice lunch at the lodge and then returned to our room.

"I'm feeling better now that I have a little food in my stomach. Would ya like some coffee?" Clark asked in his humble apologetic tone. He didn't usually apologize for being grumpy; instead, he would offer to make coffee.

"Yes, please." I happily accepted his peace offering as I gazed at the flickering red embers.

He set two steaming ceramic cups on the table and sat next to me on the couch. "I must admit, this place is pretty cozy."

"It's nice to not have to be on for anyone. I figured that we could just hang out here the rest of the afternoon and evening, since we have plans tomorrow," I said, still mesmerized by the fire.

"I like that plan." He raised his coffee cup for a toast, and I tapped mine against it.

Since Clark wasn't a fan of playing in the snow, I arranged for us to try something new: snowmobiling. Leaving the rental office, Clark followed a short distance behind me to the trailhead. The smell of gas and the high-pitched whine from the engines were slight intrusions to the peaceful trail. Thick snowflakes blanketed us as we tore through the woods up the mountain. We finally stopped near the top, turned off the obnoxiously loud machines, and just enjoyed the peaceful silence for a while. It felt good to be away from everything and everyone. As the cold started to get to us, we raced each other back down the mountain and to the rental office. Our two-hour adventure was a success: no damage to the machines, and no injuries. Win-win.

We returned to our cabin with just enough time to get ready for our dinner reservation. We sat in the dimly lit, elegant dining room to share our anniversary dinner at a corner table. Through the window adjacent to our table we could see the reddish sun setting behind the snowcapped mountain. The restaurant was buzzing with people talking and laughing, yet I felt as though we were all alone. Nobody needed anything from us, except the waitress, who asked what we wanted for dinner.

We had a chance to reminisce over the past few years as well as contemplate what the future might hold. For once, the conversation did not focus only on Jeff, as we dreamed about time as a family and plans for the girls. It was a beautiful weekend, the perfect end to a good holiday season.

CHAPTER 52

Three-Year Anniversary

SOON AFTER CLARK AND I returned from Winthrop, the girls' school break was over, and I refocused my attention on Jeff's worsening condition. His pain had increased again, and his skin looked dusky, with purplish-red stretch marks streaking across his abdomen and the sides of his torso. I called Dr. Smith asking for advice on how to manage Jeff's symptoms. As usual, he prescribed the same generic statement: "I'm not sure what you want me to do. The cancer is probably causing the changes."

Yet the urine test we'd had done a month earlier hadn't shown significant changes, which made his statement all the more confusing. I asked him to do an MRI, but he didn't think it was necessary, since the results wouldn't change his opinion.

I understood that we wouldn't do much with the results from a big-picture standpoint, but I needed to know what, if anything, was actually going on so we could figure out how to manage his day-to-day issues. We were giving Jeff a lot of pain medications for what we assumed was cancer-related pain. However, if the pain was unrelated to the cancer, then perhaps it was treatable. Or as the hospice nurses suggested, perhaps the pain medications, steroids, and itch medications could be making things worse. But if the tumor was in fact growing, then the path we were on made sense.

Not to mention that for the past three years, Jeff's condition had been misdiagnosed on several occasions, so I wanted to be as thorough as possible. Besides, the results might give my family some peace about Jeff's future.

A week passed. Frustrated that I didn't know how best to help my brother, I called Dr. Smith, yet again, to persuade him to schedule an MRI.

"Hello, Tammy. The nurse said you needed to speak to me urgently."

"Yes. Jeff is in more pain, and I really think it would help to know if the tumors are growing. Please, can you order a final MRI so we can know for sure what is causing the pain?" I begged.

He cleared his throat. "As I said last week, Tammy, I only order MRIs when I can do something with the results, like remove a tumor or fix something," he said sharply.

"Dr. Smith, I don't believe you have any idea how difficult the past three years have been on Jeff, as well as the rest of us. When you decided to do the surgery, you gave us a five-year prognosis. And then, after surgery, you changed it to six weeks. Not only did the surgery leave him blind, but every day he has experienced challenging and painful symptoms. Do you not remember that at the year mark, you asked Jeff to let you do an MRI for your research project, and he agreed? And now you can't do this for us so we know for certain that it's not something else causing these symptoms?" I took a breath, and he remained silent.

I continued. "It's so difficult"—my voice cracked—"not knowing how long this will go on, or how much more difficult things will get before Jeff passes." I swallowed hard. "I don't think I'm asking for too much."

A moment of silence passed, followed by a heavy breath. Then, softly, Dr. Smith spoke. "I'm truly sorry this turned out the way it has, and that it has been so difficult. Jeff is very lucky to have all of you caring for him. Let me see what I can do, and I will get back to you."

Either Dr. Smith had forgotten we had honored his previous request for an MRI, he was apologizing in his own way for his mistakes, or I had finally simply annoyed him into considering the tests. Regardless, I was pleased.

"Thank you. I can't tell you how important this is to all of us. We just want to know what's going on." I pushed down the urge to cheer.

"You're welcome, and I will call you in the next few days," he said kindly.

Fortunately for us, Dr. Smith ordered the MRI, a urine test, and a blood draw a few days later. We completed all the tests, and the only thing left to do was wait for answers.

The day after the third anniversary of Jeff's surgery, I received the call from Dr. Smith. Though I was eager to get the results from Jeff's tests as soon as possible, I was sort of relieved that he didn't call on Valentine's Day—that would have been too weird.

"Hello, Tammy," Dr. Smith said in a soft voice. "Well, the MRI showed that Jeff's tumors have doubled in size, and they're bumping against his organs."

My heart raced. "OK."

"His blood work is not looking good either. His testosterone and cortisol levels are very high, and there is really nothing we can do to correct them."

"I understand. How long do you think he has left?"

He spoke slowly, struggling to find the right words. "At this rate, I expect less than six months. Some of the tumors will start to interfere with his organs, and that is what will take him."

"Thank you. I—I'm grateful that we have some answers. At least we now know for sure that our focus needs to remain on managing his pain."

"You're welcome, and please don't hesitate to reach out to me if you need anything—" His voice caught abruptly. "I truly am sorry things turned out as they did."

"Thank you, Dr. Smith."

I hung up the phone, unexpectedly stunned by the news, yet also relieved that I wasn't missing something that could have been causing Jeff's symptoms. Even though I realized that I had zero control, knowledge was power, and I felt a bit more empowered now that I had a better understanding of what was happening. At the same time, I felt my heart beating in my stomach.

Sitting on the edge of my bed, I called my mom and told her the news.

"Well, I guess we just have to keep on going with what we've been doing already. All we can do is make the best of every day."

I was surprised by her calm response. "I know. But it still hit me hard," I said.

She continued, ignoring my words. "I feel a sense of relief that at least we know what is causing everything."

I resisted the urge to cry. When we hung up, I felt sorry for myself. It was great that my mom was being logical, but I needed her to ask me how I was feeling about everything. Some days I just couldn't be strong for everyone. Sometimes it would be nice to be asked how I was doing and what I might need.

Downstairs, Jeff and Christine were having their weekly meeting. I figured it was a good time to tell Jeff about the call from Dr. Smith. That way, Christine could also relay the information to the nurses when she got back to the office.

Christine's soothing voice met my ears as I entered the rec room, where they were sitting. Jeff and Rusty were curled up at the end of the couch, while Christine sat in the recliner near them.

Subdued, I sat down next to Jeff. "Hi, guys."

I patted Jeff on the leg.

"Hello," Christine said. A warm smile spread across her face. "How ya doing?"

"Hi," Jeff said. "What's up?"

"Well..." I cleared my throat. "I just got off the phone with Dr. Smith." Alerted, Jeff snapped his face toward me. "He said that the tests showed that the tumors have doubled in size, and"—Jeff took a deep breath in through his nose, exhaling slowly as I softly continued—"the blood work also shows the cancer is growing aggressively."

Christine lowered her eyes as she nodded at me.

"Did he say how much time I have?" Jeff asked, his voice flat and emotionless.

"He said probably six months or so," I said. "But who really knows."

"Yeah, only God knows," Jeff said assertively, and then he paused as if deep in thought.

Christine waited quietly for a moment before she spoke, leaning toward him a bit. "What are you thinking, Jeff?"

"Well, at least we know what's causing all my symptoms, and we have some sort of measuring mark," he said calmly.

Christine smiled softly. "Uh-huh."

Jeff's brow narrowed as he gathered his thoughts, and then he continued. "It's like my mind is in a whirlwind, like in a dream state. The emotions don't feel real."

My hand rested on his shoulder as I waited quietly for his thoughts to become words.

He said, "I wonder what tomorrow will bring. I know that God tells us to live for today, but it isn't so easy."

Well-practiced at active listening and asking probing questions, Christine empathized. "It really is a challenge, Jeff. Sometimes this type of news causes people to ponder what they want to accomplish with the time they have left, or what they might want say to those they love."

Skillfully, she stopped just short of turning her observation into a suggestion or a question. No pressure, just an opportunity to share if Jeff wanted to.

And he did. "I know I want to accomplish one thing for sure—I want everyone to learn what I've learned. I want them to be reassured so that when it's their time to go, they'll know where they're going. There's no way out of it. We all die and go somewhere, and we have the option to make the choice as to where we wanna go."

Rusty disrupted Jeff's monologue as he repositioned himself, eventually resting his head on Jeff's thigh. Once his dog was settled, Jeff sat up tall, and his voice became livelier as he continued. "I'm excited to be in heaven. I'm eager to meet Jesus, the master himself. I won't be reading his words anymore; I'll be walking with the author. I'll be able to see again, and I'll finally be out of pain."

Feeling emotions bubble up inside me, I avoided speaking so I wouldn't interrupt Jeff's stream of thoughts.

Christine gently placed a hand on his shoulder. "You seem to have a real sense of peace."

"I do, for the most part. Right now, I'm counting my blessings for being able to take care of myself. I can still feed myself, dress myself, walk, and even wipe my own butt." He chuckled. "I've been in the place where I couldn't do that before, and I might get there again."

"Does that scare you?" Christine asked.

"Not really. I try not to focus on that part. Instead, I'm thankful for my comfort, my moments without pain, and for all my family. I try to remember that today I have food, shelter, and clothing. I remind myself and others that our loved ones are here and will likely be here tomorrow, though there is no guarantee. I remember how I took all this for granted, and I now I want to help others learn to be grateful without having to go through all that I am." He sighed deeply and then leaned back against the couch.

Christine reached across the end table and gently placed her hand on top of Jeff's. "Thank you for sharing your thoughts with us. I'm sure your sister would agree; you already have made an incredible impact on this world. Whatever you do from here forward is icing on the cake."

A weird mixture of sadness and joy swirled inside me. "You amaze me—your perspective seems so healthy."

"I agree," Christine said.

"Well, I can't take the credit; it's all God. I only hope and pray that these past three years that God has extended my life, has been an example of how God has changed my life. I hope that the people around me have realized that life is not to be taken for granted."

That night I heard Jeff talking into his recorder much longer than usual. He journaled for what felt like an hour.

"It is February 15, 2003.

"My three-year surgery anniversary was yesterday. It seems hard to imagine it has been that long. I was told that my cancer is raging full force; the tumors are double in size, and my blood work is way out of whack. The Cushing's disease is also back, which means my body continues to change. My stretch marks are back, I have general body aches, and now I have shivering episodes. I still have pain, and I'm more short of breath.

"I'm not sure if it was helpful to have them predict when I will die, even though I already had a sense that I have about six months, perhaps a year at the most. I wish I could describe what it's like knowing that you're dying—it's so unreal. There are days when my mind won't let me focus on anything, and

I even have a hard time praying. Some days it's hard to think about the cancer, family, or anything because when I start to really focus, my mind starts to wander. I think it's a gift from God that I can't focus too long on anything. Sometimes I feel like I'm on the verge of breaking down at any time, but then the feeling vanishes. While other times, I feel excited that I will soon meet all the people I have read about in the Bible, get to see my Grandma, and my friend Keith.

"The news has presented a new challenge—in that it's difficult to feel the family's emotional changes. I sense a lot of depression because this time is so different. I don't want anyone to blame God for my death, or wonder 'why him,' because we live in a fallen world. I don't want anyone to feel obligated to come visit me out of pity or guilt; I only want people around who want to be around. As my friend Keith once said, 'I don't want to be an altar for people to lay their guilt offerings upon.' I don't want people to feel sorry for me.

"After all, what would have been better—my old life or my new life? I have grown closer to God in these past three years than the thirty years prior to that. I didn't take the opportunity that I should have when I could see and wasn't sick. I would go to church sometimes and maybe read a few pages out of my Christian books, and that was it. I wasn't walking with him. I'm not perfect now, but I do hope that people can see something different in me. I want them to know that Christ can get them through anything.

"There is something that I can't explain. I lost everything I had—my job, my home, my car, my independence, my dignity, and my health. I don't prepare my own meals or go to work, and I am dependent on others. I was like a brand-new baby when I woke up in the dark—it was like I was reborn. I had to learn how to walk again, feed myself, bathe myself, dress myself, even how to wipe my own butt again. Yet I can maintain a positive attitude, smile, joke, and laugh. That is a supernatural thing; it is nothing I do. I'm not crazy—it is a gift from God, which makes it unbelievable to think that Jesus Christ doesn't exist. If someone would have asked me how I thought I would handle it if I was to wake up from the surgery blind and still sick, I would have told them I would likely kill myself. I had no idea that my life could be like it is; only God knew that.

"I am so grateful for God's gift and the relationships I have acquired. The growth of my relationship with my family and friends is unbelievable. God gave me a second chance, which is a rare opportunity. I hope that I really did live my life different this second time around. I tried to practice what I preached, or what Christ taught. I don't think I have any unresolved conflicts or other issues. I hope I used the time that God gave me wisely, and I will continue to use from today forward to impact people.

"The homeless ministry will continue, thanks to all the people who support it. The ministry isn't about me; it is about following Christ when he says we should give to the poor, love thy neighbor, and love your enemy. The people who participate in the Sack Lunch Sunday ministry are just as important as I am. I don't want anyone to think that I am the 'main guy,' because without everyone else's support, there would be no ministry. My life does have meaning now, even though it is shortened. I am pleased that I was able to use my life for some benefit. It not only helps the people we serve; it brings joy to all involved. I plan on leaving money for donations and to help people with food, bills, or other stuff. It may even inspire someone else to contribute, which then will create a trickle-down effect. Who knows how the little bit of money I leave will grow and what type of impact it may have.

"I am physically and mentally tired, so it's a positive thing that my suffering is coming to an end soon. I'm not struggling to save my own life; I am struggling to improve other people's life through my struggles. I also want to continue to improve my Christian walk and my relationship with Christ. It's not about religion; it's about a relationship. Christ is a real person, and although we can't see him or hear him, we can learn about him by what we read and experience. I read the whole New Testament, and now I'm trying to get through the Old Testament.

"I want to be remembered in good ways; not as someone who was in a crabby mood, depressed, or sad. I want people to smile when they look back on my journey. I hope that people will get something valuable from my experience—faith. Jesus made it possible for me to cope and find the positives in my situation. I did not do this on my own, for I didn't know it was even possible. That is not to say that I don't get gratification or a good feeling when I do what I do, but my focus isn't on me alone. I don't want the glory or to be patted on the back, because I am doing these things for Christ. That's all for now."

CHAPTER 53

Funeral Plans

It was an unusually nice spring morning, and the sun was beaming through the window onto Jeff's lap as he sat in his favorite chair listening to the television. "Is it nice outside?" he asked.

"Yeah. Can you feel the sun?" I asked, loud enough that he could hear me over the television.

"I thought it felt warm, but I wasn't sure. Maybe we could go for a walk or go swimming?"

"It's a great day to get out—not a cloud in the sky. Let's go for a swim and then go get coffee at the coffee shop," I said.

It had been a routine for us, and one that I had been missing since Jeff's condition deteriorated. He hadn't been interested in leaving the house, so it was encouraging to hear him ask to go outside.

Our swim was somewhat short, because Jeff's energy level dropped quickly after getting into the pool. As we were leaving the parking lot, he reminded me about our plan to go for coffee. When we got to the coffee shop, Jeff already had his mind made up as to what he would be drinking.

"I want one of those mocha ice drinks," he said.

"OK, and how about sitting outside, since it's so warm today?"

"Sounds good to me," Jeff said, looking content as I guided him to one of the hard iron chairs.

He scooted his chair up to the round wrought-iron table and propped his chin in the palm of his hand. He tilted his face toward the warmth of the sun as it seeped through his pale, balding head. Though his eyes could no longer see the bright rays washing over him, it was evident he remembered their warmth and comfort.

"Here's your drink," I said, interrupting his peaceful moment.

"Thanks, sis." He lifted the straw to his lips.

Sitting across from Jeff, I was suddenly struck with gratitude—gratitude for having a moment with my brother and for being able to look around and take in the beautiful surroundings. As the sun filtered down through the maple trees, a mixture of sunlight and shadows danced across our table. Pink buds and light-green leaves decorated the potted plants lining the patio. Wafts of fresh brewed coffee and pastries passed by us as people buzzed about their day.

"It is so nice outside today. I love spring days like this," I said.

"Yeah, me too. The sun feels so good. It makes everyone seem happier—I can hear it in their voices as they walk by," he said, with a tone of happiness in his voice.

After several minutes of small talk, Jeff said, "So you know I've been doing a lot of thinking since we got the results of my tests…"

"Uh-huh…" I said.

"Well, it made me realize that my clock really is ticking, and I better make sure all my stuff is in order."

"OK. I'm listening." My full attention was now on Jeff.

"So I've been thinking about the whole funeral thing we talked about before, and I realized that I want to have some input as to how it goes."

"That's awesome. I love that idea."

"I had some funny ideas about it last night." He tapped his index finger against his lips and then continued. "I mean, let's face it. Not everyone gets to participate in their own funeral. I feel sorta lucky," he said, trying to keep a straight face.

"That's true," I said, playing along. "It's a real privilege. So what'd you come up with?"

"Well, I figure I may as well have some fun with it, since I can't avoid it. So one thing I know for sure is that I want laughter, not just sadness. Mostly I don't want people to have to sit through a boring service, where everyone is crying. We need to make it light and add some humor," Jeff said.

"That might to be a bit challenging, since not everyone has our twisted sense of humor. But I guess since we've been able to laugh through the whole journey, we may as well smile at the end. I don't exactly know how we can do it, though. I mean, after all, it's not really a laughing matter that you're dead." I giggled, and so did Jeff.

He swallowed a sip of his mocha. "I've been thinking of some songs I want played, and I like that song by Sarah McLachlan, 'In the Arms of an Angel.' And for sure we need to play 'Thank You' by Ray Boltz."

"Yeah, I love both of those songs."

We took turns offering suggestions of other songs that might be fitting, and then, suddenly, Jeff got a huge grin on his face.

My tone deepened. "Oh dear. I can see it in your face—you're up to no good."

"I have the perfect song." Drumming his hand against the tabletop, he started humming the tune to the song "Another One Bites the Dust."

"No way," I admonished, trying to act serious. "We are not going to play that song at your funeral. Can you imagine how rude people would think we are for being so crass?"

Smirking, he said, "Hey, it's my funeral—you can just tell everyone I picked it out."

"That's not happening." I obnoxiously slurped the bottom of my coffee cup, trying to distract him.

Ignoring my halfhearted rejection, he started singing. "Another one bites the dust"—tap, tap, tap—"and another one's gone, and another one's gone..." He bobbed his head side to side, and his voice swelled. "Another one bites the dust."

Amused, people smiled as they passed our table.

"Jeff, stop—you're killing me," I pleaded. "And people are staring."

His belly was bouncing up and down as his words tumbled out. "Can you imagine what people would think..."

We cracked up even louder.

"Yeah. They'd think your family was crazy."

"In fact..." He paused, having difficulty forming words. "I wanna have it playing as people are walking out..." He took in a deep breath. "You know... so it uh...sticks in their memories."

I slapped the table, struggling to catch my breath. "I actually find the whole idea hilarious, but I'm not convinced it would be appropriate."

Jeff leaned his back against the chair. His face relaxing, he said, "Hey, if someone's offended, then we know they weren't around enough to know who I really am. I'm counting on you."

"We'll see. We gotta get going now." I acknowledged the onlookers with a smile and a nod as I guided Jeff back to the car.

Though Jeff was in pretty good spirits, the small outing had exhausted him and left him needing to sleep for a while after we got home. While he was napping, I called my mom to share his plan. We laughed about the idea and avoided any serious discussion about the topic of Jeff's funeral.

It had not been forgotten, however, and later that week when I was dropping Jeff off at Mom's house, she wasted no time bringing it up.

"So, Jeff, Tammy tells me you have some special music planned for your funeral?" Mom playfully asked.

"Well, I figured we may as well do things different all the way through to the end. I've even been thinking about the food we should have—you know, like all my favorites."

Mom shook her head, shooting a smile in my direction. "So what foods are you thinking?"

"I wanna have some chicken wings, meatballs, Aunt Robin's trailer-trash hors d'oeuvres, and maybe you could make your famous potato salad." He licked his lips. "And Tammy can make her special pumpkin roll. Midge can bring her blueberry buckle, and Aunt Mel can make her clam dip."

"Sounds like a good spread…" Mom started to laugh. "But remember, Jeff…you won't be there to enjoy it."

Without missing a beat, Jeff said, "Well, I guess people will just have to make some samples of their dishes, so I can try it and make sure it's good enough."

Amused, I asked, "So, what, are you gonna have people interview to make food for your funeral?"

"Sounds like a brilliant idea, don't you agree?"

CHAPTER 54

Trying Times

TWO MONTHS HAD PASSED SINCE the funeral discussion, and Jeff's physical, mental, and emotional state had deteriorated significantly. He was much weaker and was starting to disengage from almost everyone besides the immediate family. He was having more pain, which meant he had to take more pain medication. As a result, he spent much of the day dozing in and out of wakefulness.

Jeff's words were diminishing both in frequency and content, and his lack of vitality made it difficult for him to engage with those around him. His personality was changing—he didn't joke around as much and seemed more serious. It was getting harder for him to concentrate, and he felt more tired. His memory was becoming fuzzy, and he easily lost track of the days. We still enjoyed occasional lunches out, though his appetite was diminishing. He no longer could eat a full meal, so we always shared one. He also complained that food just didn't taste the same—a normal symptom of cancer as well as the dying process.

When Jeff did find the energy to talk, the focus was no longer on teaching those of us left on this earth, but on preparing for his journey to heaven.

Mid-July, Jeff began waking up every forty minutes or so through the night with pain; therefore, I too was awake to administer additional pain and sleep medications. The pain medicine was making him extra drowsy but did little to keep his pain under control.

The sharp stabbing pain in Jeff's side eventually became so severe that we had to transfer him to the hospice center for two days so they could start him on one of their strongest pain protocols. Thankfully, Terry went there before and after work, providing much-needed support to me and to Jeff. He always added a splash of humor and a sense of normalcy, which helped during such stressful times. He teased Jeff about being a "drama queen" and trying to get attention, leaving the nurses in stitches as well. Even though Jeff was foggy from the medication, Terry could tease a smile out of him.

Eventually, the new medication regime dropped Jeff's pain level from intolerable to manageable. He felt relieved, at least for a time. Despite feeling happy to be home, his anxiety was fairly high. He was scared that the medications might stop working again and that the excruciating pain would return. Making things even worse for him, the different medications caused him to poop his pants, leaving him very embarrassed. It had been over three years since something like that had happened—a scary reminder of what might occur ahead.

While Jeff struggled with his fears, I struggled with mine. My life seemed to be on overload. The girls still needed to be taken here and there, and they would much prefer that I be the one at their side. Though they were as understanding as could be expected, they were also somewhat frustrated with the uncertainty of the situation.

I felt trapped. On one hand, nothing felt as important, or necessary, as taking care of Jeff—he needed more of my time, help, and attentiveness. On the other hand, nothing seemed as significant as being fully present for the needs of my husband and girls. I missed taking the girls shopping, to dinner, and to the movies. I didn't even have time to work with Clark in the yard, which was one of the things we enjoyed doing together. I so often asked God how I could possibly give enough to both.

Different from the first time we thought Jeff was dying, there was no longer a question that the end was near, though nobody knew exactly when. The fact that it wasn't in plain sight only added more angst. I was well aware of the fact that the time I spent focusing on Jeff necessarily meant I was missing important pieces of my girls' lives. Either way I looked at it, the sacrifice often felt unbearable.

CHAPTER 55

Fish Lake Reunion

Jeff and I were excited that my brothers, parents, and nieces would be joining us for a camping trip to Fish Lake. I had spent the day before gathering the supplies we would need and driving around town for what we were missing. The musty sleeping bags were stretched across the front-porch railing to air out for the night, while fishing and camping gear was piled in the garage to be loaded right before we left. I prepared an extra-large bowl of potato salad, a family favorite, to accompany the hamburgers and hot dogs we had signed up to bring.

The kitchen table served as the staging area for all the food, condiments, and essentials.

"Mom, didn't you buy some special treats for us?" Chelsey asked after searching through the bags on the table.

"You'll just have to wait until we get there to find out."

"Please, can you just tell me if you got powdered doughnuts?" she pleaded in an exaggerated sweet voice.

"Nope. It's a surprise." I snickered, pretending to hide something behind my back. She tried to sneak around me to see what I was holding until I finally surrendered.

"OK, OK. I have your doughnuts," I said.

She threw her fist into the air and exuberantly squealed, "Yes!"

"Now go get ready for bed," I playfully demanded. "We have to get up early so we can finish loading up."

Chelsey happily took off upstairs, leaving me to finish locking up the house so I too could get to bed.

Exhausted from spending the day preparing and packing for our early-morning departure, I crawled into bed and then reached over to my nightstand to turn on the monitor. As I had done every night since Jeff moved in, I listened for reassurance that he was quietly resting. I could hear his mattress squeaking as he rustled around to get comfortable. Tired but alert, I waited for the echoes of his movements to stop so the quiet buzz of the monitor could lull me to sleep.

A commotion coming through the monitor startled me awake. I squinted at the clock, and 2:00 dimly reflected back. I listened carefully for a moment and then got out of bed. I stumbled into Jeff's room.

"Hey, buddy, what's going on?" I mumbled, flipping on the light.

Jeff was sitting on the side of his bed, Rusty watching his every move. Painstakingly, he tapped his open hand across the top of his nightstand, grumbling, "I can't find my pain pills. I thought I had two right here. Maybe I knocked them onto the floor."

Agitated and whimpering, he momentarily held his breath, his eyes tightly squeezed shut. He cautiously expelled the air, agony emanating from his face.

I picked up the two little white pills from the floor and quickly pressed them past his pale lips. "These should help," I said, pressing his trembling hands around his water bottle. He took a big sip, threw his head back to open his constricted throat, and downed the pills in one gulp.

I carefully lifted his legs up on the bed and propped a pillow between his back and the headboard. Rusty stretched a paw across Jeff's thigh, causing him to wince.

"Get down, boy," Jeff said, gently pushing Rusty away.

I gently sat next to him. "The pain is out of control, huh?"

"Yeah. It has never been this bad before. I don't know what's going on." He moaned.

"Let me get you a cool washcloth for your forehead."

"Thank you," he said faintly as I stepped out of the room.

I could hear him sucking air through his clenched teeth. I draped the wet, cool cloth over his hot forehead and then settled beside him. I placed his sweaty hand in mine, and we sat silently.

His labored breaths vacillated with each wave of stabbing pain. I felt helpless.

"If those pills don't bring you some relief, I can give you two more in about twenty minutes," I said.

Quivering, he mumbled, "OK."

"We'll figure out something to get you comfortable. I promise." After lifting the washcloth off his head, I walked toward the door.

He panicked. "You aren't leaving me, are you?"

"No way. I'm just rewetting your cloth. I'm going to stay with you the rest of the night."

I placed the fresh cloth over his heavy brow. "I'm just going to give you two more pills now; there's no need to wait."

"Yeah, I think we better, because this isn't getting much better." He opened his mouth for me to drop in the pills.

I crawled onto the bed. "Hopefully we can get a little rest before morning."

There was plenty of room on Jeff's big king bed for me to settle in for the night. Rusty lay quietly between us, inching himself as close to Jeff's side as Jeff could tolerate. The pain pills that allowed Jeff and me to get a few hours of sleep wore off around the same time the rest of the family eagerly bounced out of bed.

"Can you please get me some more pain pills?" Jeff asked.

I flipped on the light to search for more pills. My sleepy eyes recoiled from the brightness, forcing me to pause for a few moments. Once my eyes adjusted, the grimace that encompassed Jeff's face was clear to see. A surge of adrenaline startled my mind out of its slumbering state, making my stomach feel queasy. I felt an urgent need to find relief for Jeff.

I helped him lift his head off the pillow so that he wouldn't choke as he washed the pills down his throat.

"Try to rest for a bit. I'm going to call the hospice nurse and have her come out right now," I said.

"Will she be able to help?"

"For sure. This is what their specialty is—pain management. They have options that we haven't needed until now. I'll leave your door open, and I'll be back in just a bit."

Weary, he said, "OK. Hurry back."

I opened the garage door to inform Clark and the kids about Jeff's new development.

"Morning, Momma," Kendra hollered while setting a bag into the van. "What time are we leaving?"

"I'm not sure yet. I have to make a call to Uncle Jeff's nurse—"

"Are we still going?" Her wide smile disappeared.

"I think so, but I don't know for sure."

Her chin fell to her chest, and her shoulders slumped forward. Long brown hair covered her downtrodden face as she stared at the floor, muttering and sighing.

Clark came around the corner and into the garage. He glanced at his deflated little helper leaning against the door.

"What's going on?" he asked.

Kendra answered before I could get a word out. "Something's wrong with Uncle Jeff, and we probably aren't going now."

He looked at me, bewildered. "What happened?"

"Jeff's pain has been out of control all night. The pain pills are barely touching it. I'm calling the hospice nurse to see what options we have."

I walked toward my crushed little girl and pulled her into my chest. I wrapped my arms around her and held her close. I didn't want to let go. I needed to let go so I could call the nurse. I hated adding yet another disappointment to the list of many since Jeff had moved in. My eyes burned, and my constricted throat barely let me speak.

"I think it will all work out, honey…" I cleared my throat. "I'm going to do my very best to get this handled so we can still go."

She moved her head up and down against my chest, affirming she understood.

"Come on, Kendra. Help me finish loading so Momma can go take care of Uncle Jeff," Clark said while coaxing her out of my arms.

The hospice nurse arrived within an hour of my call and evaluated Jeff's condition. His blood pressure was high, and his pain bordered on unbearable. She determined that he would need stronger and more frequent pain medications.

She contacted the doctor, and the decision was made to put an IV line in Jeff's arm, attached to a pump that would deliver morphine directly into his veins. The specialized IV procedure required a trained nurse; therefore, hospice contracted with a different company to handle such procedures.

I begged the nurse to find a way to have someone come out today so we could keep our camping plans and I could avoid disappointing my girls once again. Her request for an urgent visit was accepted, and the IV nurse was scheduled for noon. Unsure of how long the procedure would take and reluctant to be too hopeful that things would go smoothly, I informed the kids that there was a fair chance that we would still be able to make the trip. I wanted desperately for us to go and was feeling confident we would be able to.

The hopeful news was met with excitement, and it motivated them to help Clark finish loading the van. An ecstatic buzz emanated from the kids as they gathered their music players, art supplies, movies, and favorite blankets to take on the journey.

"Are you wearing my blue sweatpants?" Chelsey hollered down the stairs to Kendra.

"No. I'm in my cozy flannels. You should wear yours too," Kendra exuberantly said.

Her blue-and-yellow duffel bag in hand, Chelsey flopped on the couch near Kendra. Clothed in matching red-and-black flannel pajamas, they discussed the items each was bringing and what movies they planned to watch during the drive to Fish Lake.

A knock on the front door interrupted their chatter. "Mom, the nurse is here," Kendra said.

"OK, you girls go watch TV with Dad so the nurse can do what he needs to do with Jeff."

I swung the door open and welcomed the middle-aged, slender nurse into the house. "Hello. I'm Jeff's sister, Tammy." I extended my hand.

"Hello. I'm Tom, from Evergreen." He gave me a firm shake.

"We are so grateful you squeezed us into your busy schedule. We can't thank you enough," I said.

He looked into my eyes, his brows elevated, and smiled slightly. "Well, let's hope I can take care of this so you all can take your trip."

"Jeff is in here." I led him down the hall and into Jeff's bedroom, where Jeff was resting on his bed with Rusty burrowed into his side.

"This is Jeff and his best buddy, Rusty."

Hearing his name, Rusty leaped from the bed to greet Tom. Tom reached his hand down toward Rusty's wet nose, allowing Rusty to welcome him with a few wet licks on his palm.

"OK, Rusty, that's enough." I tapped my leg, signaling for him to come to me.

"I'm not sure if the hospice nurse told you, but Jeff is blind. So you'll need to explain to him what you're doing and what you need him to do."

"Yes, she did tell me." He stepped toward the bed and set his hand on Jeff's shoulder. "Hello. I'm Tom, and I'm here from Evergreen to put a special IV in your arm so we can get you some pain relief."

"OK," Jeff said, wincing from the pain.

"So if you have any questions as we go, please don't hesitate to ask. I will explain everything I am doing before I proceed."

Jeff nodded his head.

"He's been in awful pain and hasn't had much sleep," I said.

"Well, Jeff, I think the IV medications will bring you some relief."

"That's good…because I don't know how much longer I can take this pain." Jeff groaned as he turned onto his back.

"Would it be OK to use this nightstand to lay out my supplies?" Tom asked before placing his bulging duffel bag down.

I quickly cleared the space and watched intently as he removed medical paraphernalia from the bag.

"The type of IV I'm going to put in your arm is called a peripherally inserted central catheter, usually referred to as a PICC line."

Jeff turned his head toward the rustling papers and plastic wrappers as Tom continued. "First I will inject some medicine to numb the area, and then

I will be placing a thin, hollow tube into a vein above the bend of your elbow. I will thread it through the vein until it is in the right place."

Tom paused and turned toward me. "Would you mind having Rusty wait outside the room so I can lay out the sterile tray? I wouldn't want him to accidently bump it."

"Not at all." I opened the bedroom door and leaned my head around the corner. "Chels, I need you to come and get Rusty."

Chelsey happily retrieved Rusty after poking her head into the bedroom, her face contorted as her eyes scanned over the numerous medical supplies carefully placed on the table.

"We'll be in here for a bit, so keep him from scratching at the door," I said.

"OK," she said, but then she leaned into my ear and whispered, "do you think we will still be able to go?"

I nodded my head as I shut the door.

Tom washed his hands of Rusty's kisses and then proceeded to carefully and deliberately open a sterile package containing gloves. As he stretched a glove over his hand, the latex snapped against his wrist. Lying on his back, Jeff squirmed silently as he adjusted the pillow behind his slightly elevated head. Random involuntary puffs of air escaped his pursed lips, followed by slight jerky movements in his torso and legs.

Looking like a surgeon, Tom methodically cleaned the inside of Jeff's left forearm, and then he placed a sterile blue cloth over Jeff's arm with a round hole exposing the injection site. The aroma of antiseptic hung in the air. Explaining each step as he went, Tom informed Jeff that the needle would sting a bit as it penetrated his arm, but he shouldn't feel the catheter that would be left in his vein.

"Tammy"—my eyes moved away from the ticking clock at the sound of Tom's voice—"could you hold Jeff's hand against the bed and make sure he doesn't flinch during the process?"

I sat next to Jeff on the bed and held his hand securely between mine. "OK, I got it."

Tom placed one hand under Jeff's extended arm and held the sharp syringe in the other. "OK, Jeff, you will feel a poke now, and it might burn for a few seconds. Here we go."

He proceeded to poke the needle into Jeff's arm, triggering Jeff's eyes to squeeze shut and his jaw muscles to tighten.

"It's almost over, buddy," I sympathetically mumbled through my own clinched teeth, rubbing the top of his hand with my own.

"OK, Jeff, I will let that set for a few minutes to get numb, and the rest should be fairly painless. It's important to stay still, though," Tom said. He reached his latex-gloved hand toward the sterile tray and grabbed a foot-long piece of tubing with a needlelike point at the end.

I brushed my hand over Jeff's wet cheek, closed my eyes, and prayed silently.

"He's almost done…hang in there," I whispered.

"Here we go; I'm ready to insert the catheter. It's really important that you hold very still."

Sitting on the side of the bed, Tom poked a large needle through Jeff's skin and into a vein. He carefully threaded the white catheter through the vein toward Jeff's heart. Jeff didn't flinch.

"OK, the tough part is over, Jeff. You did great," Tom said while placing white tape across the inside of Jeff's forearm to anchor the three-inch piece of rubber tubing protruding from Jeff's bandaged arm.

"You did great," I said.

"I need to confirm the placement of the catheter with this little machine, and then your part will be done."

"Thank you." Jeff sighed.

Upon confirming that the hollow tube was in the right spot, Tom turned to me, giving me a nod and a pleasant grin. "Now comes your part, Tammy. I need to show you how to work the pump and how to maintain this IV."

I had observed this same procedure many times during my work in the hospital, but it was not in my job description to take care of it or know what to do with it. I felt a bit overwhelmed as Tom unloaded the rest of his duffel bag. Bandages, alcohol wipes, and syringes covered the nightstand.

"How soon can I get some medication? Remember…we skipped my last dose?" Jeff asked with a sense of urgency.

"It won't be much longer. I promise," Tom said.

"Can Rusty come back in now?" Jeff asked.

"Oh yes, I'm done with the sterile part now."

I opened the door. "Rusty, Rusty…come on, boy."

Chelsey followed Rusty into the bedroom and walked toward the end of the bed. Rusty hopped up on the bed and sniffed around before burying his head between Jeff's chin and chest.

Chelsey patted Jeff's foot. "How are you doing, Uncle Jeff?"

"I'm OK. Thank you," he said with a slight smile.

"We're getting close to being done, honey. It should be less than an hour." I nodded my head toward the door.

Barely out of the room, she announced, "They're almost done."

Her excitement was palpable even in the bedroom. Jeff smiled.

"OK, we better get a move on it. We don't want to disappoint those sweet little girls," Tom said as he pulled out a quart-size bag of clear liquid from the nearly empty duffel bag and dangled it in front of me.

"Now this…" He snickered, swinging it back and forth. "This is the happy juice."

My eyes sparkled. "That's what we're counting on."

Tom proceeded to instruct me how to connect the bag of fluid to a long tube and then connect the long tube to the piece hanging from Jeff's arm. He showed me how to set up the pump to deliver a certain amount of morphine per hour.

The advancing clock periodically interrupted my focus and caused me momentary worry about whether we would be able to leave as planned or would have to leave the next morning.

Tom checked the connections and then opened the line to the catheter that would deliver Jeff some expected relief.

"You should feel something quickly, Jeff," Tom said confidently.

Jeff's face slightly relaxed. "Oh yeah, I feel that." He exhaled a heavy breath.

"How long will this stuff last?"

"The goal is to keep you comfortable twenty-four hours a day. It may need to be increased from time to time, but you shouldn't have the severe pain episodes like you had last night," Tom said while packing up his belongings.

"Remember, it is very important to wrap his arm in Saran wrap and tape it tight before he takes a bath—you really want to keep the IV site dry. If you have any complications or questions, please do not hesitate to call us. Someone will be available twenty-four hours a day to help you."

"I will," I said.

He flipped the duffel bag strap over his shoulder and gave Jeff's hand a squeeze. "Take care. I hope you feel better soon, and I hope you catch lots of fish."

Jeff held on to Tom's hand and lifted his eyes toward him. "Thank you so much for coming out on such short notice. I really do appreciate it. I feel better already."

I walked Tom to the door and thanked him again for being so accommodating. The clatter from the door closing initiated an onslaught of questions.

"Can we leave now?" Kendra asked, a hopeful smile lighting up her face.

"We are all packed up and ready to go," Chelsey said, with an equally vibrant grin.

"I'm ready now too," Jeff excitedly yelled from his bed. His words brought instant relief to my tense shoulders, and my breaths became easier.

"It's kind of late. Maybe we should just plan on leaving early in the morning," Clark bellowed from the other room. His loud voice pierced the bubble of exuberance.

"No, Dad," the girls said simultaneously, their eyes searching mine for reassurance.

Clark's hearty laugh relieved the momentary doubt. Enjoying teasing the girls, he appeared pleased with their reaction. The Fish Lake trip would proceed, even if it happened to start a few hours later than planned.

The trip would be the first time our core family had camped together in many years. Gary and his two daughters, Terry and Peter, my family, and Mom and Dad would be creating one last memory. Jeff was excited to go, and he was determined that nothing would stop him. I had some apprehension about taking him two hours away home, but I had faith that since God worked out the details, he would keep us safe.

It was a crisp Saturday morning, with orange rays of sunshine looming over the jagged mountains surrounding the blackish-green lake. Fishing poles and tackle boxes in hand, Dad and Clark meandered down the long wooden dock. The preparations for a day of fishing began as they pulled the tarps off their boats. Jeff was resting in Mom and Dad's motor home while the girls were snuggled in our tent.

The scent of pine trees and damp dirt permeated the air. I sat on the weathered picnic table, surrounded by tall trees, waiting for the silver coffee pot to percolate on the camp stove. The quietness of the morning was interrupted by the brotherly banter between Gary and Terry.

"We'll start breakfast, since we'll be back with our limit before you guys even catch your first fish," Terry said as he tucked a jar of fish bait into the pocket of his heavy blue coat.

"Ha ha. We'll be resting in the motor home by the time you get back, so you can go ahead and serve us in there," Gary said as he grabbed his orange tackle box from the table.

"Peter and I will go with Dad, and you two can go with Clark," Terry said.

Peter said, "I'm not much of a fisherman, so I'll do the cooking"—his nose puckered—"as long as I don't have to clean the fish."

Like a well-oiled machine, Clark and I prepared the boat for the morning competition. He routinely managed the motors and tackle, while I packed the food, the blankets, and a thermos of hot coffee. We had been through the drill many times before, as fishing together was one of our most coveted activities.

Wearing his tattered flannel jacket and brown stocking cap, his traditional fishing attire, Clark stood tall behind the wheel of our little boat and waited patiently for me to untie the ropes from the dock.

"So the first boat to catch its limit wins—is that how we're playing this game?" I shouted at Terry from the bow of our well-worn yellow boat as he swaggered down the dock toward Dad's boat.

"We'll be waiting for ya," he said as he stepped off the dock and into Dad's boat.

The mixture of gasoline and oil polluted the air as both boats pulled away from the docks. The engine rumbled as Clark pushed down on the throttle, but it paled in comparison to Terry's booming voice as it reverberated across the lake: "Let the games begin."

The morning fishing excursion didn't end so well for Gary and me. We were met at the dock by our very proud older brother. He waved his wrist and elbow back and forth through the air as if he were in a victory parade, his exaggerated grin forecasting the taunting that was soon to come. Bragging rights were always granted to the one who caught the most fish and the biggest fish.

"Well, hello. Glad you found your way back." His sarcastic words reached us before the boat was even docked.

"We decided to give you guys this round." Gary paused and looked my way, one eye twinkling and the other squinting. "There's a lot more fishing to be done, so enjoy your small victory while you can." Our raised hands slapped against each other as if we had planned to lose all along.

A red-and-white checkered tablecloth adorned the picnic table where the shared bags of food and treats were placed. My two nieces and my girls giggled across from one another, white powdered sugar spilling out of their overstuffed mouths as they sampled all the goodies. A few steps away, Jeff and Mom sat near the radiating fire.

Logs and twigs crackled and popped, causing thick waves of smoke to weave through the campground. A black pouch hung from a strap around Jeff's shoulder, a somber reminder of his need for continuous pain relief. He silently absorbed the sounds and smells around him, a noticeable change from his previous chatty self.

"Momma, can I go fishing with you guys?" Kendra mumbled through her doughnut-stuffed mouth.

"Of course you can. We'll be leaving after Dad and Grandpa get up from their naps."

"The girls and I want to stay here with Peter," Chelsey said, and then she took a swig of milk and gulped the last bit of food down. "We're going exploring in the woods."

"That sounds like fun. Maybe you'll find some treasures," Mom said.

The afternoon outing included Jeff, Kendra, and Mom on our boat and Terry and Gary on Dad's. Clark and Dad had restocked the boats and prepared for a most memorable outing. Mom and I walked on either side of Jeff and carefully guided him down the narrow rickety dock. Kendra could be heard trash talking her Uncle Gary and Uncle Terry about who would catch the most fish.

"Hi, Jeff. Ya ready to go catch some fish?" Clark called out from the boat.

"I think so." Jeff hesitated.

"You're almost there," Mom said.

"Hey, you made it." Clark said, securing Jeff's foot as he cautiously stepped down into the boat.

"OK, Jeff, I'm gonna have you sit right here," Clark said as he gently backed Jeff up to the seat behind the captain's chair.

"Whew, I made it," Jeff said. An elusive smile spread across his puffy pale face.

"You feeling OK?" I asked.

He raised up his two thumbs. "Yep. Let's get this show on the road. We have some fishing to do."

Clark made his way toward the rear of the boat to set up Jeff's pole. The boat rocked back and forth as the current gently moved us down the lake. I helped Kendra put orange bait on the sharp hook, and she knew exactly what to do next. Through the years, fishing had become one of her favorite hobbies. Mom had prepared her own hook, using her self-proclaimed "special green-and-blue bait."

"OK, all the fishing lines are in the water," Clark said.

"Jeff, get ready for the big one," Mom said.

The dark-green water glistened as the hot July sun danced across its surface. Trolling across the placid lake, we all watched and waited patiently as the tips of our poles bobbed up and down. Not only did I love the scenery around the lake, but it was also a place filled with many of my favorite family memories.

Mindlessly gazing, out of the corner of my eye, I saw Jeff's pole bounce aggressively. An inquisitive look covered his face. "Start reeling, Jeff—you have a fish," I yelled excitedly.

His eyes squeezed shut. Grinning from ear to ear, he turned the crank as fast as he could manage.

"OK, OK, you can stop reeling—the fish is in the boat," I said.

We all laughed.

"How big is he?" Jeff asked.

"He's a good one—about a foot long," Clark said. "Do you want to feel him?"

"Sure," Jeff said tentatively.

Clark held the fish out and slid Jeff's hand down its body. "Wow, he's a fat one," Jeff said, quickly wiping his slimy hand on a towel.

The lines went back into the water, and the fishing resumed. Kendra and Mom both caught their limit, allowing us the bragging rights for the afternoon.

Immediately after we returned from our fishing excursion, Jeff fell asleep in the motor home. His endurance for any kind of activity seemed to be diminishing rapidly. The narcotics made him feel extra drowsy, so it was difficult for him to think clearly at times, which added more worry for Mom and me.

The alarm on my phone went off, reminding me to change Jeff's medicine pouch. I gently patted his arm, startling him from a deep sleep.

"Hey, it's time to change your medicine," I said softly.

"OK. What time is it?" he asked, slightly dazed.

"It's almost dinnertime. It might be a good time for you to have your talk with Gary," I said, knowing it was a goal he had for the trip.

"OK. My brain feels pretty foggy, so could you remind me of the key points I wanted to say?"

Recalling our many discussions about Gary, I reminded Jeff what he had shared with me. "Well, first off, you wanted to let him know that it's OK that he hasn't been as involved as others, and that you don't want him to feel bad about it."

"Oh yeah. And I wanna apologize for not taking the time to get to know him before I was sick…" Jeff's words slurred and then halted momentarily. "I feel bad about that. It's also my fault that I didn't prioritize that time, and I don't want him to feel guilty that he didn't either."

Finishing, I zipped the canvas medicine pouch. "OK, I'm done. Shall I get Gary now?"

His chin bobbed against his chest as he dozed off for a few seconds, and then he sluggishly answered. "Yeah, I better get it out while I still can think."

I summoned Gary to the motor home and then left so they could have some privacy. Gary wasn't in there long, and he was crying when he came out.

Blubbering, he walked toward Mom and me. She jumped up from her seat and wrapped her arms around him.

"It's all gonna be OK," she whispered into his ear.

His head buried in her shoulder, I heard him say, "I'm sorry I haven't been more involved. I've been so selfish."

He then hugged me. Barely able to get the words out, he said, "I will try to be around more to help."

"That would be good, because he probably doesn't have a whole lot more time." I choked up. "I'm just glad he was able to share his thoughts with you."

The trip proved to be a time of healing, reconnection, and fun for our family. It allowed us to mostly focus on living instead of dying.

CHAPTER 56

Dying Thoughts

"I FEEL LIKE I HAVE lost a bit of independence with this new machine because I have to carry a backpack-type bag with pain medications everywhere I go. The tubing feels a bit confining, but I am sure I will get used to it. It's a bit of a hassle since we have to wrap the IV site so it won't get wet during my bath. It is a step up from a pain-management standpoint, but a step down from an independence standpoint.

"I am trying to take today for today; I don't think about tomorrow. It's hard to focus on God with all my physical symptoms, because my mind just wanders and won't stay focused.

"Food that once tasted good doesn't taste good anymore. Salty foods don't taste salty, and sweet foods taste bitter. I wish my dad would stop bugging me about eating, because I don't feel hungry. Tammy tells me that not eating is part of the normal dying process. I guess it is also normal that family tries to feed the sick person out of love. Christine and I talked about it too, and she said the same thing. She's gonna talk to my dad to help him understand.

"During my last session with Christine, she told me that some people like to leave letters for their family to read when they are gone. I liked the idea but didn't know what I would say. She asked me some questions about my relationships with my family and then suggested I could write down how things have changed since I got sick. That part was pretty easy when it came to talking about Dad and Terry, since my relationship with each of them got way better since I got cancer.

"My dad and I really got close after his fire. It has really helped our relationship that we have experienced similar losses. He has some understanding as to what it is like to have to struggle with the simple things in life, like buttoning your shirt. He asks more about my day and how things are going for me. I really love my dad, and I am grateful for the relationship we have now.

"Terry and I weren't very close as we were growing up because of our age difference. He comes over for dinner and to visit. He is really funny and makes us all laugh. He likes to cook, and I like to eat his food. I don't know how he is coping with my illness. We don't talk about it.

"Things didn't change much for mine and Gary's relationship since I got cancer. It's OK, though; I don't have any hard feelings.

"It was hard to leave letters to Mom and Tammy—it got super emotional. I've always been close to my mom and sister, and even more so since I got sick. I wouldn't have made it this far without them, and I am so grateful for the care they gave me over the past three years.

"Good night."

CHAPTER 57

A War Zone

ONCE SUMMER BEGAN, JEFF SLOWLY drifted away from most activities. No more swimming, coffee runs, or trips out to the movies—everything just took too much effort. Though he was less interested in outside activities, he still managed to make our lives pretty exciting—or stressful, depending on the situation. During those times, Mom and I exchanged phone calls several times a day. Our daily reports became our lifeline as we shared everything from sorrowful moments to funny tidbits.

One morning, I answered the phone, expecting it to be my mom calling with her typical morning report. And as expected, it was her. But instead of saying good morning, she emphatically announced, "I could have put your brother out of his misery this morning."

Though there was a joking tone in her voice, I could hear her alarm and hoped it wasn't anything too terrible. "What happened?"

"I went in to get Jeff up and saw blood all over the bedsheets and a towel on the floor. I was absolutely petrified," she said, seemingly amused.

"What the heck is going on over there? Is Jeff OK? What happened?" Questions tumbled over one another on their way out of my mouth as I struggled to understand the joke. Jeff had a variety of unusual symptoms, but they rarely included blood dripping on the floor.

"Yes, yes, we're both fine. You know how Jeff hates those little moles and skin tags he gets? Well, he decided to cut one off with his scissors. The damned thing bled everywhere, and of course he couldn't see how bad it was, even though he felt that his arm was wet. He used his towel to dry his arm but apparently didn't realize that it was still bleeding." After another bout of laughter, she continued. "I could have shot the little bugger."

"I bet you did freak out. Did he just feel awful?" I asked, concerned for both of them. Jeff could be clueless, and it was frustrating for my mother when his carelessness affected his health.

"He should have. I thought he was dead."

Most of the time, the problems Mom and I dealt with were little ones much like that—relatively simple events that happened as we cared for my extremely ill, blind brother. However, every once in a while, we came across something more severe.

The very next weekend, I received a similar call from Mom. Hearing her slightly giggle as I answered, I anticipated that she and Jeff had had another humorous mishap.

Bypassing any typical greetings, Mom said, "You won't believe what I just did."

"Oh, great. What's going on now?" I asked. Mom didn't sound nearly as concerned as when Jeff had tried to cut off his mole, but there was clearly something fishy happening.

"Well, I just got Jeff out of the bath and went to cut the tape off his arm, and uh…I, uh…accidentally cut his IV line." She barely managed to finish as she cracked up laughing at Jeff hollering in the background.

"She just wanted some of my morphine."

This set off another round of giggles in my mother; she tried to contain herself and finish the story. "Morphine was flowing everywhere, but I finally got the tube clamped off."

I could still hear Jeff heckling her. "Just admit you were trying to suck morphine from the IV tube."

She tried to push the laughter aside. "I don't know what to do now, though—I figured you would."

Amused but concerned, I asked, "Did you cut it before or after the connection?"

"It looks like it's before the connection—the tube closest to the IV site."

"Oh, shoot. There's no way they can reconnect it. They'll have to put in a whole new PICC line." My disappointed tone dampened the fun.

"So what do we do then?" she asked, her laughter dying away.

"Well, I'll have to call the nurse and have the IV company come out and put in a new line. For now, just keep it clamped off."

Sensing she felt bad, I tried to lighten the mood. "And don't try to sneak any for yourself. I can't leave the two of you together for too long, or all hell breaks loose."

In light of yet another faux pas, I quickly realized that regardless of whether or not we sought out challenges, they seemed to find us on a fairly regular basis. I reflected back on the days when we didn't have the house set up for Jeff's blindness and Jeff tripped over things, and even walked into doors. I remembered a recent day when he accidentally took his night pills in the morning, knocking him out the whole day. It seemed like a month couldn't pass without some sort of problem; thankfully, they were usually more humorous than serious.

CHAPTER 58
A Night of Horror

I COULD FEEL MY OWN mental well-being deteriorate along with Jeff's declining health. I felt depressed often, and at times relieved that our shared journey was clearly at its end. The monotony of each day made it difficult for me to find any positives.

Jeff spent much of his day sitting on the couch, dozing in and out of sleep. He no longer journaled at night and seldom engaged in deep conversations. His breathing became increasingly shallow and labored, even with little activity. I attempted to walk with him, but instead of walking our usual mile, he could only walk up the driveway and back before becoming completely exhausted.

Food didn't appeal to him much anymore, causing his weight to drop precipitously. I remembered that it hadn't been long ago that his main focus had been on his next meal. I longed for those lunches on the back patio, just Jeff and me, with plenty of time to talk about life, gratitude, and God.

Pain had become the constant factor in Jeff's daily routine. I worked relentlessly with the nurses to find the right balance between minimal pain and maximum wakefulness. Just when we seemed to find a nice balance, something would change. His breathing would get worse, his pain would increase, the medications would cause him to itch like crazy, or he would be too sleepy—something always caused us to have to change his medication regime again and again.

We settled into a fairly predictable routine. I tucked Jeff into bed and placed the monitor on his nightstand next to his sleeping pill and water.

Only then could I make my way upstairs to catch a few hours of sleep before he whispered my name, asking for some help getting to the bathroom. Our nightly routine had become pleasantly predictable. Just as a new mother sleeps in a semialert state, I slept with an ear listening for his nightly call. A trip to the bathroom, a short chat about how he was feeling, and then back to sleep usually completed our night. I cherished those rare occasions when we had particularly special talks during our midnight rendezvous—when we would reflect on the meaning and purpose of our life here on earth.

It had been another hectic summer day: driving the girls to and from their friends' houses, managing Jeff's worsening pain, doing house chores, and preparing meals. I was exhausted not only from the day's activities, but from not having enough sleep the night before because Jeff was awake a few times during the night with a stomachache. He seemed fairly comfortable when I tucked him into bed, so I finally headed up to bed myself.

I drifted off into a deep sleep, and sometime afterward I was slightly aroused by a nightmare—I heard moaning and crashing sounds that almost felt real. Only half-awake, I desperately tried to fall back to sleep. Then another crash and more moaning startled me again. This time it seemed less like a dream and even more real than the last. I heard another moan, and bleary-eyed, I scanned my room trying to make sense of the noises. The lights on the monitor rapidly blinked as indecipherable moaning sounds eerily echoed through the speaker. My heart began to race as I cleared my head to listen carefully. Then I heard Jeff's faint voice. "Taaaammmy—help me." I frantically jumped up and sprinted down the stairs, flinging Jeff's bedroom door open.

"Oh my God! Clark...Clark! Help!" I screamed in horror at the sight of Jeff's seemingly lifeless body lying on the floor between the bed and the door. One leg was bent at the knee under the other, diarrhea smeared his legs and the floor, his arms sprawled to the side of his body, his grayish face was pressed against the hardwood floor, his lips were a ghastly bluish-purple color, and his faint breath could barely repeat my name. "Tammy..."

"Jeff, Jeff, I'm here," I wailed. I reached one arm under his limp body, pulled him onto my lap, and cradled him in my arms. Residual vomit leaked out of his mouth as I propped his head against my chest.

"What's going on?" Clark called in a panic as he sprinted around the corner and into the room.

"Clark, Clark, I think he's dying." I wailed hysterically, begging, "Help me, Lord. Please don't let him die…" My words dissolved into blubbering. "I didn't hear him call for me. I didn't hear him."

Quickly, Clark knelt on the floor next to me and placed his fingers on Jeff's neck to check for a pulse. "He's still alive; he's still with us."

A gasp of air came out of Jeff's mouth, and then a faint murmur. "I tried to call…but you didn't come…I can't stand up…I keep falling…" His words faltered, and then his face went blank, his head slumped over my arm.

"No. Jeff…Jeff, stay with me…" I rocked back and forth with his head on my lap. "Don't go now, Jeff, please, not like this. I'm so sorry I didn't hear you. Please don't die." I frantically begged louder. "Help me, Lord. Please don't take him today, not like this."

"Help me lift him up to the bed," Clark said, slipping latex gloves over his hands.

"I didn't hear him call for me. I didn't hear him," I repeated, as if the words could fix everything.

"Come on, let's get him up," Clark said urgently. "Tammy, I need you to focus. We need to help him now."

I started to move Jeff's lifeless body off my lap so I could help lift him to the bed. "Wait. Put on some gloves first so you don't get poop on your hands." Clark's practical tone of command stopped me as he dangled gloves in front of me. The gloves wouldn't help my already-soiled hands, so we carefully proceeded to lift Jeff's limp body onto his bed.

I rechecked Jeff's pulse, and it was slow and faint. Unconscious, his listless body was soaked with vomit, urine, and poop.

Pulling off Jeff's pants, Clark asked, "What happened? Why was he out of bed?"

"I don't know. I just heard some commotion through the monitor, ran downstairs, and he was just lying here," I said, my hand shaking as I struggled to get Jeff's shirt changed. "He must have called for me, but I didn't hear him." My teeth clinched together as I tried to force a deep breath.

"It's not your fault, Tammy. It's gonna be OK," Clark repeated, his composure beginning to break as well.

Clark started wiping up the floor while I cleaned Jeff's body. Haunted by Jeff's cries for help, I wept, trying to make sense of what had happened.

"By the position of his body and the trail of urine and feces, it looks like he fell, then tried to grab the bed and get himself back up. Then he must have collapsed again," I said. My mind relentlessly replayed the initial images and sounds of Jeff's pleas, leaving me sickened and broken.

Carrying a large green garbage bag stuffed with soiled towels, Clark momentarily left the room. He quickly returned with the phone in his hand. "I'm gonna call the hospice nurse. Do you wanna talk to her, or should I just tell her what's going on?"

Distraught, I blubbered, "I can't talk, not right now. Just tell them we need a nurse to come out as fast as possible."

Calm and collected, Clark called hospice, and they informed him that the on-call nurse would be out within the hour. While we waited, Clark helped me roll Jeff's limp body to the opposite side of the bed so we could change his soiled sheets. I noticed red marks on his arms and legs from falling, and my stomach filled with nausea. I propped his head on the pillow and pulled the clean sheet over his naked body.

The night only seemed to get worse after the on-call hospice nurse arrived and confirmed my worst fears. She said that his blood pressure was really low, and the fact that he wasn't responding really worried her. She removed the blood pressure cuff from his arm, and her eyes met mine. And then she looked away as she empathetically told me that she believed his body was too sick to recover.

Clark immediately wrapped his arms around me, and we cried. The nurse briefly placed her hand on my shoulder and then continued her work. She looked over Jeff's body, assessing what might have caused the crisis. Moments passed before Clark and I were able to compose ourselves.

When we were calm, the nurse explained that she thought one of his tumors might have been bleeding, and the loss of blood was what caused him to pass out and fall.

In a fog, I heard her words, but nothing she said mattered. The only thing I could focus on was the fact that I hadn't heard my little brother the one time he needed me most. My worst thoughts flashed through my mind—he must've been terrified as he called out my name, struggling to make sense of what was happening, and I slept through it all. And now Jeff was dying. Was this really how it would all end? Why hadn't I woken up? We had been through too much together—to end like this would haunt me. I feared my guilt would overshadow all the good memories.

I hovered over Jeff constantly for two straight days, anticipating his final breath. Mom and Dad stayed at our house so they could be near Jeff as well. Since he had been misdiagnosed so many times, we almost couldn't accept that he was actually dying. The nurses and social worker were incredibly supportive as they tried to prepare each of us for the dreaded moment.

My favorite hospice nurse, Pam, was finally back from her days off. She was like the little sister I never had. Whenever she would come to the house to check on Jeff, we would spend time talking and sharing about our lives. She was usually very bubbly and always honest about Jeff's condition. I had learned to trust her assessments above all others.

Pam entered Jeff's bedroom to evaluate his condition; I followed close behind. My eyes were glued to her every move as she lifted the blanket away from his chest, then his legs. She methodically checked Jeff's breathing, heart rate, blood pressure, and reflexes. I quietly waited for her to answer all my unasked questions.

She pulled the covers over Jeff and pointed to the door. I walked out, and she followed. Talking in a quiet voice, she explained to my mother and me, "His legs are starting to mottle, turning a grayish blue, which is usually a sign that the blood flow is slowing down. Since he hasn't eaten or drunk anything for the past three days, his urine output is negligible, and he isn't responding." She took a breath. "It doesn't seem that he will make it much longer. These are all the signs we look for at end of life." I had heard nurses say those same words to many of my patients when I worked at hospice.

"Are you sure this is really it?" my mom asked tearfully, staring off into the distance.

"Yes. All the signs point in that direction. I'm so sorry." Pam hugged Mom, and they continued to talk for a few minutes while I returned to Jeff.

Pam joined me at Jeff's bedside as I held his limp hand between mine and prayed. I felt desperate for even the smallest grain of hope. She lovingly rubbed her hand across my back as I wept. I struggled to accept the situation, especially since I hadn't helped him when he needed me most.

"You know you couldn't have prevented this," she said quietly.

Swimming in guilt, I muttered, "He wouldn't have fallen, though, and he certainly wouldn't have felt alone."

Pam quietly sat next to me until I was done crying. She had to leave to see other patients but promised to return in the afternoon to check on Jeff again.

Later that morning, I told the girls that it was very likely that Jeff would never wake up and that he really was dying this time. They both cried, and then they told me how Christine had encouraged them to write Jeff a letter if they had anything they wanted to tell him. She had informed them that many people believe that the dying person can still hear even though they are unresponsive. The girls took her advice, and each wrote a letter to Jeff, but they didn't want to read it themselves because they were too uncomfortable. I agreed to read their letters to him.

Several family members and friends came to say their final goodbyes, even though he didn't seem to be aware of their presence. When everyone left, Mom and I sat on Jeff's bed, crying, talking, and sharing memories as we watched his every labored breath.

Day four of our vigil started with the rising summer sun peeking through the wood blinds. I rested beside Jeff in his big king bed, as I had done since he slipped into a coma. Lying on my side facing him, with Rusty nestled between us, I watched Jeff's chest sharply rise, then fall as his lungs and heart continued to fight to survive. I was so thankful he was still alive. As I had witnessed with my past clients, the dying process could take days, and sometimes even weeks. I usually would be praying for it to only take days so that those around the dying person wouldn't have to be in such pain. But considering how much guilt and sadness I felt about not being able to comfort and protect Jeff when he was falling and so afraid, I begged God to not take him anytime soon. I wanted another chance, a chance to make things right. I wanted to feel at peace when Jeff took his final breath. No part of me had peace. My brain ached from so much crying, lack of sleep, and too much thinking. I was filled with a sadness that hurt me to the bone.

I so desperately wanted God to wake him up, and I yearned for the smallest sign that Jeff was fighting to stay alive. Having steadfastly observed his breathing patterns every night since he had gone into a coma, I noticed that his breathing rhythm was a bit more regular than it had been.

As I crawled out of the bed to go to the bathroom, Rusty jumped over Jeff to follow me. Out of the corner of my eye, I thought I saw Jeff twitch. A shot of adrenaline rushed through me as I turned to see if he really was moving. Standing at the side of the bed, I watched to see if he would move again. He didn't.

I left the room, disappointed, and used the bathroom. I let Rusty out front to go potty, and then we both returned to the bedroom. Rusty immediately jumped back onto the bed, bumping Jeff's legs as he nestled next Jeff.

I again thought I saw Jeff twitch. I stopped what I was doing and stared at his still body. Moments passed, and then he moved his arm from his side toward his chest. I felt my heartbeat increase. I reached down and squeezed his hand, waiting eagerly for something to happen. Several minutes passed, and I got no response. I let go, crushed, and walked out to get some coffee.

When I came back in his room, I noticed that his legs were in a different position. I knew better than to get my hopes up. I couldn't think straight. I felt extremely tired and trapped in my head.

"Tammy? Is that you?" a frail voice uttered.

I spun my head around toward Jeff, unsure if I was dreaming or hallucinating.

"Is that you, sis?" In the quiet, his words reverberated in my head.

"Yes, it's me." I sat on the edge of the bed, my heart pounding.

"Can you hear me?" I asked, my voice deceptively calm, but fearing it was all a dream.

"Yeah, I hear you," he said clearly.

All the pain left my body at once as I sat next to him, mumbling, "Thank you, Jesus. Thank you."

Confused, Jeff moved his hand on top of mine. "What's going on? What time is it?"

Unable to contain all my emotions, I struggled to form words. "You… you've been in a coma…for four days." I sobbed joyfully, kissing his forehead and hugging him.

"What happened?" he asked, slightly dazed. "I remember calling for you, and I kept falling down."

I shook my head in disbelief, relief overshadowing my guilt. Joy mixed with my horror for the first time in four days.

"I can't believe this. You need to make up your mind whether you're living or dying," I teased.

His eyebrows lifted slightly. "I know one thing for sure—I'm hungry for some McDonald's."

"What is this with you and McDonald's every time you're about to die? Remember the first time you came home from the hospital? We weren't sure if you were going to live through the night, and McDonald's was supposed to be your last meal."

"So what happened? Where were you…" His voice faded.

My head dropped. "I didn't hear you. I'm so, so sorry. The nurses think you're bleeding internally, and it's making your blood pressure drop. That must have been why you fell down."

"Oh…" Jeff took a minute to process, his mind still foggy. "That sounds pretty bad."

"But you're awake now. That's all that matters." I hugged him again. "I need to go call the nurse. I'll be back in two seconds."

As soon as I closed the door, I ran toward the stairs, yelling at the top of my lungs, "He's awake. He's talking. He wants McDonald's."

Hearing all my commotion, Clark rushed in from the garage. "What's wrong? What happened?" he yelled, assuming the worst.

"He's awake. Call the nurse; I want her out here ASAP," I shouted back in his direction.

Mom and Dad quickly made their way down the stairs. "What? He's talking?" Mom demanded as she pushed past me, reluctant to take my word for it.

They opened the door to Jeff's room and immediately saw him turn his head toward the sound.

"Tammy?" he asked. "Is the nurse coming?"

"No, it's your mother," Mom cried, leaning over to hug him.

Emotional, Dad whispered, "I'm here too."

Clark entered the room, car keys in his hand. "The nurse is on her way. Tammy said someone wants McDonald's. I'm taking orders." His jovial voice echoed throughout the quiet room.

"I want a cheeseburger, fries, and a chocolate milkshake," Jeff said, clearly oblivious to the fact that he had not eaten or drunk anything for four days.

"That might be too much on your system," I said.

"Let the boy eat whatever he wants," Dad said, wiping his eyes with his sleeve.

"OK. Well, as long as you eat slowly. I'm sure Clark will finish what you don't want." I shrugged.

Clark grinned. "Sounds good. I'll be back in a bit."

Mom helped me put a shirt on Jeff while he lay in bed. We didn't dare have him sit up. Within an hour, Pam arrived and was stunned to see Jeff so awake. There was no medical explanation for his sudden recovery.

CHAPTER 59

The End Is Near

AFTER THAT TRAUMATIC EPISODE, I suffered extreme guilt, sadness, and fear for not hearing Jeff's cries for help and for not supporting him in that moment. Despite everyone's words of comfort as they tried to help me get past my angst, I couldn't quiet the sound of Jeff's haunting voice calling, "Taaaammmy—help me." The flashbacks freely played through my head. I was horrified then, and the replay in my mind left me equally traumatized every time I heard it.

Jeff continued to decline at a slow and steady pace. He worried every time I had to leave him, scared that something bad could happen and I wouldn't be there. I shared the same worry, which was why I tried to leave him only when I absolutely had no choice, such as when I had to work or care for the girls. I hardly slept because I was so nervous that I would miss Jeff's call. I kept the volume of the monitor on high and also put a loud whistle on Jeff's nightstand just in case I wasn't next to the monitor.

Each passing week seemed more challenging than the one before. Aside from help with his medical needs, bathing, and dressing, Jeff also required help getting around the house, and he no longer could be left home, for even short periods. Thankfully, several friends and family offered to help with Jeff's care so I could spend more time with the girls. One of our longtime family friends, Sharon, started coming to my house once a week to sit with Jeff so I could do other things. She was soft spoken, calm, and like a second mother to us. Her presence was comforting to me, and I was relieved Jeff was comfortable having her stay with him for an hour or two.

By the end of September, Jeff required oxygen around the clock and large amounts of pain medications. He was too ill to travel to Mom's house, adding additional pressure to our already tight schedule. Since Dad had returned to work and Mom couldn't drive to my house because of her anxiety, we didn't have a regular visitation schedule. Mom would come over whenever one of her friends or a relative was coming out. Otherwise, she and Dad would visit on the weekends when Dad wasn't working.

Clark and I did our best to manage everything, but each week became more exhausting as we juggled work, kids, Jeff, chores, and occasionally a moment for each other. I took vacation days, days without pay, and occasional sick days from work to care for Jeff when his health worsened. I tried to utilize all the help that hospice offered, but sometimes it was more work to have the nurses' aide come out because I would have to wait on her schedule, which meant Jeff would have to lie in bed waiting for help to get bathed and dressed for the day. It was quicker and easier for me to just get it done, even though it was one more thing I had to do. Pam and the other nurse, Joan, were seeing Jeff at least three or four times a week, and Christine was over twice a week to provide support to Jeff and our family.

They all urged me to hire more help, but I found it so difficult to let go of caring for my brother. It had been my responsibility for so long, and often it was easiest for me to just do it. Plus, the idea of training someone new made me exhausted. And Jeff wasn't comfortable being left with just anyone, which made me feel even worse. It wasn't that he was being difficult; he just felt safest when I was with him.

I talked to Jeff about needing to hire some help so that I could spend a little time with the girls. He suggested that Jessica, one of the girls' friends and Patrick's little sister, help out. Jeff was comfortable with her because whenever she came to our house to play with the girls, she would often sit and talk with him, or just watch TV with him. Jessica had her own health issues and was very interested in all the medical issues happening to Jeff. She was very mature for being only twelve and was excited to be helping. Her visits freed me to spend time with the girls, even if it was just to go upstairs and watch a show with them—uninterrupted.

Between Sharon and Jessica, I was able to spend a few hours a week focusing my attention just on the girls, but it still wasn't enough. The girls tried to be patient and supportive, but they too were getting frustrated by not having a sense of normalcy in our lives. About to turn fifteen and sixteen in less than two months, both girls were ready to focus on things other than Jeff's looming death.

I understood their struggle but found myself helpless; I had no control over when it all would end. Even though being Jeff's caretaker was becoming extremely exhausting, I wanted nothing more than to be with him through the end. The joyful days of being his caretaker had left me and had been replaced with a grim sense of duty. I knew I would miss him terribly, but I couldn't stop wishing for the end of Jeff's suffering and an end to the pressure I felt from everyone.

October brought with it not only drastic changes outside, but a definite change inside our home as well. I finally succumbed to the overwhelming pressure and hired another family friend to help me manage all my responsibilities. I took a leave of absence from work because Jeff's deteriorating health left us believing he had less than a couple of weeks to live. His pain had increased dramatically, his breathing was becoming more compromised, and his appetite was dwindling significantly from the nausea.

Throughout Jeff's illness, my goal had always been to have him die at home, in his own bed, with me and his faithful dog at his side. It never occurred to me that I would have to sacrifice so much of myself to make that happen. My family's approval was paramount for me, and the very *thought* of disappointing any of them, let alone knowing it was a reality, sent waves of panic through my body. I felt out of control. I was torn between wanting to be a "good" mom and wife and wanting to finish the journey with Jeff. I secretly worried about failing each of them, the people whose love and approval I so desperately needed and wanted.

Yet to fail Jeff by not being there for him would have felt worse. I justified putting Jeff's needs ahead of my girls, Clark, and my work because he needed me most. Clark and the girls could care for themselves, but Jeff had no one else. I kept putting them off, thinking that it wouldn't be long before Jeff was going to pass, but then another day would come, requiring more time and devotion. I needed help to be able to balance Jeff's needs with my family's, but at the same time, I did not want it. I just wanted everyone to understand.

Jeff had been waking up several times a night with extreme pain. I ended up sleeping in his bed, fearful I would miss his calls for help. I increased his pain medications as high as the machine would let me go, but it still wasn't enough. I couldn't get him comfortable no matter what I tried, so I called Pam to see if she could come over. Even though it was her day off, she had asked me to call if something happened.

The girls were sleeping in because they had Jessica over for a sleepover, and they had all stayed up late. Since it was a Saturday morning, Clark was mulling around, cleaning up and offering help with whatever I needed.

I gave Jeff a sponge bath and was getting him dressed when I heard a faint knock on his bedroom door.

"Come in," I said.

"Good morning. Is it OK for me to come in?" Jessica asked softly while standing in the doorway.

"Sure, you can. I'm just finishing up." I pulled the blanket over Jeff's chest.

Her sweet smile faded to a slight frown when she saw the grimace on Jeff's face. Her big brown eyes narrowed as she looked in my direction.

"He's in a lot of pain," I said. "Pam's on her way."

"Oh. I'm sorry, Jeff." She rubbed her hand over his arm. "Can I get you some water or something?"

"Yeah, that would be nice." He shuddered.

I gently rubbed my hand over his head. "Hang in there. Pam should be here before long. Try to slow your breathing down just a bit so you don't start hyperventilating."

He took a sip of water, and then Jessica set the glass on the nightstand. "Can I do anything for you, Tammy?"

"Maybe you could sit with him so I can run upstairs and get out of my pajamas."

"I'd be glad to."

About a half hour later, Pam knocked at the door. I welcomed her in and quickly ushered her to Jeff's room.

"He's been in severe pain on and off for the past two nights, but last night was by far the worst," I said as she pulled her stethoscope from her bag.

"Hi, Jeff. What level is your pain right now?" she asked, holding the round metal end of her stethoscope against his chest.

Wincing, he pushed a heavy breath through his clenched teeth. "It's about a nine."

Jessica and I watched helplessly as Pam took Jeff's pulse, checked his bag of pain medications, and then turned up his oxygen. Jeff squirmed, trying to move away from the severe pain.

"I think we need to transfer him to the hospice center so we can try some new pain medications. The doctor thinks we need to switch from morphine to methadone, and we can manage that better at the hospice center. We should take him there and see how he does. Depending on how things go, we can talk about bringing him back home if that's what you decide."

Breathless, Jeff asked, "Are you sure they can make this pain go away?"

"Yes. That's why I want to move you. We can give you some drugs that can only be given at the hospice center. I know you're suffering, Jeff." Pam's eyes got watery as she cleared her throat. "I'll do my best to make this happen as fast as possible."

I pressed my damp cheek against Jeff's, and whispered, "I will be with you the whole time. You won't be alone for even a moment."

He nodded and then softly mumbled, "I can't take the pain any longer…" Tears trailed down his cheek. "Please, make it go away."

Initially, I feared that by moving Jeff I would be letting him down. I promised him I would try to keep him home to die, but my reluctance to move him was immediately abolished. The decision was out of my control. I trusted the hospice team implicitly, especially Pam.

She began phoning immediately for an ambulance to transport Jeff, since he was no longer able to make the short walk to the car.

I sent Jessica upstairs to get the girls so I could explain to them what was happening and to ask Clark to put the dogs in the garage so that when the ambulance team arrived, there would be less commotion.

Barely awake, Chelsey stumbled into Jeff's room. "What's going on, Momma? Is Uncle Jeff OK?"

"His pain is out of control, so we're transferring him to the hospice center, and I'm going with him."

Kendra patted his leg sympathetically. "I hope you feel better."

"I'll take care of Rusty for you, so don't worry about him," Chelsey said.

Despite his agony, Jeff mustered a slight smile and said, "Thanks, guys. I appreciate your help."

Jessica's mom, Colleen, arrived just as the ambulance pulled into the driveway. She had been a big support throughout the time Jeff had been living with us. I had counted on her on many occasions to help with the girls, and she was quick to offer help with whatever was needed now that I would be going to the hospice center with Jeff.

"Jessica and I will come up to the hospice center later this afternoon, so call me if you need me to bring you anything," Colleen said.

"I got Jeff's stuff packed, but I forgot to pack a bag for myself. Maybe you could bring my stuff with you. The girls know what I'll need," I said as I rushed around to get the last of Jeff's things.

Clark helped the ambulance crew move the gurney through the doorways and out the front door. He squeezed Jeff's hand just before they lifted him into the ambulance. "I'll see you later." He swallowed hard but couldn't keep from weeping. "I...I'll be praying."

He quickly walked into the house, and I followed. I wrapped my arms around him, burying my face in his chest. The girls rushed to our side and wept with us. I squeezed them tight and then kissed each of their foreheads. Torn between wanting to stay wrapped in my family's arms and staying by my brother's side, my body quivered as I suppressed my need to go.

Sensing my struggle, Clark thoughtfully said, "It's OK. Go. We're going to be OK. I got the girls; you go and help Jeff." The girls reluctantly nodded, and they kissed me goodbye.

CHAPTER 60

Goodbye, My Little Brother

THE AMBULANCE RIDE HAD AN eerie familiarity to the one we had made nearly four years earlier, when we made the journey *from* the hospital to my house, when he was expected to die within weeks. A small part of me wondered if this really was the end.

Clark called my mom and dad and told them what was happening. They arrived at the hospice center shortly after us. It took some time to get Jeff settled and for the unit nurse to complete her assessment. Since Pam only worked with outpatients, she would no longer be the one in charge of Jeff's care. But she planned on participating however she could.

Shortly after we settled Jeff into his room, the doctor arrived. She was a pleasant woman whom I was only vaguely familiar with from my work at the hospital. She said hello to my parents and me and then stepped toward the side of Jeff's bed.

"Hello, Jeff. I'm Dr. Bell—"

Whimpering, Jeff abruptly interrupted. "Can you please make this pain go away? I can't take it any longer."

Dr. Bell placed her hand on his. "I will do my best. Pam and Joan have been telling me that you have really been in a lot of pain—we are going to switch your medications. I will do everything I can to get you feeling better."

I followed the doctor out of the room to reiterate what had been going on and to get a clearer idea of what her plans might include. Even though I knew in my head that only God knew when Jeff's final day would be, I still found myself asking the doctor if she had any idea how long Jeff had to live. Though she believed that he only had a few more days, the daily uncertainty was so difficult to endure.

That afternoon Colleen and Jessica arrived. I had them bring Rusty up, anticipating it might help Jeff feel a bit more comfortable. My girls decided they didn't want to come to the hospice center. They expressed that they couldn't handle everyone's sadness, and they didn't want to see their uncle's suffering any longer.

Jeff woke up from a short snooze and was slightly confused about his whereabouts. Mom reminded him that we were at the hospice center, and I told him that Colleen and Jessica had arrived.

"Did they bring Rusty?" he asked.

Jessica lifted Rusty onto Jeff's bed. "Yep. He's right here."

Rusty nestled his head into Jeff's chest while Jeff rubbed his hand up and down Rusty's back. Sniffles could be heard as we noticed Jeff's teary eyes.

Choking up, Jeff whispered, "You've been a good companion…" His words dissolved into sobs. Rusty moved around, pushed his black nose into Jeff's cheek, and then licked his face.

"Ouch. That's enough, boy." Jeff gently pushed Rusty's leg off him. "Can you get him down now?"

Dad lifted Rusty off the bed and held him on his lap. Scratching Rusty's ears, Dad somberly stared at the floor.

"I think it's best if you guys take him to your house, Dad," Jeff said. "It's just too hard for me, and he doesn't understand why he can't snuggle with me. It makes me sad to be leaving him."

That evening everyone left, and I spent the night with Jeff. I wasn't leaving his side, knowing that it was possible that he could take a sudden dive. The next day, my parents drove their motor home to the hospice center so they too would be close by when their youngest child took his last breath. Family and friends showed up throughout the day to offer support, bring food, and hold vigil. Colleen and Jessica delivered coffee each time they visited, while Midge brought my favorite treats. I stayed in the room with Jeff, while others came in and out. Jeff was mostly heavily sedated from the pain medications, leaving him oblivious to whoever was there.

Four days passed, and the medical team was still struggling to keep Jeff's pain under control. They had him on methadone and several other medications to help him relax. Though he was so sedated that he no longer talked to us, his facial contortions revealed that he was still experiencing occasional pain. As before, his heart rate began to slow, his blood pressure dropped, and he wasn't eating or drinking.

Day five, then six. Each passing day was a day closer to the end of our time together. The addition of yet another medication finally seemed to bring Jeff the comfort they had promised. His facial muscles relaxed, and his breathing became less labored. No longer aroused by pain, he seemed to stay in a deep and peaceful sleep.

Desperate to be there when Jeff died, I continued my vigil in his room. I could hear laughter and crying outside his room, where there was a large rec-room-type space for families to gather. My parents, Terry, a few other family members, and friends gathered to support one another through Jeff's final hours. People came and went quietly through Jeff's room, paying their respects and offering me support. Though people meant well, I found myself selfishly wanting to be alone with my little brother. Exhausted, I drifted in and out of a fog, tuning out the processional as I watched Jeff's chest slowly rise and fall.

In my daze, I found myself reflecting on some of the other people I had witnessed pass from this world to the next. I flashed to my grandparents, several friends, and many clients. I was grateful to be with them, but especially grateful to have the chance to be with Jeff as he was dying. It was not only because I had told him I would not leave him, but because I selfishly wanted to be with him—I yearned to witness his transition from this life to the next. For me, each person's final moments are the start of a journey. There's often a sense of peace, sometimes even a smile, a profound silence that marks the end of this life. But at the same time, the silence seems to contain an essence of hope, as if the person is headed for a new beginning.

My thoughts were abruptly interrupted by a change in Jeff's breathing. His breaths became increasingly sporadic, and my experience told me that it was the time—today was the day. I wanted to let my parents know in case they wanted to be in the room with me.

I opened the door, poked my head into the family room, searched for Mom in the crowd, and motioned her to come to me. We stood in the little hallway just inside Jeff's room.

"I know you told Gary that Jeff wasn't expected to make it through the day, but someone may want to let him know that Jeff only has a few hours left, in case he wants to be here."

She gave a disappointed sigh. "I'll have someone call and let him know."

A few minutes later, Mom entered the dimly lit room, walked toward Jeff's bed, and sat beside him while I perched on the other side. Jeff looked peaceful as his head rested on a white pillow. A sheet and pink blanket were pulled up to the top of his chest. His arms were to the side, and his hands rested safely in ours. Mom and I sat silently, watching Jeff sleep.

I eventually broke the silence. "I don't know if you want to be here when he dies. If that would be too difficult, you may want to go soon. It's OK if you want to be outside with Dad. He's already said he couldn't handle being in here."

Somberly staring down at Jeff's hand in hers, she said, "I don't think I can handle it either, but will you be OK being in here alone?"

Neither of us looked up, making it easier for me to be honest. "I prefer to be alone, unless you want to be here." I didn't say it, but I had the thought that it felt right that I would share these last moments alone, just Jeff and me. All through this journey, I had been the one closest to him.

She leaned down and kissed Jeff's pale lips, then hugged his limp body. No mother should have to experience such agony, yet she did it with as much courage as she could muster. Mom and I clung to each other at the end of Jeff's bed. I watched her leave the room, and then I quietly sent up a desperate prayer. "Please, God, don't let anyone else in. Everyone has had a chance to say goodbye. I want to be left alone now."

The curtains to the outside were open, yet little light came through the gray sky. The room was peaceful even though sorrow was setting in. Depleted, I crawled on the bed next to Jeff and whispered into his ear, "You can go home now. We're all going to be OK." I struggled to get the rest of the words out of my heavy heart. Rocking back and forth, I gazed out the window, searching for enough peace to allow me to finish my thought.

I rolled toward Jeff again and whispered, "Go be with Jesus and be in peace. I'll miss you, and I'll do my best to never forget all that you've taught me…" My words disintegrated, and all I could utter was "I love you. I love you so much."

I laid my head on the pillow next to him and held his hand for only a few more minutes before his breathing appeared to stop. He then took another breath. A longer pause, a deeper breath, and then he was gone. Without warning, draped over his limp body, I let go of every emotion I had in me, emotions that had been building up inside me for the past four years—agony, joy, pain, and relief, all in one. Time seemed to stand still to finally allow me the opportunity to empty my soul.

Oblivious to their presence, I shuddered when Mom put her hand on my shoulder. "It's going to be OK, Tammy. Jeff is in a better place," she whispered as she wrapped her arms around my exhausted body.

When I looked up, I saw Dad and Terry hugging each other as they wept at the end of Jeff's bed. The four of us embraced one another in a group hug, an expression of unity—united in sorrow, united as a family, united by sharing in Jeff's journey.

Gary entered as the others were leaving the room. "Sorry I missed it. I had to go to my daughter's soccer game," he said. As soon as he saw Jeff's body, he began to cry, offering other reasons for his absence. I didn't hear them—I didn't have it in me.

I slowly gathered my and Jeff's belongings, finished the last of the paperwork, and then left Jeff's room, knowing that I had given all that I had and that I had received much more in return.

CHAPTER 61

Another One Bites the Dust

EMPTY AND SLEEP DEPRIVED, I crawled into my bed for the first time in seven days. I slept deeply the night of November 1, 2003. It was done. I felt numb. A part of me was gone, and I didn't know exactly how I felt about it. I did know that I would have to wait until after Jeff's funeral to figure out how my life would be affected by the loss of my brother—my buddy.

My girls heard me finally stirring, so they slowly opened my bedroom door, and seeing the whites of my eyes, they crawled into my bed next to me. With me sandwiched between them, we talked briefly about Jeff's passing, but they quickly switched subjects. They eagerly told me about all the exciting things coming up at school. Feeling numb, I tried to muster some enthusiasm about their upcoming school dance by smiling and saying all the right words. I wanted to feel excited with them, but I couldn't force myself to *feel* much of anything. I nodded and listened as they rambled. I eventually did *feel* something—I felt glad to be home, and I felt grateful that Clark and the girls were there for me.

Clark called up the stairs for me to come down for coffee time. I had missed my coffee time with him over the past week. It had been a long, emotional week, and I was looking forward to a restful day at home with just my family.

I felt as if I were on autopilot the days following Jeff's death. My feelings vacillated between relief and sadness. It felt strange to drop the girls off at school and not have to rush home to care for Jeff.

They liked that part and wanted to me to pick them up every day from school, just as I used to, and go places such as shopping or the coffee shop. They shared that after the funeral, they were excited to have their friends over again, since there wouldn't be so much stress and sadness over Jeff.

Clark also seemed relieved that life would be back to normal, back to how it had been so long ago. Though he was supportive and understanding of my grief, several times during our morning coffee time he commented on how nice it was for me to not be distracted by Jeff's needs.

I couldn't blame my family, but I also couldn't move on from the whole experience so easily. I cried off and on during the day, mostly when I was alone—it just felt better to let it all out rather than try to hold myself back when others were around.

I still woke up startled a few times at night, glancing toward the nightstand to check the monitor, which was no longer there. Usually I was able to fall back asleep, but a few of the nights, my mind played tricks on me and convinced me I had heard Jeff calling for me—triggering jolts of adrenaline through my veins.

Mom and I talked several times a day throughout the week, often reflecting on how weird it was to not have to take care of Jeff. She and Dad cried throughout each day building up to the funeral, which they both were dreading, especially Dad. He was more emotional than ever before and had a hard time keeping from crying, even in front of people.

The few days leading up to the funeral were especially hectic as we organized all the various pieces. Mom focused on arranging the food, while I focused on the service itself—speeches, music, and programs. Aunt Robin, Aunt Mel, and several others planned on making Jeff's favorite dishes, just as he had requested when he was planning his funeral. Mom had a list of all his food requests, and she was busy assigning dishes to others who volunteered to bring something.

I met with Pastor Bill to discuss the details about the church and his message. He had met with Jeff several times over the past few months to discuss any final thoughts Jeff wanted shared at his funeral. While Pastor Bill prepared his part, I was busy writing the eulogy. Chelsey and Kendra decided that they wanted to share something at the service as well, so they also started working on their speeches. Terry agreed to close the service by sharing Jeff's final wishes.

It was the day before the funeral, only six days since Jeff had died, and the girls wanted to read their speeches to Clark and me for final approval. Chelsey stood in front of the crackling fireplace as if she were on stage. Rusty was curled up next to me on the couch, a stark reminder that he was without his best friend. Kendra sat on the arm of Clark's leather chair, her legs resting across his lap. The air felt heavy.

Chelsey's eyes lowered, and she began to read. "My uncle Jeff has had a huge impact on my life. He moved in with us when I was only twelve years old. At first I was anxious about having him there because he was so sick, and he was only expected to live for about six weeks. I was never around a sick person like that before, so it was sort of uncomfortable. It only took me a few days to adjust to having him there. And as you all know, he didn't die, and with each passing year, we became closer and closer." She paused, looking up from the white lined paper that she held firmly in her hands.

"Keep going; we're listening," I said.

"He became one of my best friends. He listened to me when I was anxious and down, he understood me like no one else, he encouraged me, and he taught me important lessons about life. I learned how to give people the benefit of the doubt, to not judge, and to be kind to others because you never know what they might be going through. Uncle Jeff was always willing to lis-ten to me and Kendra, whether we were excited, frustrated, sad, or whatever. He never made me feel like I was bothering him. In fact, he seemed to really like that he was helping me." Again, Chelsey's eyes met mine. She frowned. "I'm sorry; I don't mean to make you sad."

Clark said, "It's OK, Chels. Mom's gonna cry no matter what. You know your mother—it's normal for her when things are emotional—and this is gonna be especially hard."

"Dad!" Kendra glared at him, smacking his leg.

"What? I'm not trying to be mean; I was just sayin' it so Chelsey wouldn't feel so bad," Clark explained sincerely.

"It's OK. Dad's right. Everyone knows that emotional stuff makes me cry, especially now." I wiped my eyes. "So keep reading, Chels. Your words are beautiful."

She looked down at her paper and continued. "Another thing my uncle Jeff taught me was to never give up. Even though his life was turned upside down from the cancer and blindness, he kept a positive attitude and was able to laugh through the hard times. I learned the importance of being grateful for all we have and to not take our health for granted. He showed us what is important in life—that it's not about what clothes you wear, who your friends are, or what you have—it's about finding the positives, being true to yourself, and loving others."

She swallowed hard, and her voice cracked as she continued. "Uncle Jeff touched so many lives since he became sick. He not only gave to the homeless people every month, he also gave to whoever would take the time to talk to him. Even my friends who got to know him have said that he has changed their lives. God puts angels like Uncle Jeff on earth to show us how to do it. I love you, Uncle Jeff, and I will never forget all you have taught me. I miss you already." Barely able to utter the last word, Chelsey plopped next to me on the couch and buried her face in my bathrobe. I wrapped my arms around her, and we wept together.

Clark pressed his trembling lips together, trying to keep from bawling. Kendra wiped her sleeve across her eyes as she silently stared at the floor, purposely avoiding eye contact.

After a few emotional moments, Clark said, "OK, Kendra. It's your turn."

"Maybe I should wait for a while," she mumbled.

"We may as well get it all out now," I said lightheartedly as I reached for the tissue box.

"Seriously, I'm sure we'll all be bawling by the time Kendra's done," Chelsey said.

Still sitting next to Clark, Kendra unfolded her neatly typed speech and flipped through the pages to the beginning.

"OK." The corner of her mouth turned up sheepishly as she cleared her throat. "OK, here it goes. Uncle Jeff has changed my life forever. I never would've thought that this is how it would end up, but all things happen for a reason. I think God used Uncle Jeff to help all of those around him. These past four years have been some of the most impactful that I will likely ever experience. My uncle Jeff was an incredible man..." She paused, glancing toward me and Chelsey.

"Sounds good, honey. Keep going." I nodded.

Clark listened with his eyes closed as she continued. "He taught me so much about life. He taught me integrity, love, patience, perseverance, kindness, and inspiration. But most of all, he showed me how to take every day as it comes and make the best out of it. As most of you know, we took him in as a family expecting for him to have six weeks to live. We all thought…why not give a little…at least we can spend more time with him. Well, after those six weeks turned into years, you might say there were days that were pretty frustrating, even for him."

Chelsey slightly bobbed her head up and down, gazing at the fire as she listened.

Kendra flipped the page. "Throughout the years there were many times when I was ready to give up on this whole journey. I just wanted it all to be over and for my life to be back to normal. But it will never be normal like that again because we've all been changed by Uncle Jeff. He has left a lasting impression on our lives. One of my favorite things about him was his humor. I loved that he was always able to laugh about the unchangeable fact that he couldn't see, like when he would send my mom to the bathroom to change the light bulb for him." Her eyes twinkled as she glanced at me.

I mustered a half grin.

She continued to read, and as she turned to the last page, her eyes welled up. "It takes a special person to turn such a tragedy into a gift, and I believe that is why God chose Uncle Jeff…" She squinted. "I believe that Uncle Jeff wanted to impact people's lives the way God impacted his—and as far as I can tell, he succeeded. Although our house will feel empty for a while, I would rather Uncle Jeff be in a better place. He no longer has to suffer and feel the pain. Best of all, he can see again. And when I die, I will be most excited to see my Uncle Jeff at heaven's gates. I love you, Uncle Jeff, and want you to know you will never be forgotten." She buried her head against Clark's chest, launching a full-on family sob fest.

"Tomorrow ought to be a real blast," I said as the sobbing subsided. "You guys did a great job. I'm really proud of you both."

"I'm sure there won't be a dry eye in the room," Clark said.

Chelsey raised her eyebrows, her voice elevated. "What if I get anxious and can't get up there tomorrow? I don't wanna go up in front of a bunch of people if I'm too emotional."

"Don't worry. Peter said he would read your letters if you wanted him to," I said.

"I wanna read mine," Kendra said confidently.

It wasn't hard to imagine that Kendra would likely do well reading in front of a tearful crowd, since she never let people outside our family see her emotions—unlike Chelsey, who sometimes couldn't help being emotional whether people were around or not.

The girls left to finish the photo boards they were putting together about Jeff's life, and I retreated to the office to finalize the eulogy—a final goodbye to a part of my life I didn't ever remember being without.

It was an overcast Saturday morning, exactly two weeks from the day Jeff was transferred to the hospice center—the day Jeff left our home for the last time. I rushed around, gathering a few last things before Clark and I had to run out to meet my parents and Pastor Bill at the church.

Only a few blocks from my house, we pulled up to the dated brown church. A large, colorful stained-glass window hung behind a tall wooden cross—a pleasant sight for such a somber event. Clark pulled open the heavy wooden door, and just as I entered, my dad reached out and pulled me into his arms. It was a rare experience to console my father.

As Mom came around the corner, she hugged Clark. My dad finally let me go, and then Mom reached her arms out toward me. I held her as she cried, doing my best to stay strong. Her cheek pressed against mine, she said, "I hope I can get through this day. It's already been a rough morning. I never expected to have to attend my child's funeral."

"I'm so sorry, Mom." My words stuck as my throat constricted. "I know it's gotta be hard; I can't even imagine."

Mournfully, she whispered, "You don't even wanna."

"We just have to get through today," I said gently.

Pastor Bill swung open the sanctuary doors, a welcome distraction from the heavy emotions. He invited us to follow him so we could begin our preservice meeting. I wrapped my arm around Mom's shoulder and walked with her into the large room. We discussed the details of the service, such as where to set the picture boards the girls had made, where to put the food tables and food line, and where to place the programs.

Carrying grocery bags and two large flower arrangements, Terry and Peter arrived just in time for Peter to learn how to manage the sound system and to hear the final details about the service. They gave Mom a quick peck on the cheek as they brushed by to set their stuff down so they could join us.

Dad quietly hung in the background, working hard to keep himself together. We finished the short meeting and had about one hour before the service was to start, which left me with just enough time to run home, change clothes, and pick up the girls.

When we returned, several family members and close friends were already working to set up the food tables. Midge hugged me as I entered the kitchen. She smiled as she pointed to her dish of Jeff's favorite blueberry buckle coffee cake, and she had even made an extra one for me to take home, just as she had promised Jeff she would. Welling up with sadness, Aunt Robin was able to muster a smile as she unwrapped her "trailer trash" hors d'oeuvres. People brought their special dishes exactly as Jeff had requested—meatballs, chicken wings, potato salad, cookies, and more. Smiles, stories, and laughter filled the foyer as each person set his or her food on the long cloth-covered table. Just as Jeff had hoped, the laughter overshadowed the sadness, at least for a short time.

Friends and family packed the pews, waiting for the service to begin. Soft music played in the background as my parents, brothers, and our families filed into the front two rows. Tissue boxes were placed sporadically under each row. All of Jeff's requests were about to unfold—the sermon, the music, and the food. Pastor Bill stood behind the wooden pulpit, his subdued expression giving way to a half smile as his compassionate eyes met my parents', then mine and Clark's, and then my brothers'. He took in a deep breath and then gently released it as he reached into the pocket of his black suit.

"Welcome. I am Pastor Bill, and I have had the precious gift of meeting with Jeff throughout the past few years, and I am honored to share his words of wisdom with you today. It is not often the case that someone is such an active participant in their own funeral, but Jeff considered himself *lucky* to have the opportunity to do so." Smiling, he raised his dark eyebrows and shook his head as he emphasized the word *lucky*.

The somber aura quickly dissolved as sporadic laughter rumbled through the room.

The pastor continued. "Jeff and I spoke many times about the message he wished to have shared at his funeral. He loved the parables in the Bible and often related them to his journey with cancer and blindness. He frequently thought of himself as having two separate lives—the one before his sickness, compared to his life after getting cancer and going blind. Using the lessons from the parable of the great banquet in Luke 14:15–24, Jeff came up with his own message—and of course it includes food, as you might have expected." Pastor Bill looked up from his paper, acknowledging the muffled affirmations.

"Jeff compared his 'two lives' to two different tables at a banquet. He referred to his life after cancer as Table One and his old life as Table Two. He elaborated on how Table One would have a lavish spread of not only the best foods, but the best people. Not necessarily the richest or most successful, but the humblest, kindhearted, and loving. Those invited to sit at Table One would include people who give of their heart freely, as well as share their time, joys, and sorrows."

Pastor Bill paused and walked from behind the pulpit to the front of the stage.

His voice lowered. "Table Two would have an average spread of food, and sitting at the table would be those people too busy to share of themselves. Not necessarily bad people, just those who spend their time primarily focusing on themselves. Seldom are these people helping or thinking of others, and rarely do they mingle with those who sit at Table One."

Reflectively, the pastor paced across the front of the stage. The tapping sound from his shoes striking the wood floor penetrated the silent sanctuary.

Gazing out at the crowd, he continued. "While Jeff wanted to share this parable with a smile on his face, he also hoped each of you would have the opportunity to consider at which table you might find yourself invited to sit. He also wanted me to point out the main difference—which is *selfless love*.

"You see, those at Table One will always be there for you and will always be sharing with others. Those at Table One have discovered that the miracle is not always about a cure—it is not the destination. The miracle is the journey. It is about what *really* happens along the road of life. It's about feeding the homeless, sharing your time, giving to others, and loving selflessly. The kind of selfless love that Jeff's family demonstrated to him each and every day of his entire journey, the kind of selfless love they showed to others, the kind of selfless love that is inside each one of you just waiting for the opportunity to present itself."

Aside from the sniffles and creaky benches, the sanctuary remained quiet as the people listened intently to Pastor Bill passionately deliver Jeff's message.

"Jeff acknowledged that most of his life he sat at Table Two. His diagnosis of cancer, subsequent surgery, and loss of sight became his turning point. He eventually opened his heart completely, strengthened his faith in God, and gave of himself selflessly. Once seated at Table One, Jeff quickly worked his way to be the chairman." With a dramatic tone, Pastor Bill said, "That was God's answer to Jeff's prayers. *That* was Jeff's cure."

Standing front and center, he silently and methodically acknowledged the guests from one side of the room to the other before he concluded. "So at whatever table you find yourself, we invite you to join us at Table One today. At this table, the laughter and tears are heartfelt, and the love is genuine and selfless. We come together as one and celebrate the life of the chairman of the table—Jeff. Thank you."

A gracious applause filled the room as Pastor Bill took his seat. I wiped my eyes and looked to Clark for approval that my makeup wasn't dripping down my cheeks. A wad of tissue in one hand and my speech in the other, I walked toward Pastor Bill and leaned down to give him a quick hug before approaching the pulpit.

I looked around the room, recognizing every person there; I felt loved and supported. I took a moment to compose myself.

"I feel blessed to have each and every one of you here with us to celebrate Jeff's life. I would like to take some time to tell you about my little brother and to share how he has changed my life." Trying to avoid smearing my mascara, I dabbed my eyes carefully. "Whew. I'm going try to get through this without blubbering, so bear with me."

I glanced at Pam, who shot me an encouraging thumbs-up, and then I began. "Jeff was born on December 20, 1968, and is the youngest of four. Ever since we were young, Jeff always had a special place in my heart. I have fond memories of the days when we shared a bedroom—he would usually end up in my bed so that the monsters wouldn't get him." Some of the guests echoed my amusement with a few chuckles.

"I remember one particular day when I was walking Jeff to kindergarten. I was kicking a can along the way. He tried to kick the can too, but being a bit uncoordinated, he fell and hit his chin on the curb. His little yellow coat quickly turned red with blood, and I carried him all the way home. I remember another time when we were swimming in a lake, and he fell out of the tube. He couldn't swim, so I frantically swam out and saved his life."

Trying to be a good speaker while maintaining my composure, I quickly looked up from my paper before continuing. "When Jeff was ten years old, he was diagnosed with an inoperable tumor on his brain in the pituitary gland, and the doctors told him that he could die if it grew. I vividly remember that day because Jeff came into my room and we prayed together. We talked about how God can heal people, and we even talked about dying. He asked me what heaven was like, and in my fourteen-year-old wisdom, I assured him that it was greater than going to Disneyland."

I playfully pointed to my temple as I joined everyone's amusement at my logical explanation.

My smile dissolved as I looked down at my speech. I read, "Jeff struggled through much of his adolescence and early adult life with depression and anxiety. I always tried to 'fix' him and make things better for him. I helped him with his schoolwork, I let him hang out with me and my friends, I tried to help him make friends, I took him to fun places, and often brought him to church with me. But since Jeff was pretty resistant to change, he made my 'job' a lot more challenging." I grinned while turning the page.

"I see now that throughout my life, God had been grooming me for my most important duty—to walk with Jeff to his final and eternal destination. When Jeff was first diagnosed with cancer, he was so scared because he knew he would meet God and would need to answer for the way he had lived his life. He would need to explain why he dumped his ice cream cone on the little girl's head at the ice cream shop." I paused, waiting for the laughter to subside. "And he would have to account for writing on the walls at the high school, and perhaps a few other things."

"His greatest fear was that he would have to explain away his selfish nature. You could say that Jeff didn't have much joy or peace in his life, and he wasn't confident of his final resting place. He was a Christian, but he often said that he wasn't 'walking his talk.'"

As I hesitated, whispers could be heard as parents quieted their restless children. My jaw clenched as emotions began to well up inside me. I drew in a deep breath and willed myself to stay focused.

"I must admit, I almost missed the final leg of mine and Jeff's journey together. Right after his surgery, I asked God to stop the pain—to give Jeff a break from all the suffering and to take him home. I begged God to let him die. I mean really—Jeff wasn't the happiest guy around before—and I could only imagine what he would be like blind and struggling with cancer. What I know now is that I almost missed the real purpose and meaning of Jeff's life.

"For it was through his suffering that I learned that one could lose every material possession, could lose their total independence, and all that we have been taught to be important in life, and yet somehow end up happier and full of peace."

Trying to stay engaged, I looked out toward the people, but their sadness only made it more difficult to contain my own. I blinked my eyes rapidly a few times to clear the burning tears and noticed Clark slowly raising his hand up and down—my cue that I was nervously talking too fast.

I nodded at him and then proceeded. "Jeff laughed more, loved many, shared much, and played the game of life like none other. Yes, his blindness was frustrating and difficult, but as you might recall, he coped by using humor. His favorite thing to do was to tell me I had a booger in my nose…which all too often led me running for the bathroom."

Amused, the crowd laughed and cried as I playfully and joyfully shared other stories about the funny things Jeff had done over the past three years, including Jet Skiing, bowling, going to the movies, fishing, and even reading menus upside down and backward. I felt I was honoring Jeff's wish to have his funeral include humor.

I flipped to the last page of my eulogy, and when I saw the words, my smile quickly faded. I swallowed hard as I spoke with conviction. "When the doctor told us that Jeff only had six weeks to live, I didn't think twice about bringing him home to die. Of course, I would be honored to care for my little brother during his final days. Wow, did God have a different plan. I know that you may think that I have done much for my brother—that I cared for him and helped him in his time of need."

My eyes blurred, and my throat thickened. "But that's not what I see today…I see that Jeff cared for me. He unconditionally loved me and supported me. He listened to me when I was down and was always there to pick me up. He paid back all I ever gave and more.

"Jeff's journey taught me that God truly does answer our prayers, but in his own time frame and in his own way. Jeff's life taught me that God truly does use *all* things for his good. If Jeff had died when I begged God to take him home, I would've missed the chance to witness not only how great and unique my brother was, but how God can turn even the darkest of circumstances into light."

Contained weeping and sniffling permeated the dimly lit sanctuary. My composure was cracking. Pastor Bill discreetly set a box of tissue on the stool behind me. Holding hands with Dad, Mom stared off into the distance, occasionally patting a tissue against her puffy eyes. Terry nodded, mustering an approving smile.

"This is the blubbering part I was worried about," I said, wiping my nose.

Leitha smirked, disappointedly shaking her head as she pointed to her tear-filled eyes. She wasn't one to ever cry in front of people.

It was a brief relief before the ending of my speech. "Though Jeff was born sighted, he lived a life blinded by depression and loneliness. He longed to find true happiness and joy, but he was never able to see beyond the challenges in his life—beyond the dark clouds. It wasn't until he became blind that he was able to see the many gifts he had been given. I truly believe that if Jeff hadn't become blind, then he wouldn't have experienced such a changed faith and the determination to live his life differently. Jeff received spiritual sight through his physical blindness.

"Many may look at Jeff's life and believe that God didn't heal him, but I see it differently. He experienced more joy, peace, and purpose over the past four years than he ever did in the previous thirty. In fact, I believe that we have all seen more clearly since walking in Jeff's darkness. God healed not only Jeff's spirit, but many of ours as well.

"I have always known that *faith* meant believing in that which cannot be seen. But now that I have been an eyewitness to God's miracles as he helped my brother see the light through his darkness, and my father be transformed through fire, I have learned to have *faith* in the unimaginable—in things that we can't even comprehend. I believe that miracles are often hidden in our unanswered prayers—and for that I am eternally grateful. Thank you."

Amid whispers and compassionate smiles from my family and friends, I exhaled deeply as I grabbed my papers and tearfully walked off the stage. Terry gave me a quick hug as he walked past me onto the stage.

He bent the microphone upward and swiped his fingers below his eyes. "Thanks a lot, Tammy. I sure hope my makeup isn't smeared." A roar of laughter encouraged him to continue. "Some of you might wanna ask yourself that same question, if ya know what I mean." He winked at the usual victims of his jokes, Kendra and Jessica.

"In all seriousness, we want to thank you for being here. I want to let all of you know that Jeff planned every part of this funeral, from the food to the music. And as many of you know, Jeff sort of had a sick sense of humor, so don't judge our family as we conclude this service. After the last song is played, we invite you to meet outside for something special. After that we will gather in the foyer to enjoy some of Jeff's favorite foods. We hope you can stick around."

Terry's face lit up as he continued. "It was with great joy that Jeff chose this last song, so just keep in mind that we are simply honoring our little brother." His cheeks lifted with his wide grin as he walked toward the stage steps, the first few notes of Jeff's favorite song by the band Queen increasing in volume as he returned to the pew.

The thumping bass, percussion, and guitar drowned out the eruption of laughter as the song "Another One Bites the Dust" blasted through the sanctuary. Laughing and crying people rose to their feet as Terry led our family down the carpeted aisle that separated the two sections of pews. I stood by the sanctuary doors, hugging and thanking people as they made their way outside; some shook their heads in disbelief, while others were still cracking up. Regardless of their reactions, everyone seemed to embrace Jeff's humor as they made their way to the only unplanned portion of the funeral.

The outside air was cool, but thankfully the drizzle had abated just at the perfect time. Everyone gathered around several wooden cages filled with thirty-four snow-white doves. Aunt Robin had made the special arrangements and kept it a surprise from everyone except from Pastor Bill.

Emotionally, she explained. "I thought this would be a beautiful way to honor Jeff's life. The first thirty-three doves will be released to represent the years Jeff lived on this earth. The last dove represents the new life he has in heaven." She closed her eyes and placed her hand over her mouth, unable to finish her thought.

Standing beside her, Pastor Bill put his arm around Aunt Robin's shoulder and then elaborated. "The dove represents the Holy Spirit in the Christian religion. It is used as a sign of hope and peace. As the doves circle around us, let us reflect on how Jeff left us with hope, peace, and yes, even laughter."

He and Aunt Robin took a step back as the owner of the flock of doves came forward. I reached out for Clark's hand, then my mom's. Slowly everyone linked hands and silently waited for the doves to be released.

The owner knelt in front of the wooden cages and lifted the latches. She then swung open the doors one after another.

A mass of white filled the air as the doves fluttered up toward the gloomy sky. They gracefully circled the church where at least two hundred of Jeff's friends and family had come to pay their last respects. After circling three times, the doves flew away. She then opened the door, and the last dove was set free. All alone, it circled the church twice before flying off into the distance, joining the other thirty-three—a beautiful yet gut-wrenching sight.

Weeping and humbled, I silently thanked God for the transformational journey from darkness to light, from pain to hope, from prayer to miracle.

THE END

Tamura Arthun

EPILOGUE

NOT A DAY HAS GONE by over the past fourteen years that I haven't reflected on the lessons I learned from Jeff and our journey together. I didn't want my brother's struggles and triumphs to be forgotten, and most of all, I wanted to share how taking care of my brother for four years transformed my faith. I wanted nothing more than for my brother to find peace, and though it may not have come in the way I expected, it happened nonetheless. As a result, I learned that faith is about believing great things can come from tragedy—even when we can't fathom such an outcome.

Not long after Jeff's death, I felt compelled to share our journey with others. I spent months transcribing every word from his tape recordings into written form. Once his voice was on the paper, I spent the following years painstakingly writing, editing, and rewriting—determined to memorialize our story.

I want others to know that when we embrace the dying process, we can live more freely. Done well, it can heal, instill peace, and inspire us to live our life with intention. I learned that when we allow ourselves to expand our perceptions of healing, great experiences can emerge. The transformation of Jeff's wounded soul proved to be as valuable as the restoration of his physical body would have been.

Jeff's prayer was that he would make a lasting impression even after he passed, and through the actions and attitudes of many people, his prayers are still being answered. Each year since his death, my mom and I gather friends and family together to honor him as we deliver hundreds of lunches to the homeless in Seattle. Jeff's Sack Lunch Sunday program continues to teach humbleness and gratitude to all who participate.

Though I had to make many sacrifices along our journey, such as losing valuable time with my daughters during their formative years, I now get to see how God used that loss for good. Chelsey and Kendra face life's struggles with a renewed perspective—anything short of a life-threatening event is considered an inconvenience, not a "real problem." They both have an appreciation for the basic things in their lives, such as their eyesight or their ability to care for themselves. Reflecting on the lessons Jeff's life and death taught them, they are now able to find joy in the small things and hope during the tough times.

Many of us witnessed how God's grace changed Jeff's bitterness into gratitude, but my father may have experienced it in a way that none of the rest of us could. During his own brush with death and subsequent physical challenges, he admittedly may not have recognized the blessings along the path. The emotional and spiritual transformation he went through as he recovered alongside Jeff continues to bring him peace despite the pain and scars that remind him of the fire that nearly consumed him.

I hold so dearly the memories written on these pages, and I hope they inspire others to see the light through their darkness.

ACKNOWLEDGMENTS

BLIND AWAKENING IS A LABOR of love dedicated to Jeff's extraordinary journey. Fourteen years ago, I started *Blind Awakening* by transcribing every word from Jeff's seven original tape recordings. I wept and wrote. I grieved and laughed. I was brokenhearted, and I was healed. I learned not only about grief, but about how to express my and Jeff's thoughts and feelings onto the pages of what is now *Blind Awakening.*

I would like to give thanks to all my friends and family who provided love and support to me, Jeff, my parents, my brothers, and my children during the most trying times of our lives. We would not have made it through this journey without your help, love, and sacrifices.

To my precious daughters, Chelsey and Kendra, thank you for sacrificing four years of your life to support me and Uncle Jeff. I know it wasn't always easy, and you may not have felt you had a choice, but you rose to the occasion with grace and strength. Uncle Jeff was blessed by your selflessness. I will be forever grateful, and I can only hope that your lives have been enriched by the experience. I am proud of you both, and I am blessed by the love and dedication we share. Thank you for your unconditional love.

Clark, I hope you know how thankful I am for your selflessness, care, and support during such a tough time of our life. Thank you for allowing me to care for Jeff, free of guilt and feeling loved along the way. I trust that you and Jeff are watching us from above.

Tracy, Kelli, Aaron, and Bobby, thank you for the love and acceptance you have shown me since the day I married your father, and for all the support.

Bobby, thank you for being there for me at the hospice center when Jeff passed away; your presence meant so much to me.

Kylie and McKenna, your uncle Jeff always appreciated his time with you. Your kindness and love toward him never went unnoticed. I know you were both affected by all that took place, yet you were still able to find the good. Thank you for your support and love through it all.

Aunt Robin, you have always been there when I needed you most, and there are no words to express my gratitude for you. Jeff felt comfortable whenever you stepped in to give me a break, which brought me enough peace to get away. I love you, and I am thankful for the incredible bond we share.

Mom and Dad, we made it through together. I am grateful for all the sacrifices you made for all of us kids growing up. These trying times were doable because of the love and commitment we share.

Terry, your ability to bring laughter and happiness into my life is invaluable. I am grateful that whenever you are around, the situation feels a little lighter. Jeff loved his time with you and was grateful for the effort you made to see him. Peter, your calm and friendly demeanor has brought great balance not only for Terry, but the rest of us as well. Jeff really enjoyed his talks with you. Also, thank you for being one of my beta readers. Both of you helped make Sack Lunch Sundays a success, which meant the world to him.

I want to thank my dear friend Midge for always sticking by my side—for going to every doctor appointment with us, for weekly lunches, and for helping me make life better for Jeff and the girls. Your friendship is priceless! John, your weekly visits with Jeff provided comfort, guidance, and encouragement. Your friendship with him meant more than words can express. Thank you for making time for him.

Sharon, your weekly help was invaluable, and I am grateful to you. Whether you were helping with laundry or visiting with Jeff, you brought us so much peace. The girls, Jeff, and I felt comforted by our time with you.

Christopher, you are like a son to me and a brother to the girls. Jeff considered you family, and he loved the time you guys shared. Your friendship to him, Chelsey, and Kendra during such trying times was cherished by all. I love you, and I am thankful for your sweet soul.

I want to thank Aunt Mel and Terry S. for making time to visit Jeff, and for all the help with the homeless project. Also, thank you for supporting me and helping me whenever I needed it.

Allison, Jeff loved it whenever you would come over to Mom's house to visit. He was grateful for your time and your willingness to entertain him. You are so special to me, and I am thankful for all the fun memories we share.

Katie, despite having little kids at home, you made time to come over for visits with Jeff, and he was always grateful for his time with you. Thank you for the love and support we have shared through the years.

Cindy, Jeff always enjoyed your visits and was grateful for the fun you brought to his life. He especially enjoyed bowling with you and the boys and being the recipient of your Secret Santa gifts.

Scott, I appreciate you for driving Jeff and/or his medicine to my house when transportation was an issue. Jeff always loved your special delivery of homemade cinnamon rolls. Your help with the homeless project and regular visits brought Jeff a great deal of joy.

Brenda, your home-baked cookies always left Jeff anticipating what his selection would be for the following week—peanut butter, snickerdoodle, chocolate chip. It was a highlight in his day when you would arrive, bag in hand. Thank you for your friendship and support.

Ardy, your care near the end allowed me to spend precious time with my girls—I am grateful. Thank you for all you did for us and for Jeff.

Mark, when you showed up at my door late at night, you showed me the true meaning of unconditional friendship. Your help with Jeff and with the homeless project meant the world to both of us.

Colleen, thank you for being such a great listener, helping with the girls, and sharing your time with me and Jeff—we always had a good laugh. You were there from the beginning to the end, and I am forever grateful.

Jessica, though you were just a little girl, you helped in such big ways. Jeff always enjoyed your talks and your insatiable curiosity. I appreciate the time you shared with him and the help you were to me.

Patrick, spending time with Jeff and taking him to the movies made him feel like just a normal guy hanging with his buddies. Thank you for making his days a little brighter. The poem you wrote for him still hangs on my wall—a priceless tribute I will always cherish.

Chrissy, your bubbly personality was just the thing Chelsey needed during those trying times. Your friendship helped her get through it all. Jeff appreciated your talks and the kindness you showed him.

Leitha, your friendship and nursing advice helped me be a better caregiver for Jeff. Working with you was one of the highlights of my workday; you made me laugh and provided much-needed respite. Thank you for being such a supportive friend throughout the years.

Gene, thank you for keeping me sane when times were really tough. You have stood calmly by my side through my greatest struggles. Your wise counsel and unconditional friendship are priceless to me. I am grateful for all you did then and do now.

Linda, I can't thank you enough for being such a wonderful friend and sister-in-law. You have been by my side through so much. You and James were there for Kendra during one of the most difficult times of our life. Your home was a place of comfort for her, which made me happy. As a beta reader for *Blind Awakening*, you provided invaluable encouragement and feedback. I am so thankful for your friendship.

Julie, your home was a safe haven for my girls when they just needed to get away. Thank you. I appreciate the love you have shown to them and to me throughout the years.

Lori B., our three kids have been through a lot together, and I am grateful that we had each other to help them through it all. Thank you for your help and support throughout the years. I could always count on you and Joe to be there for us.

Lindsay and Lori, Kendra was so blessed to have your love and support growing up. You made life fun and provided her a special place to get away. I am truly thankful for the friendship you gave to her and to me.

Frank, from childhood through death, you and Jeff experienced a heck of a ride together. You were a true friend to him, and he was so grateful to have you in his life. Thank you for always being there for him, and for all you did to support his homeless project.

Dave, Jeff always looked forward to your dinner outings and interesting conversations—thank you for sticking by his side and being a true friend.

To my coworkers at Evergreen Hospital, I want to thank you for your support, encouragement, and genuine care for me and my family. Evergreen Hospice services exceeded all our expectations. The physicians, nurses, and other staff showed compassion, competence, and kindness. Jeff died peacefully in the hospice center, and the care we received during that time was stellar. Thank you to all who helped care for Jeff and our family. I have always felt honored to be an employee and a patient of such an excellent program.

Pam, you are the most amazing nurse. You are always thinking outside the box, and as a result, your patient care is excellent. Your compassion, competence, and advocacy made a significant impact on Jeff's quality of life. I am grateful to you for all that you did for him and for the close bond we continue to share.

Joan, your advocacy and nursing care gave Jeff and me hope and comfort. Thank you.

Chris, your compassionate counsel provided relief and peace to both Jeff and me. Your mentorship when I was a new social worker gave me the foundation I needed to follow in your footsteps. I admire and respect you and feel blessed by the time we shared.

This book has been through many changes, and without the editing, feedback, and encouragement from several people, it would not be what it is today.

I want to thank Carol Pederson, my longtime friend and mentor, for her honest and (sometimes) hard feedback. She spent hours critiquing the initial manuscript, and she not only helped make it better, she has helped me become a better version of myself since the day we met.

Jessie Byron spent many months editing and critiquing my words and ideas, helping me articulate my thoughts on the pages of this book and holding my hand to the finish line. Always only a phone call away, she encouraged me and gave me the confidence to keep going. Thank you for your dedication to help me see my dream through to the end. I am forever indebted.

Ellie Byron and David Byron also provided editorial feedback and constructive input during the final phases of the book. They challenged me to articulate my ideas, and when I couldn't, they made helpful suggestions. Thank you for your support and encouragement. I am truly grateful.

Stephanie G., Dr. Amy, and Debbie, thank you for being beta readers and giving me helpful feedback. I appreciate your support and encouraging words.

Shirley Thomas, thank you for your editorial feedback, support, and encouragement. Your input was very beneficial.

Garrett Alwert, thank you for reading my manuscript and giving me professional recommendations on how to make it better. Your input gave me the guidance I needed to take the necessary steps to publish my book. Thank you for taking the time to share your talents with me.

Robert Dugoni, thank you for taking your sacred time to read my manuscript. Your constructive feedback and encouragement have given me the con-fidence to jump. I admire and respect you not only as an author and teacher, but as man who hasn't forgotten his roots and who gives back to others. I am beyond grateful for all you have done for me and for *Blind Awakening*.

To the other people too numerous to mention who have helped me along the way, please know that I am forever grateful for your contributions.

To my amazing husband, Ray: you are my greatest cheerleader and the wind beneath my wings. Though Jeff was gone when we met, you have made it possible to bring his story to life. Your hours of reading, editing, and rewording this manuscript have been priceless. The sacrifices you have made to support me in making this dream a reality are too numerous to count. Since 2010, you have prioritized helping me complete *Blind Awakening*—sacrificing our vacations, weekends, and days off. I am thankful for your dedication to me and to Jeff. Your actions define unconditional love and dedication. I love you from the depth of my soul and I am so thankful for the amazing love we share.

Finally, to my little brother—the one who changed my life forever—I hope you rest in peace knowing that you have changed the lives of many and that you were the example you hoped to be of how God could use all things for good. Your final request was that you would not be forgotten and that the lessons you learned through this journey would be shared with the world—it is done.

ABOUT THE AUTHOR

From her earliest childhood, Tamura Arthun was dedicated to helping others. After graduation from the University of Washington with a Master of Social Work, she spent a career in hospice and critical care, counseling dying patients and their families. Even her background didn't totally prepare her for becoming the primary caregiver for her younger brother Jeff as he experienced terminal cancer and blindness. Jeff's surprisingly positive attitude made her realize all over again the importance of faith, and she shares that faith with readers in this remarkable memoir.

For more information on Tamura Arthun, and to view Jeff's *Sack Lunch Sunday* video, go to www.tamuraarthun.com